THE WRONG GOODBYE

Toshihiko Yahagi

THE WRONG GOODBYE

Translated from the Japanese by
Alfred Birnbaum

MACLEHOSE PRESS
QUERCUS · LONDON

First published in Japan as ロング・グッドバイ (*Rongu Guddobai*)
by Kadokawa Shoten in 2004

First published in Great Britain in 2021 by

MacLehose Press
An imprint of Quercus Editions Ltd
Carmelite House
50 Victoria Embankment
London EC4Y 0DZ

An Hachette UK company

A CIP catalogue record for this book is available from the British Library.

ISBN (HB) 978 1 52940 097 7
ISBN (TPB) 978 1 52940 098 4
ISBN (Ebook) 978 1 52940 096 0

10 9 8 7 6 5 4 3 2 1

Designed and typeset in Minion by Libanus Press Ltd
Printed and bound in Great Britain by Clays Ltd, Elcograf S.p.A.

Modern life is often a mechanical oppression and liquor is the only mechanical relief.
Ernest Hemingway

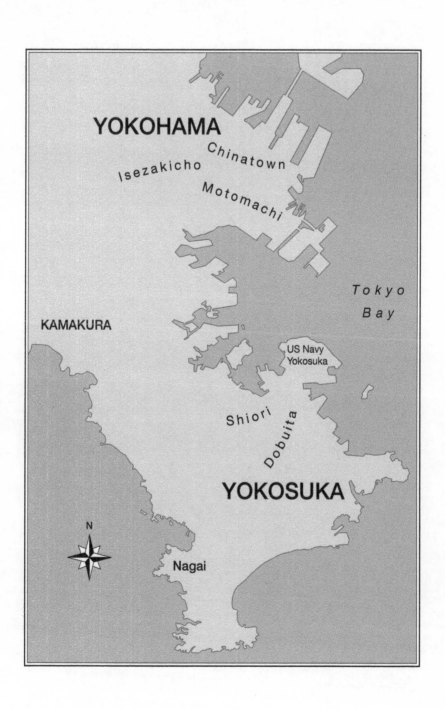

1

I first crossed paths with Billy Lou a few nights before midsummer in the wee hours close to daybreak. Wearing a leather-collared flight jacket, he was slumped on a pile of boxes down a dead-end alleyway, serenading the cockroaches.

What a lousy day it had been. Barely a burnt-out flicker of sun, and nightfall left a dull pallor in the sky. High tide came and went, a salty wind blew in and licked the hilly Miura coastline like a queasy cat's tongue.

For three whole days my detail of local detectives had been staking out a prefab somewhere in the sticks, Kanagawa Prefectural Police's idea of an important assignment. Tomorrow or the next day or a decade from now the murder suspect might've chanced by. But then he stumbles into a routine questioning up in Tokyo and is arrested just like that. Some grunt patrolman nabbed him at 9 p.m. while we kept up our surveillance well past midnight in a watermelon patch.

By the time we finally shoved off it was going on two in the morning. I was famished. My body craved something warm. Heading north, any number of family restaurants beckoned, but I held out. That was my first mistake.

Passing the gate of the Yokosuka US Navy base, I pulled to a stop and walked over to Dobuita Street. Here I'd come all this way for a thick slab of steak and a heap of fries, but there wasn't a light on anywhere. Those happy-hour days were ancient history, gone with the A-sign bars of the Allied Occupation.

What lured me into the alley wasn't his crooning. It was the neon sign, a steaming hamburger with the bright red words WE NEVER CLOSE—though the shop's name was half missing, and push or pull the grimy door wouldn't budge.

That's when I heard his voice. It startled the hell out of me, but there he was, all cheekbones and jutting chin. A wave of dark hair fell across a broad forehead, over bushy eyebrows. Definitely a foreigner, but from where? The pilot shades on his nose and carrier crew pin glinting on his collar above some embroidered emblem were GI issue, but he looked more like a movie extra perched there on that garbage heap.

I turned to leave when he suddenly popped open his eyes and waved with a slurred "Morning, buddy."

I should never have given the clown an opening, but for some reason I answered. "Still a few hours to morning. And where do you get off calling me buddy?"

"Sorry, sir. Back in Nam, day starts early. It'd already be 'Good morning' time."

"Back where?"

"Just flew in from off Haiphong. What a place to land, eh?"

An alarm went off in my head—*Leave now*. I retreated slowly toward the street.

"Hey, where ya going?" his voice chased after me.

He looked harmless enough, still you never can tell. I kept walking and shouted over my shoulder, "To look for some food. A man's got to eat."

"Wait!" He leaned forward, causing the pile of boxes to sway and throw him down with a nasty bang. An empty bottle broke.

I knew I'd regret it, but I went back to lend him a hand. "Drink so much, you'll be lucky to land anywhere."

"Me? I'm not drunk. You say you come for a meal?" He shook his hand free, wobbled a few steps, then leaned on the door to exhale a stale breath. "So who the hell are you?"

"A customer. This your place?"

"Yeah, yeah, I heard you—the man's gotta eat." He pulled something out of his pocket and tapped Morse code at the keyhole.

For some reason the lights were on inside. A long formica-topped counter faced four high-backrest booths. The mirror ball wasn't spinning, but the jukebox was aglow. He stepped behind the counter, switched on the radio, and started singing a "Summer Wine" duet with Nancy Sinatra as he prepped some eggs. Five minutes later he took a breather and tossed me a can of beer, then poured some red wine into a saucepan and took a swig straight from the bottle.

After another ten minutes, he set two plates in front of me. There was a nasty scar on the back of his right hand, but it didn't seem to bother him. One dish looked something like a Spanish omelet, the other tasted like chorizo and beans and garlic, but had no chorizo or beans or garlic in it that I could see. Whatever, it hit the spot, nice and spicy.

While I was eating, he stretched out on the counter and dozed off. I'd just finished and lit a cigarette when a clunky relic of an ice machine began to rumble.

"Makes round ice cubes," he spoke up on cue. "Real Fifties Americana, built to last." He tossed a scoopful into a bowl and pounded the balls with a meat tenderizer, then filled two glasses with the crushed ice and Havana Club. He passed one to me, I couldn't refuse. The place was hot and stuffy with the air con off. I drank my rum and said nothing.

"So who *are* you anyway?" he asked again, eyeing me suspiciously. "And why're you checking up on me?"

"Futamura's the name," I said, rising to go. Why would anyone be checking on this joker, I thought, but kept my comments to a brief "Thanks, how much do I owe?"

"It's on the house, and this isn't even my place. Come sunup, it'll be Sunday. And I don't work weekends. Not in a dump like this."

"But you have a key, don't you?" I just hoped he had a reasonable explanation.

He produced a penknife. "Time was I could get a drink anywhere in this town on an empty pocket."

Before the flyboy could pass out on the counter again, I sat him up straight, turned off the gas and lights, then lent him a shoulder out to the street. The entire block between the highway and Dobuita was covered with demolition tarps. Beyond that towered a new high-rise hotel with a heliport on top. As if people needed that shit.

The ace cleared his throat and laughed when we reached my car. "Yeah, yeah, I get the picture. Take me to Yang. Got a bone to pick with him."

"Yang?"

"Don't play dumb," he said. "I don't know how things go in Taipei, but this here's Yokosuka, home of the Seventh Fleet, and I'm an American citizen . . ."

"Listen, I only stopped in for something to eat," I said impatiently, hoisting him by the arm again. "You got a place to go, I'll drive you. I owe you one, but if you want to stay that's fine too. End of conversation."

I unlocked the passenger door and pushed him in. How did I get myself into these situations? The sooner I got on the road, the sooner I could drop him wherever. At the sound of the engine revving, he began to mumble groggily. "That a four-cylinder G60 I hear? None of Yang's boys would drive a number like this."

"Where to?" I prompted, ignoring his ramble. "Which base?"

"Yokohama. Between Chinatown and Osanbashi."

"You're on, but don't think you're getting special treatment. I'm only giving you a ride because I'm going that way."

I started the car, a Volkswagen Golf I'd bought second-hand seven years before. The paint job and driver's seat showed some wear, but otherwise the package was mint. The area outside Shioiri Station, however, was a mess. The old brownstone Imperial Navy Noncommissioned Officers' Club that went on to serve fifty more years of postwar R&R had succumbed to a wave of new development, dwarfed by yet another hotel-theater complex. The shipyard on the Pacific side was now a shopping center. Pedestrian bridges crisscrossed between megastructures. All you could make out of the harbor behind wouldn't have filled a washbasin. The route north was fretted with turnoffs, the sky plastered with road signs. I took the elevated bypass to the expressway and floored it almost nonstop all the way to Yokohama.

He was staying at a place called Palm Brothers House, a residential hotel with maybe the nicest facade of all the old buildings along Motomachi. If you can put up with bad plumbing and an excruciatingly slow elevator, they throw in housekeeping and concierge service for next to nothing in these places.

"Much obliged," were his first words when I opened the car door. "Never been treated so nice when I been plastered."

Wasted as I was myself, I saw him into the lobby and handed him over to the middle-aged receptionist who woke at the sound of the doorbell. "After you picked the lock and cooked for me? Don't mention it."

"Yeah, well . . . what was your name again?"

"Futamura. Eiji Futamura."

"No Jap ever told me his full name before." He may have had more to say but wasn't the sort to grovel. He mussed his hair, then reached out to shake my hand like a kid who couldn't tame his arms and legs. Maybe he was brought up that way, no thanks to anyone, forever acting up, always standing his ground. A tongue-tied American, now that was a first. He didn't even tell me his name.

After a long fumbling hesitation, he extracted a hundred-dollar bill from his wallet, then backed off like a scolded child when he saw my reaction. "Course I knew you wouldn't take it," he said, sliding the Franklin across the reception counter instead. "This is for you, from Futamura-san here. Thank him if you want."

The receptionist bundled him into the elevator. "He's not such a bad person," the guy told me once the doors had closed, "if he didn't drink himself silly."

He could have been talking about me. I just smiled and left. The sky behind Yamate Bluff was already bright. As I raced up Motomachi away from the promise of sunrise, for some reason I remembered the car I had when I was a young rookie. My old pride and joy, a cantankerous beast of a Skyline sedan with a three-stroke carb that sounded like a bugle charge. Why hadn't I thought of it till then?

Suddenly a car was honking at me. Work thirty hours straight, then drink till dawn, anybody's bound to lose it.

2

The next time I bumped into the flyboy, he was wearing a blazer and regimental tie—to a ballgame at Yokohama Stadium, of all places. He also had a split lip. It seems an offhand comment about the New York Yankees erupted into a shouting match with some black guy sitting next to him in the stands.

The game itself was dull by comparison, hardly any action by the top of the eighth, so I left early and the blazer tagged along. We steered clear of the Chinatown crowds and walked toward the harbor along the ginkgo-lined waterfront by Yamashita Park to the old wing of the Hotel New Grand. He stopped at the stone steps and peered under the portico. "Hey, they got rid of the revolving door."

"Ages ago. Some developer brought in a new manager and redid the place."

"Even the bar?" he said indignantly. "Let's pass. I think I've had enough excitement for one evening."

We circled around to the rear of the hotel where all the seamen's flophouses and Jewish trading firms had made way for upscale condos. A fancy department store down the deserted block behind the Prefectural Concert Hall was the only place that seemed half alive, but the light behind stained glass at the Karlingchen Hofbräu still looked inviting. It was an old haunt, with a long bar separated from the dining area by a swinging door straight out of a western.

"I'm overdue thanking you," he said as we claimed two stools. "The name's Bonney. William Lou Bonney, but you can call me Billy."

"Bonney? I thought you might be part Japanese."

"Way back, yes. My old man's mother was from here before she shipped to the West Coast. His father was named Bonney."

The Hofbräu's proprietress was an elderly white lady with dull silver hair tied back in a bun. Hilda had been here as long as I could remember, had probably stood behind the counter since before I was born. Short but sturdy, she'd have looked better in an SS uniform than in her frilly apron. What were we drinking, she wanted to know.

"First, vodka," insisted Billy. Hilda pushed a shot glass his way and he threw it back to sterilize his mouth, his face screwing up at a sting of pain. There was blood on the rim of the glass.

Next he asked for a Papa Doble.

"You mean daiquiri? So why you not say double daiquiri?"

I had to agree with her on that score but hastily ordered another of the same, in case she served me castor oil. "Tell me, why'd you have to go and pick a fight?" I asked. "That guy must've been twice your size."

"Them jimbos always play dirty."

"Hey, is that any way for a New Yorker to talk?"

"New Yorker? Not me, I was born in Alameda. Lived a year in San Diego and Long Beach too, but Pasadena the longest of anywhere."

"So did you go to college back East?"

Billy shook his head and tapped a finger on the brass bar rail. "Didn't go to college anywhere, but I know my game. And I know foul play when I see it."

"I played college baseball, the catcher who never got a hit. I only got up to bat twice in a real game. You have leagues and playoffs in the Air Force too?"

"Navy. Flew an LTV F-8 Crusader in Nam. They call the F-8 a second-rate fighter plane, but who are they kidding? Forty percent of the MiGs downed by the Navy were F-8 hits, even though there were a helluva lot fewer of them than F-4s. Know why?"

"Haven't a clue." Nor the foggiest idea why he was telling me this.

"An F-8 is half the size of your F-4 Phantom. Tighter turning radius, no afterburn trail. But the F-4 traded cannons and cornering for computer-tracking missiles—like missiles are supposed to be for air-to-air combat? Your F-8 was the last honest-to-goodness fighter, and with it ended the age of dogfights. Witness the Gulf War."

Billy lit a cigarette and watched the smoke drift toward the ceiling. When our drinks came, he downed his double daiquiri in one go. "Real fruit in this," he said approvingly.

"What does he say?" Hilda said in kraut Japanese. "He does not like it?"

"How's it taste?" I translated, nudging Billy's elbow.

"Give Castro a sip, he'd defect here and now."

"He says it tastes great." And he probably never went to Key West either.

"Americans usually complain I not use Welch's."

I didn't bother translating.

"What's about Welch's? You use bottled juice?" snapped Billy. "Speak English?"

"With all respect, I refuse to talk *mit dies Hanswurst*." Her hazel eyes quickly lost interest in us. With a vague shake of the head, she huddled down behind the counter with the previous month's *Women's Week*.

Again I had to sympathize with Hilda. "You sure talk big, even for an American."

"This is Japan, isn't it? Aren't I entitled?"

"It's a different Japan today, pal."

He frowned and ordered another drink, nodding at his empty. The old barmaid clucked her tongue as she got up to get the blender.

"And one for me too, make it *doble*," I added, then turned to Billy. "There was some trouble you had—with a Mr. Yang. You clear that up?"

For once he seemed startled. He set down his glass and stared wide-eyed. "I must've blown things out of proportion. Wasn't nothing at all, it's over and done with. Yang's an old buddy of mine.

A generation apart, but comrades in arms. Say, Futamura," he said, quickly changing the subject, "any chance I left my phone in your car?"

"Had to have been in that bar in Dobuita. There wasn't anything in my car."

"Take another look, will you? If it's lost, fine. Anyway, already got a new one."

"I'd say you were lucky not to lose your skin."

He laughed and took out a brand-new mobile, insisting we exchange numbers. I told him I didn't have one, which earned me a wiseass smirk.

"Don't give me that look. A mobile would only give me grief."

He sighed in disbelief. "So what do you do on the job?"

"We've got phones at work, but they keep changing the numbers for some reason." I handed him a card with only my name and home number on it.

"Okay, I won't pry. Just don't *you* ask too much about *my* line of work," he said, examining the back of my card, "because Japanese generally do."

Some things are better left blank. If anyone at a bar asks what I do, it's always: "I'm a civil servant. A routine office job." Where others can overhear, the Department is "the company" and the Precinct a "local branch."

We drank to our health, another three rounds each.

"I'm a professional drunk," said Billy, as he raised his glass. "Some Joes'll tell you they're only social drinkers. Famous last words. Keep at it and who's to say what's pretend, least of all yourself, eh?" He absently massaged the scar on his hand. Only then did I notice it went clear through to a mark on his palm. I didn't ask how he came by it.

"I'm not in your league," I said. "My Asian liver wimps out every time. Must be why the Eskimos were such pushovers, trading Alaska for whiskey."

"Inuits," corrected Billy. "Eskimo's a racist word."

My pager began to beep in my breast pocket. The LCD flashed a code for emergency duty. "Sorry, work calls."

He beat me to pick up the tab and left the bar when I did. A damp wind was blowing in from Osanbashi Pier. He scribbled his number on a matchbook he dug out of his blazer, saying, "Give me a call on the weekend if you're in the mood, okay?"

"Sure thing," I said, though who was to say we even had tomorrow coming. He gave me a firm handshake and wandered off toward the harbor.

I beat a path to Headquarters only to be saddled with hours of trumped-up desk work. Someone must have been watching the televised game and seen me sitting behind the backstop. It was late when I got home. I poured myself a nightcap and turned on the sports news. The game had ended with the same stalemate score. I switched it off. Nothing to do, but I didn't want to turn in just yet, so I kept drinking.

It wasn't liquor I needed. What was it about this bullshit artist that bothered me? I'd only met the guy twice, both times by chance, but I couldn't get him out of my head. A Yankees fan born and raised in California who goes to a ballgame in a monogrammed blazer? Already by my college days everyone was in jeans and T-shirts. Dark hair and eyes, claims to be a quarter Japanese, but badmouths blacks. Why would a South Bay kid be putting on East Coast airs and drinking Hemingway gimlets like a phony *yanqui*? His whole getup belonged to the era of radiator-spired movie theater marquees and duralumin diners, of the romantic leads in those Technicolor thrills-and-spills I'd watched as a boy on Saturday afternoons.

In this day and age, guys like him had to be homos, or crossdressers who wore bras under their suits and shoplifted to relieve their stress. This ace was no Ivy Leaguer. Hell, he wasn't even white. But the weird thing was, there was something about him I liked.

3

A body had washed up between the blocks of a breakwater not far from Yasuura Station in Yokosuka. Male, mid-forties, probably Indochinese from the pronounced cheekbones and shape of the nose, five days gone. Little decay or damage for a sea find. Fingerprint search turned up no match. There was a concussion on the back of the head, but not from a beating or even anything fatal. The bullet scar on his butt wasn't recent either; moreover the wound appeared to have been treated by a doctor.

The seawall in question jutted out between a fishing port and a fly-casting spot beside a strip of family restaurants, cash-and-carry outlets, and a prefab housing lot. A broad, landscaped boulevard traced the boundary where landfill met an enclave of old houses that once were pleasure quarters. The road saw a lot of car and foot traffic. No place for a drunk to saunter along, much less an immigrant. The coroner wrote it off as an accidental fatality, drowning due to heart failure.

A former detective named Sato got wind of this. He had retired from the force years before, but re-enlisted as a liaison for victim affairs and was always showing up uninvited at Yokosuka Precinct. Sato went to the crime lab and looked over the photos of the corpse. Just as he suspected, the trouser fly was unzipped. The stiff could have taken a piss off the seawall, slipped, and fallen in. In most cases like this, he explained, the zipper is open. However, drowning victims suck in water, which displaces the air in their lungs, causing them to sink to the bottom, where they proceed to decompose. They don't fill up with gas and float to the surface. Don't rookies these days know anything?

Sato's criticism turned to outrage when he learned the medical examiner hadn't even checked for alcohol in the blood. He went straight to his old boss, the Precinct Chief, and remonstrated. More precisely, his well-chosen words were: "You're still using that quack? You off your rocker?"

Osaka, with almost nine million people, has fifty medical examiners on call to its police force, whereas the whole of Kanagawa Prefecture—with roughly the same population—has only three. One of whom, a Dr. Kito, was not exactly known for his skill or ethics. He conducted some three thousand postmortems a year, or roughly half the cases involving dead bodies. On average, one in three cases, or one thousand bodies, required autopsies. All this on the side of treating patients at his private clinic.

It later came to light that Kito had students and nurses do the cutting, and merely reported their observations verbatim. Once he even let an undertaker who brought in the corpse assist with the postmortem, then let him dispose of the body afterwards.

The police, for their part, thought him a useful dupe, willing to write up death certificates on demand, unlike sticklers who might insist on opening a formal case. And whenever the friendly undertaker was entrusted with a corpse, he'd leave that Precinct a little offering of beer coupons. So these Kito concessions were on the rise.

Three years on, the good doctor was arrested for tax evasion. One postmortem pays twenty thousand yen. An autopsy, fifty thousand. A tidy income of close to a hundred million yen per annum went into his back pocket for more than a decade.

Even when he was still on active duty, Sato had never approved of Dr. Kito. So now he sounded off to the Chief and got him to order an independent autopsy. The findings were alarming: the lungs had shriveled, the blood in the heart that ought to have been a dark muck was bright red. The cause of death was determined to have been hypothermia—the stiff froze to death. If human body temperature goes below 28°C, blood circulation immediately slows and fails to reach the brain. The body automatically shuts down. But this was around the end of June. A person could hardly even catch cold sleeping out in the open.

Time of death is hard to estimate for a corpse that's been frozen and thawed. There was no sign of suffering, no marks to indicate he tried to fight or put up any resistance. Further details showed up: rips on the back of his clothes, skin scraped off his knuckles. With no vital responses, skin peels easily. Possibly he'd been laid out on something colder than ice and the back of his hands and slacks had stuck, then tore when he was lifted away. They sampled dirt from under his fingernails, but found no toxic substances anywhere. Very little alcohol in the blood either.

It was looking more and more like a case, but still not enough for us investigators from Headquarters in Yokohama to come on board.

Then, over the weekend, a television production company asked if it could do some interviews at Yokosuka Precinct, and someone leaked word of the incident. And not just to a press club crime reporter, but a prime-time media commentator. The Chief panicked. Come Monday who knew what sensationalist charges might flash up on the evening news. He had no choice but to preempt any potshots and launch a full-scale homicide investigation, calling in everyone from administrators to us First Division flatfoots.

The initial briefing went on for ages even though there wasn't much to tell. Most personal effects had been washed out to sea. No wallet, let alone a phone. The pocket of his polo shirt yielded only a bus ticket purchased at Shioiri Station and a faded scrap of a receipt from a convenience store nearby.

We set about harassing every resident and worker within a kilometer radius of the station, completely encircling the Shioiri district centered on Dobuita Street. But like the old Momoe Yamaguchi pop ballad lamented, streets here run steep, even if you hardly get a glimpse of the sea anymore. Sharp hillsides cut through the town, making it a pain to trudge around questioning people.

A brawny newbie from Headquarters and I took the north side of Midorigaoka and part of Otakimachi, minding everyone's business along Honcho-dori—the official name of Dobuita. The "brothers" from the base call this strip "the Honch" and the girls who flock here to pick up sailors all mimic the mispronunciation. The *dobu* ditch is long gone, as are the *ita* slabs of shipyard steel that covered it. The street is now paved with pastel flagstones, embellished here and there with handprints and reliefs.

The town suffered a slow death after the Vietnam War when the dollar plunged below two hundred yen. Topless bars folded left and right, discos fell silent. Only lately has business revived, though the clientele has changed. Especially by day, the place has become a mecca for tourist outings. Young kids, high school girls, and pensioner groups swan past retailers selling military uniforms, furniture stores flying 7th Cavalry flags, and curio shops offering Lotfe bombsights. Portrait studios that catered to sailors on shore leave have taken down their velvet pictures of geisha girls and hung up Hiro Yamagata posters. Tailors who used to specialize in "Yokosuka jumpers" embroidered with dragons and tigers now sell Gore-Tex parkas and Edwin jeans. Battalion badges and authentic tour-of-duty pins make nice souvenirs.

A local detective ran interference for us, priding himself on his connections with the yakuza families who control these parts. But after three days of pointless probing, I fabricated an excuse to send him and the newbie back to base. I had a far more useful "in" for goings-on in Dobuita. Who'd be the wiser if I did a little poking around on my own after hours?

I left my car in a pay lot facing the main road, switched off my pager, and strolled back to Dobuita. The real night was just beginning. The air took on a different smell, the neon lights a different color. Folks milling about the narrow, snaking street walked a different stride.

Ten years ago, when US troops deployed from here to a latter-day conflict, Dobuita got a new lease on life. Of course not everything went back to the way it was. Salarymen began to frequent eateries in high-rise amusement complexes, an increasing number of shops were converted into karaoke bars and *izakaya* pubs. Hostess clubs fell off dramatically, but in their place "nice girls" now hung out in the area for a fun evening.

Amidst these changes, Private Princess was something of a relic, an old-school venue where escorts in plunge-back dresses still entertained customers. As I walked up, I saw a beautifully restored midnight-blue Ford Mustang waiting out front. "Yo-ri!" called a deep voice from the driver's seat. Curtains parted in the open doorway and out stepped a bareback girl. A hand held out a cardboard box from the car and received a few ten-thousand yen bills in return.

The Mustang sped off but the girl didn't move. Two big eyes were watching me from under silky bangs.

"Futamura!" she said, then blinked. "No fatter or thinner, same height and hair."

"Why not just keep it at 'Looking good, I see'?"

"Oh, alright." Yori smiled like a biscuit poster. "Someone die again?"

"How'd you know? I'm looking for Yamato. Any idea where I can find him?"

She tapped the tip of her nose with her index finger. "I know you're always after something, but please don't ask two things at once."

Yori used to be the sweetest princess money could buy. That was back in her teens; now she was into collecting luxury brands. And not just to pull in sugar daddies to support her folks or to send her brothers to school like in the old days. I counted the years. She had to be well over thirty.

"Come on in. I'll treat you to a beer."

"Next time. I'm on duty."

"Wow, just like a real cop."

"Tonight I *am* a real cop. But don't tell anyone."

"Not a soul." She shook her head, her hair fanning out a clean scent of soap. She wore no makeup except for bright red lipstick.

"What's in the box? If it's smuggled liquor, hide it from me."

She glanced down at the box by her feet and laughed. "Who buys booze from GIs these days? I get all my liquor and lingerie on the net."

While I fumbled for a response, she opened it. Inside were a matching leather billfold and satchel wrapped in fancy tissue paper. "Prada. Bought them on an American site and had them sent over by military mail pouch. They'd cost a fortune in Japan."

"Never thought I'd see you buying booze by computer and spending big money on brand-name bling."

"I'm not spending. I'm laying in stock. Hey, it's only a hundred yen to the dollar." The curtains parted and a girl poked her head out to say "Mama" Yori had a phone call.

Yori invited me in again, but I declined. "Sorry, I really am on duty. I got to find Yamato." There wasn't a person in this town who didn't know the old shoeshine, a busybody who kept an ear tuned to US military affairs. Even our own naval intelligence saw him as a "reliable source."

"Yamato's gone executive," giggled Yori. "Go to Daiei department store during the day and you'll see his booth. Shoe repair and key cutting. I had him do our locks here."

I let out a sigh, and she stopped smiling. "So. Someone died, right?"

I pulled out a sketch of the dead man drawn from the photos and showed it to her.

The picture took her by surprise. "Hey, that's Chen, isn't it? But what's with his eyes?" She held it up to the streetlight to take a better look.

"Chen, you say? Chinese?"

"I told you, don't ask two things at once. I answer one thing and forget the other." She looked more closely at the picture. "But yeah, when I told him he didn't look Chinese, he showed me his passport."

"Where would I go to find this Chen?"

"He runs a hamburger place round the corner. It hasn't been open for some time, even though the sign says 'We Never Close.'"

A chime went off in my head. "Hamburger place?"

"Uh-huh, right behind here. At the end of the alley that leads in from the highway. It's called Cappuccio."

I said my thanks and started walking. Yori said something to my back, but it was drowned out by a passing gaggle of high school girls. Clearly up to mischief out this late, one of them still managed to give me a dirty look on the fly. An old dog chained under the eaves of a taco stand across the way glared back at them for me.

4

The neon sign was half-busted like before, but in the twilight that filtered down to the street I could now make out the name. The bar where Billy and I did our little breaking and entering wasn't called Cappuccio—it was Kaput.

The door was locked and no one answered when I called. Short of a handy all-purpose knife, the only metal on me was a snubnose. Headquarters had instructed us all to carry handguns after a GI threatened a detective with a pistol, then stole his handcuffs, but that didn't mean I could blow open the door like in a Hollywood movie.

When I asked at the corner bakery, the man there told me the place had folded maybe ten days ago. It was often closed before that, he confided with a cocked head. Round-the-clock hours had fallen by the wayside who knows when.

I showed him the composite. The baker screwed up his eyes like a nun who'd uncovered a love letter, and nodded at the resemblance. "Pretty much a one-man operation. Young part-timers came and went, but never the same faces."

"No cook?"

"Not that I could see. He had a butcher somewhere prepare his meat, though once he did come to buy buns when he ran out. But whatever, the place was 24/7, right? He'd take on anybody he could get, all different types, Chinese or . . . hmm, don't think she was Filipina. Sometimes this woman, she'd be cleaning up at the end of the alley."

I borrowed the bakery phone and called Headquarters to let them know the name and address. "The comp's a dead ringer for a guy named Chen." I hung up before they could order me in to file a report.

Further inquiries along the main drag led nowhere. Few shop owners even recognized Chen. An electrician had seen him drive up with boxes of groceries, but nothing on a daily basis.

Back closer to Kaput, I noticed a Kelly-green Range Rover riding up on the curb, an expensive British four-wheel drive you don't see much in this town. The Y-license plate indicated a private family car of a serviceman or someone military-related. A much cheaper Jeep Cherokee decked out with flash options or maybe a Toyota Land Cruiser ought to have filled the bill. Something didn't fit.

A light flickered in the alleyway. I went up to the door and crouched down. The lock showed no sign of tampering. Just then I heard a noise inside. I slowly turned the doorknob. It was unlocked. Peering through the crack I saw a flashlight beam flick about the dark interior. A figure holding a tiny Maglite appeared from behind the counter. As the shadow knelt to check under a nearby barstool I got a good look at the face.

I stood up and knocked. "You sure must like hamburgers. Or is it a drink you're after?" I said calmly.

A flustered Billy trained his light on me.

"It's me. Futamura."

"Too many chance encounters for comfort," he said.

I could tell he'd been drinking. Tonight he was wearing a suit. No tie.

"Pure coincidence," I quipped.

"This many times, can't be no coincidence. You got a key for this place?"

"Me? What'd *you* use, that knife again?"

"Don't suppose you'd believe it happened to be open. I only just got here myself."

I took a seat on a barstool. The ace shrugged, lined up two glasses on the counter, and uncapped a bottle of Havana Club. I brushed my glass aside, a little too hard. It fell on the floor but didn't break. The floor was vinyl tile.

"'Never trust a man who doesn't drink,'" he recited in a voice flat as a debit slip. "Old Chinese saying."

"Never trust anyone. Period."

"Whoah, just like a cop."

I swallowed hard. If I'd simply nodded, I probably could have avoided most of what happened later. "You know this Chen fellow is dead, don't you?"

He gave me a dazed look and threw back his rum.

"You've had enough of that. Better stay sober tonight," I said. "So tell me, what *are* you doing here?"

"I was looking for something I left behind. I get drunk and forget things."

"The other night, were you looking for something too?"

"No, that time I was just plain drunk." He shuffled out from behind the counter, bottle in hand. I snatched it away and pulled him outside with no resistance. He hesitated a moment when I told him to lock up, but then shrugged and calmly produced a key. Once the door was secure I grabbed his arm.

"What the hell's got into you, Futamura?" He shook himself free, but then came along quietly.

I walked him up the pavement past the Range Rover—yes, it was his—toward my car, opened the passenger door, and waited. He gave me a probing look before climbing in without a word. I revved the engine and swung a hard U onto Route 16, down past the main gate of the US Navy base and around a bend to the right. City Hall came into view straight ahead, and directly across from it the Yokosuka Precinct. I pulled off onto the shoulder and turned on my hazard flashers.

"See that building?" I said. "Right now dozens of officers in there are trying to track down the person who killed Chen, and they're bound to consider you the prime suspect."

"Why me? Sure I had money problems with Yang, but that's all squared away. Got nothing to do with Chan."

"Chan? You mean Chen."

"Yeah, right," he said with an odd smirk. "The guy just kept shop. I got a key 'cause I was his best customer."

"His best customer?"

"Who else spends as much on cheap booze in dumps like that?"

The officer standing guard outside started walking toward us. Had he recognized my car or simply thought we looked suspicious?

"So everything's cool with your Mr. Yang?" I pressed him for an answer.

"Listen, Futamura. This world cranks out too many rich guys like him, but when you're dealing with a *Forbes* tycoon, you take what he pays you."

"As long as it's not dirty money."

"What money isn't dirty? It all piles up the same. I'm his pilot on call. I could never see clear to buying a plane myself."

"Weren't you two comrades in arms?"

"Yeah, way back when I was twenty and the gook was in his mid-thirties."

I took one last look at the guard and the barred windows of the station, released the handbrake, and drove off. A left turn at the first light brought us close to sea level, though the harbor was sealed off by the plastic barrier of a six-lane highway. Beyond that the only scenery was a strip of family restaurants, a discount furniture outlet, and an auto supply store. You could hardly make out the water for a prefab display lot, sales banners fluttering eerily in the gloom. The city was planning a ten-kilometer pedestrian promenade along this "beachfront." Walk your dog in a place like this, even the canine would feel like cashing it in.

"Chan or Chen, whatever, they found his body out there," I said.

"The killer can't be too smart. So close to town, near so many people. I'm kind of relieved. Yang would never pick a place like that."

"Did your Mr. Yang have any reason to kill him?"

He flinched slightly, then forced a smile, but didn't answer.

We merged into Route 16 just before a wholesale produce market. The road narrowed to one lane in each direction, the median ragged with tall unkempt palms. To the right was a seawall scrawled with graffiti. Opposite that, a suburban tract packed with uniform kennel-size homes. Traffic dropped off to nothing.

Billy finally spoke up. "So what're you saying we do?"

"You must've had business with the guy. Why else would you keep going there?"

"I told you, I lost something, honest. That's all, I swear. I'll testify to the police. *You're* the one who doesn't want to go to the cops."

It was about time I leveled with him. Time to head back to the Yokosuka Precinct and talk across an interrogation desk instead of a bar counter.

"You notice that Toyota tailing us?" asked Billy all of a sudden.

Sure enough, a pair of dimmed headlights was following right behind us, though I couldn't tell what type of car it was.

"Where'd they start following from?"

"When you hung that U, the Toyota turned with us. And when we drove away from the police station, they pulled out from a little behind us."

"Why didn't you tell me?"

"I'm no good at co-piloting."

I accelerated, but it didn't put any distance between us and the headlights. I downshifted into second, and the tailgater slowed to the same speed.

"Uh-oh. You let them know we know we're being chased." But before Billy could offer more words of wisdom, the other car—a white Crown sedan—shot forward to try to pass us on the shoulder side. Did I sense some hostility here?

The coast road ahead was all snaking curves, dips and rises. If we made it that far, I just might be able to shake them, but we still had almost a kilometer of straightway to go. And a Volks is no match for even a Toyota sedan these days.

"Turn off over there!" shouted Billy. "That side road!"

A red traffic light came into view. There are plenty of smarter people in this world, people who never pull stupid stunts like me. I whipped the steering wheel to the left, then reeled it back hand-over-fist to the right, propelling us at a gap in the median.

"Hold on tight!" I yelled, pulling the handbrake. The earth revolved on our front axle as the Toyota sped past. Next I eased into the opposite lane, downshifted and let the steering wheel right itself before releasing the handbrake and stepping on the gas—and we were in-bound back toward Yokosuka.

Or not—something else was off. The rear end didn't grab, the palm trees spun by while the engine churned in limbo.

"Oil," Billy said. "The road's all slick." He had a good eye, I'll give him that.

The Golf did a 180-degree about-face. I doubled over as the rear of the car boomeranged, digging the seatbelt into my chest. Next thing I knew we'd ground to a stop on the median strip and the windows were full of leaves. The car body seemed unscathed, though the underchassis had to be banged up bad. The engine started, the gears engaged, but no, we didn't budge. I rolled down the window—we'd rammed up onto the concrete divider with a front wheel angled off the ground.

By now the white Toyota had reversed full-throttle back to the traffic light, swerved over to this lane, and steered onto the shoulder ahead of us. I saw brake lights, then both front doors opened at once and two men jumped out. A big white guy with gray hair and a shorter Asian sidekick, both wearing suits and ties.

"Get out," shouted the sidekick, pulling a pistol from his jacket.

Angry and puzzled, I opened my door and stepped out. Could I reach my gun? I barely managed to free it from my crappy police-issue waist holster and duck behind the car door. "Don't move!" I yelled, training my piece on them.

The two men dived left and right, the sidekick still holding his show-and-tell shooter.

"Throw out your guns and get down on the ground!"

There was a pale blue flash and a gunshot echoed off into the sound of the surf.

"Billy! You hear me?" the short guy called out from behind the Toyota. His accent was American. I couldn't see the other one.

"Hey, we don't want a Little Bighorn here."

"You've got your history wrong," I put in. "The ones who got slaughtered there were US Army."

"Either way, they got an engine block for a shield, you only got a door between you and a bullet." Billy peered at me from across the gearshift. "Why'd you have to go and mess things up? You drew your gun, you should've just fired."

"There's nothing in the chamber. I don't walk around with it loaded."

"Where the hell did you get your training?"

Without a word I slid back the bolt and loaded the first of several bullets. I had my reasons for not answering, if only to uphold the Japanese police code of conduct.

A black head of hair poked above the hood of the Toyota, the gray hulk still nowhere in sight. "Billy Lou, we need to talk. We just come to, like, invite you out to dinner. Nobody told us we'd be needing guns to talk you into a meal."

Billy got out and crouched behind the car. "Lend me your gun. I'm a better shot."

"Who are those two suits? Yang's flunkies?"

"Yang doesn't hire Americans. Now hand me that Browning."

Across the road stretched vacant land with a lone advertising signboard.

"I'm going around behind the bushes. The other guy's still out there somewhere," I said. "Count to twenty and if you don't hear gunshots, turn on the high beams and run like hell for the other side. When I see the light, I'll start shooting."

I reached across and turned off the headlights. Everything went pitch black. "You just keep up your comedy routine until their eyes adjust to the dark."

He swung his arm across and clasped my wrist. "If I don't see you again tonight, let's have a drink at sixteen hundred tomorrow, the old lady's place."

"Sure," I said over my shoulder, then burrowed through the shrubs. I crawled out to the curb and looked around, but there was no sign of the hulk. No cars in the out-bound lane either.

"Okay, boys," came Billy's voice. "My friend's descended from Crazy Horse. How about you do us the warrior's honor of telling us your names?"

"I'm George Custer, my bro is Tom."

I strained my ears to the wind in the trees, breakers rushing the seawall, distant engines. Unless the guy was wearing spurs, I wouldn't hear any footsteps. I circled in closer. When Billy hit the headlights I would jump out and jam my gun in George's back. That was the plan, not accounting for Tom.

Just then a leather sole scuffed the dirt behind me. I turned and my head felt something hard, sparks raced up my nose, my neck went numb. In almost the same instant my right arm jerked up. As my mind wandered off, I heard faint lingering echoes of the shock: a duet for two slugs, the shot behind my ear and the hit to my forearm, resonating in the hollow of my skull.

I faded out before the closing notes.

5

Piglets waltzed across the dawn sky to harp music, angelic porkers from a religious frieze. The harp was a jazzy Wes Montgomery guitar riff.

His head must hurt, said one piglet with a knowing wink.

He just overheated. Hot where hit, twinkled another.

He wasn't hit. He just had a nip too much.

The piglets squealed, scattering a cloud of talcum-scented stardust.

Abruptly my eyes popped open. Light stabbed through to the back of my head, the pain was intense.

"It wasn't drink this time, Futamura," said a young woman's soothing voice. "It's your head not your liver I'd be concerned about." Yori's face floated before my eyes. I was on a bed. A fresh talcum fragrance came from her scooped neckline.

"Don't tell me I'm in your bed?" My lips were all gummy. "Wh-what time is it?"

"There you go again. I told you not to ask two questions at once. You never remember."

"Yeah, right. So first of all, where am I?"

"In my apartment. On my bed. First man ever to sleep here by himself." She slid off the mattress and gazed down at me.

I sat up halfway, turned my neck three times and groaned four.

"No bleeding, you just got yourself a nice big lump. Billy says not to worry."

"Billy? You know Billy?"

"Uh-hmm. He's my steady."

She propped me up and parted the wall drapes to call Billy's name at a door. All four walls were covered in a flowery Indian paisley. The bedspread wrapped me in more of the same flowers.

Yori returned with a moistened towel. "Billy had to head back to the base. Sends you his best."

"So how do you know Billy Lou?"

"Billy Lou? My one's name is Billy Stimwell. Tall, blond, not very handsome."

She stood up with a sigh and drew the curtain on an open closet. Neatly folded inside were my jacket and holster.

"Guess I owe a word of thanks to your Mr. Stimwell." On a hunch, I got up and checked the pistol. There were only three rounds left in the clip. I pulled the bolt, shook a bullet out of the chamber, and returned it to the magazine. I held the muzzle to my nostrils and got a whiff of gunpowder. Must have pulled the trigger when the mug hit me.

"Was this in the holster the whole time?" I asked.

"Uh-huh. When we came for you, your car was plowed into the median. There was a red triangle thingy out in the road and you were asleep at the wheel. Couldn't even tell you'd been knocked out."

I tried on the jacket, though it made me groan, and patted the pockets. Nothing was missing. On the contrary, I found more than before: an empty 9 mm casing from the fired round.

"You two didn't pick this up for me, did you?"

"Course not."

"Not that I'm complaining. Seems there's another thoughtful soul out there somewhere. Remind me to buy a Christmas present."

"For your guardian angel?"

"No, for you, Yori."

"Wow, for real?" She put her hands on her hips and announced, "I could really use some curtains."

"Let me guess, you'd like—"

"The same material. I wanted to do the breakfast nook too, but I ran out of fabric."

We stepped outside to a staircase that led down to a parapet above another flight of stone steps down to the street. All roads thereabouts ended at the commanding heights of her concrete apartment block. Encrusted with regulation white paint, it must have been a US military lookout post built in the mid-Fifties.

Amazingly, I saw my car. Someone had parked it there. "So where was it you were going with this Mr. Stimwell?" I thought to ask as I got in and started the engine. "No hotels down that way until you get to the lighthouse."

"Puh-lease. I don't do that kind of work anymore. When I say he's my steady, I really mean it. He's my steady business partner, we run a companion service."

"Got it, so what took you in that direction?"

"I got a phone call saying a friend had an accident, could I round up some strong-armed 'brothers' and come quick. But I'm not into 'brothers,' so I got Billy and a friend of his to rescue your car. Lifted up good as new." She leaned over and pointed to her cheek. "Where's my thank-you kiss?"

"Sorry, sweetheart. Too much competition with Americans named Billy for one night, especially guys who can lift cars."

Yori smiled and waved in a windshield wiper arc. I released the brake and headed down the slope.

As soon as I got to the Precinct, I scrubbed the powder burn off the gun in the cleanup room. Investigations was deserted. They were all probably out making inquiries about Kaput and its proprietor. Back at my desk, I caught the attention of the Runt, who jockeyed over on his caster chair. "Night beat, eh? Or were we maybe doing a little fishing after dark? Snooping around on your own's not nice. The Department's got eyes, you know."

"Don't know whose merchandise you're pushing, but since when did the Department become such a bargain-basement operation?"

His eyes contracted. Youngest cop in the unit, he passes an exam and makes sergeant. Taller than anyone, solid chest, still nobody calls him "Sarge." Not since Komine, our short slouching Section Chief, dubbed him the "Runt."

"Today I went to the real estate agent who handles that burger place," he said, regaining his composure. "Your Chen was from Britain."

I almost choked. "He was *what*?"

"British. The agent had a copy of his passport. The lease was in his name."

"Where'd he live?"

"He kept a change of clothes and a bedroll behind the counter."

"You're saying he lived there?"

"Can't tell for sure from just this one night."

"Who owns the property?"

"The landlord," he answered perfectly straight-faced.

"You don't know much about dealing with realtors, do you?"

"Why should I? Always lived with my family since I was a kid."

"Alright, so the name. Chen or Chan, which is it?"

"The passport has it Chen Bin-long. Used to be a Hong Kong subject, but with the reversion to China it looks like he got himself UK citizenship."

I cocked my head. Chen in Mandarin, Chan in Cantonese. So what's a Chinese Brit doing running a dump like that? "He had to have a backer. Who's the real owner?"

"Ah, funny you should mention it. Komine asked the same thing at the meeting just now."

"And?"

"And I'm looking into it."

"Praise be. You're so good at answering questions. Why Public Relations doesn't snap up talent like you I'll never know."

At that point the far door over by the blackboard creaked open and in peered a balding head. Old man Sato gave me a meaningful look, like a mother-in-law seeing whether her son's new bride had finished her chores. A summons not to be ignored.

Sato stood in the middle of the hall holding a cane in one hand and a crushed pack of cigarettes in the other, bits of tobacco flaking onto the floor. As soon as he saw me, he tossed the pack into a red plastic bucket in the corner.

"Take the exam, Futamura. You been here near as long as I was," he said without looking up. "C'mon, a lieutenant at your age? And still on regular duty? You even finished school, more than I ever did."

Sato had worked almost forty years straight in the Homicide and Violent Crimes Unit. When he retired from active service, the local paper ran a column on the "Demon Detective . . . Last of the great career snoops, he could talk the truth out of a corpse."

It was true. Sato could get them to redo a postmortem even without looking at the body. He just *knew*.

I offered him my cigarettes. He pulled one out, lit up with a paper match, and took a slow deep drag. His face lightened up a shade.

"You keep beating the pavement on your own, nobody's gonna care."

"Listen, I'm not some old-school cop. It's just my legs are too long, I get tired of sitting around."

"Not what I heard." He lowered his voice. "Seems someone rammed the median on the Mabori coast road. But when the patrol car got there, wasn't a sign of an accident."

"What's that got to do with the price of ramen?"

"They had local units do a little poking around, see if maybe somebody witnessed anything. Found out the crashed car was a dark Golf," he said, staring at me. He lowered his head in a double-chinned nod. "That's biker country, and patrols are scared of run-ins with the gangs. So residents keep an eye out and call in when something's going on."

"Like what?"

"People heard gunfire. Sworn citizen's report." He tapped his cane and started shuffling toward the stairs. "You be careful. There's license-tracking systems. Once the town installs surveillance cameras, won't be a blind alley goes unseen. Some terrible world we're making."

"They snap a picture of me loping through on horseback shooting my Colt .45?"

He stopped abruptly. "You make cracks like that, you're asking for trouble. There's all kinds of shit pent up here in the Precincts, and the bosses'd rather have flunkies who don't fuck up than detectives who catch crooks. That's the name of the game nowadays. Nothing but self-serving bureaucrats who survive by making good on test papers. The best cop is a do-nothing cop. It's all just admin and meetings."

"Tell me about it."

"Ever wonder why us police keep getting raked over in so-called scandals? It's 'cause controls are getting so tight. We're more bothered about looking good and not pissing ourselves than we are about fighting crime."

I kept quiet and heard him out. What else could I do? When I was promoted to detective, Sato was my first partner.

"I heard about your new Station Chief, Oba," he said without turning around. "Fussy type, doesn't like smoking. Got no use for ashtrays in the corridors. No smoking anywhere. None. Smokers are the new criminals."

When he reached the floor below, he opened the door to the WC, leaned in halfway, and flicked his butt into the toilet. Then, with a parting wave, he started to tap his way down the next flight of stairs. "Take the exam, Futamura. But first, wash that car of yours. Tires must be all muddy."

Yokosuka Precinct does have elevators, but maybe going up and down stairs is the only exercise an ex-demon detective gets.

6

A sleepless night dawned. Someone offered to lay out a futon in the training room on the fifth floor so I could catch a few winks until the regular investigation meeting, but I passed on it. Once I'm plugged into the office, there's always plenty of things to do.

After the meeting, I excused myself and walked three blocks to Shioiri intersection, then crossed over a brand-new pedestrian bridge with fancy columns and even elevators—nothing like tacky old Dobuita—to a huge shopping and cinema complex with a multi-story atrium under glass and a rash of bright signs for fast-food joints. All the window seats were taken well before lunchtime, mostly by young housewives and their mothers, some with fat little kids obviously used to having their way. I didn't hear one scolding voice, only resigned parental murmurs. I even saw a father, on a weekday no less. The second largest group of customers were high school kids. And third, Americans.

One foreign housewife, red hair, early thirties, was sitting alone outside a sandwich shop, sipping a cola. She was the only woman who seemed unoccupied.

"Excuse me, would you know of a locksmith stand around here?" I asked her. She wore light makeup and, from the waist up at least, still had youthful good looks.

"Hey, you must play baseball," she said.

"Well, yes, I used to, but . . . How'd you know?"

"Looks like you've been sliding home head first," she laughed.

Ah yes, I still had that scrape on my forehead where I hit the asphalt.

"You don't have to be so inscrewtable. Though I don't usually do this kind of thing." When she spoke, her tongue looked like a piece of stew meat. "Hubby'll be home before too long, so we can't take it nice and slow. How about twenty thousand yen?"

It was several seconds before I could open my mouth. "Honest, I'm looking for a friend's shop."

"Oh, that so? Shame," she said with a shrug.

I walked on without further gallantries. She really didn't seem the pro type. Maybe I ought to have been more polite.

I found the stand I was looking for next to the outside stairs. It was just a counter all of two meters wide in a window cut into a small trailer. Yamato stood before a wall of keys, heels, and power tools, wearing a red striped jacket and a Bob Hope straw boater. I'd last seen him ambling around with his shoe-shine kit, coming and going on base like he owned the place, earning himself a reputation as a stool pigeon. Not that he necessarily cooed for the police, or for the Americans for that matter. His dark sunburnt face made him look more like a bat than a pigeon.

"Yo, Bro. Long time," he hailed. "Your shoes look like shit. You crawl out of a ditch?"

"Yeah, literally," I said, examining the price chart on the counter. "How much for a shine?"

"Not worth my time. Shoes don't cut it no more."

"How's that?"

"You'd flip if I told you how much the key money runs on this piece of shit. And to make it worse, the foreigners aren't flush like before. I'd starve just shinin' shoes."

He put his boater down on the counter and I slipped in a ten-thousand spot. "Just now, a lady back there propositioned me for twenty thousand. I don't get the going rates in this town. Let me know if I'm due any change."

He eyed the bill and his face crinkled in a smile. His teeth were stained yellow, but they were still his own. Rumor had it he was the last surviving crewman of the *Yamato* who swam to safety from the sinking battleship—hence the *nom de guerre*. If it were true, he'd be pushing eighty.

"Know someone named Chen?" I asked.

"That I do. Dozens of them. Shine shoes as long as me, you meet 'em all." He scratched his nose with boot-blacked fingers, not that it spoiled his complexion. "By Chen, you must mean Tran who worked the burger bar over the road."

"Chan, Tran, whatever."

"Well, the Joe was Vietnamese. Named Tran Binh Long, for a fact. Down Saigon way, they pronounce Tran as Chan."

I made no secret of my surprise, but he pretended not to notice.

"Big man in the Liberation Front, they say. But then, after the war, the Red cadres from the North weren't too grateful toward the VC. Made them unwelcome in their own country. Turns out the only thing the Hanoi boys and them ever had in common was their anti-'Merican solidarity, no love lost for past patriots or the South. It was put up an' shut up, else exile or prison."

"But Tran had a British passport."

He nodded knowingly. "Tran washes up in Hong Kong two, maybe three years after the Vietnam War, when all them boat people left. But they don't let in VC for nothin'. Brit counterintelligence is one helluva lot slicker'n the CIA. When the Brits hand back the Territories in as much of a mess as they could make—a little goodbye gift for China—that's when Tran gets himself a Chinese name."

"Some kind of tradeoff? What did Tran have to sell?"

"Well, think about it. All those years ago? Tip-offs on the Soviet Navy, or info on former VC with anti-Hanoi loyalties, Cold War stuff like that had its uses. But by the time the Joe lands in this neck of the woods, he's all washed up, no harm to anyone."

"Why would an ex-VC come to Japan? And to Yokosuka of all places? With UK citizenship, he could've made it to Canada or Australia."

"Who knows? I heard his baby sister had a condition, hospitalized here long term. But that still don't add up. Foreigner wants treatment, Canada beats Japan hands down."

A steam whistle blew somewhere. I looked around, startled. It took me a second to remember we were near the harbor. "Any recollection of a Mr. Yang?"

"Hmm, the only Yang comes to mind is up in Yokohama. Yang Yun-shi," he said, tracing the Chinese characters on the countertop. "But more'n Yokohama, his real turf is San Francisco. Also got a foothold in Taipei. Ten years back, during the 'bubble,' he was buying up all the ocean-view properties along Sagami Bay he could get his hands on. Word is he got burned bad, but that's just talk. To be honest I don't know that much. All them Taiwan an' Hong Kong triads spring up these last few years are way outta my league."

"How about a pilot named Billy Lou? Japanese-American, probably around my age."

Yamato shook his head wearily. "Bro, how old're you now?"

"Well past the forty mark."

"You're gettin' up there. Tide's goin' out on me too." He forced a smile, then glanced at the bill in his hat. "Sorry, I ain't got change. Doncha have something smaller?"

"It's all yours, Yamato. But there's something else I want to buy."

"Let me guess. You're a bullet short for a Browning M1910."

"How the hell did you know?"

He grinned and smoothed his fingernail with a keymaker's file. "Time was I knew everything goin' on in this town. But now, let's just say a friendly military police connection tipped me off."

"So it was you who called Yori? Then I wake up in her bed and I hear somebody made it look like I was sleeping in the car. Pistol back in my holster, like they were trying to cover up the whole thing. What gives?"

"Well, you didn't want no squad car to find you down there,

but this old fart hasn't got his own wheels. I did what I could, that's all. Not a clue why them goons were after you."

"It wasn't me they were after. They had some business with this Billy Lou I mentioned. Ex-Navy pilot, regular at Kaput. Lives at Palm Brothers House in Yokohama, has some connection with Yang."

He spread his hands on the counter. "Got me there again."

I had to think. MPs obviously don't go traipsing around Japanese residential areas waving pistols these days. What more could I possibly learn here? "One last question. Does all this have anything to do with Tran? You know his body washed up near the fishing port at Yasuura."

"Sorry, but I'm right out of information." He looked me in the eye, then shook his head. "Tell you what, add on a buck and we'll see what we can do. The ten-thou tip says we never conducted any business but shinin' your shitty shoes."

I dropped a few coins in the hat, and Yamato reached under the counter muttering something about a dollar going for five hundred at the black rate in the old days. He brought out an old factory carton with .380 Auto scribbled in magic marker on the lid, broke the seal, and handed me one bullet. "What a joke. Me, a shoeshine, selling slugs to a cop. Shouldn't you better take a spare or two? You boys are such lousy shots."

As I turned to go, Yamato raised the end of the counter and came out with his old shoeshine kit. "Don't be rushing off. It'd be fraud if I didn't work for my dollar."

He started rubbing hard, pausing only when he'd finished one shoe. I heard a woman laughing from across the plaza. The same American lady was leaning on an off-white company car, teasing the man inside. Soon enough, she stepped over the guardrail and got in on the passenger side. The driver turned away, embarrassed. She pointed straight ahead and off they went.

7

I caught the train from Shioiri to Kami-Oka and transferred to the subway for Yokohama. My apartment in Horaicho is a minute away from the local station, practically at the top of the exit stairs. A quick shower and a change of clothes, and I was good to go. I looked for a taxi, but ended up walking all the way to Yokohama Park, then cut across the edge of Chinatown and made for the Karlingchen Hofbräu.

The sun hid behind clouds, but the sky was so summer bright it lit up the whole town. What is it about summer that makes the city look like a beached blonde? It was hard to believe we were between rainy spells.

There was no sign of Billy, but I was fifteen minutes early.

"Coffee perhaps?" asked the old bar lady kindly.

I ordered a daiquiri like before. I was off duty, but I'd left the car because I figured we'd be drinking as soon as he got here. She mixed my drink and let on pointedly how a good half of a pork cutlet sandwich she'd delivered to Kagacho Precinct four days before went to waste, barely touched by a suspect they had in custody. "You tell your boys, I not catering to their *Schweinereien* ever again, not even for last request."

I promised to pass on her comment, then took a sip.

At four o'clock on the nose, Billy Lou strolled through the door in a linen suit and knit tie, looking like he just stepped out of a barbershop, scrubbed and polished down to the tips of his toes. His flight corps insignia was embroidered on the pocket of a clean white shirt.

"I hope you don't think I abandoned you," he said straight out, before ordering his usual.

"I didn't feel abandoned, just groggy. What went on after you knocked me out?"

He shrugged and tapped his forehead, then a wry grin slowly spread on his lips as he raised his cocktail glass. "I only meant to borrow your gun, even if it took some doing. But just after I bopped you one, that Joe jumped out of the bushes right in front of you and my hand slipped . . ."

"So what did my bullet hit?"

"Part of my shoe. Ruined a good pair of brogues. I flipped and went after that guy's gun. You were out cold, so I did a deal with them, smoothed things over."

"I'm impressed," I said.

Billy forced a smile. "They didn't really want to get tough, you know. They helped me find the cartridge and lay you in your car. Even gave me a lift back into town."

"So who were those guys?"

"Beats me. Last night was such bad news, we didn't talk much. Sure, I asked them what their game was, but they didn't want to say and I didn't feel like pressing further." He emptied his glass. I could tell it wasn't his first of the day. "Drink up, Futamura. That's not for slow sipping."

"I thought it was your favorite."

"More of a habit. Of course, I don't dislike the stuff. Which is why I drink 'em by the dozen." He waved his empty glass, and the old lady reached over and snatched it away.

"You don't dislike it, just a habit," I baited him. "Like working for Yang, I suppose?"

"It's like this. Yes, I *do* work for the man. But as far as I'm concerned, he's just a success story with his own private plane. If he was even more loaded but didn't have that beaut of a minijet, I wouldn't have nothing to do with him."

"But weren't you two war buddies? What exactly *do* you do for Yang?"

"Like I said, I'm a pilot." He intercepted the second daiquiri in midair and downed it in two gulps without spilling a drop.

Only then did I speak. "You're a strange one, you know."

"You're not going to tell me to stop drinking now, are you?"

"We're not down on drinkers in this country. We've even got a saying: our livers give out too soon to get hooked. Money can cure a sick gut, but not addiction." My homegrown wisdom elicited no comment. "Okay, so who *were* those guys yesterday? And what's between you and Yang?"

He laid a bill on the counter and ordered another round. "You think I'm lying? They say drinking with friends you can't trust is more of a curse than a courtesy."

"Listen, I don't for a minute believe you killed Chen," I said. "I trust you, Billy."

"Better not trust fighter pilots. Looping around behind your enemy is what it's all about." He rose as he spoke. "Let's onward and upward, shall we? But first, you gotta tell me what you feel up for."

I ignored his lead. "You tell me. Were you trying to find Chen for Yang?"

Billy pursed his lips, then ran his fingers along the edge of the counter. "No, I wouldn't say that. It was more for my own sake."

The mobile phone Headquarters made me take with me that morning began to pulse in my pocket. I hesitated a few seconds, as long as I could, then put the thing to my ear and walked to the partition at the far end of the counter. I'd hardly said hello before the Section Chief's voice blasted out at me.

Get yourself back here. The case is closed.

"What's 'closed' about it?"

Whatever. The culprits came clean. It's not murder, just disposing of a corpse. Maybe there's other dust we can tap out of the woodwork, but as of now it's over and done with.

"I haven't the foggiest idea what you're talking about."

Whatever. Urgent briefing. End of conversation.

I glanced back at Billy. He'd just ordered another of his quota of twelve.

"Another the same?" Hilda growled at him, knocking over the shaker. "We serve beer and potatoes here, I have you should know." The old lady opened the ice chest and brusquely stirred up a scoopful. She really wasn't as disgruntled as she sounded.

Report back A.S.A.P.

"What's this 'other dust' supposed to mean?"

The line cut off with a loud click.

The "other dust" was an infraction of immigration laws governing refugee status, on top of a fatality due to professional negligence. The case of British subject Chen Bin-long—the name on his documents—led the authorities to revoke a license to operate refrigerated warehouses whose owner had illegal immigrants working for him and effectively left operations entirely up to them.

On Saturday, June 17, three Myanmar nationals had mistakenly locked Chen inside a minus 30°C freezer unit. The negligence charge still stood, but otherwise the district prosecutors had already written off any formal indictment. Chen had died in ten to twenty minutes, reported the crime lab. On Sunday, the workers found the body frozen solid and panicked. Shake him, pour hot water over him, nothing did any good. So they took the corpse to a seawall behind the housing showplace five kilometers away and dumped it. Country boys from the Kachin Hills far from any coast, they thought the sea would simply tow it under and bye-bye. But the body came right back. They were spooked. At wits' end, they confessed to a French colleague, who then went with them to the police.

French colleague? "*Mais oui,* I too am illegal," Père Guignard told us in florid *japonais.* If not for the crucifix around his neck, I might have taken him for some déclassé Montmartre painter in his black smock and collarless shirt.

He lived in his church, the Family of God Chapel, part way up the rise behind Shioiri Station, sandwiched between the hilltop park and the far end of Dobuita Street. It wasn't much of a chapel really, just an ordinary Fifties-style two-story wooden house with white-washed clapboard walls and a cross on the roof. We walked right past it at first without even noticing.

It was a sweltering night. The chapel office was cramped and the lack of air con made it seem even smaller. Tacked up on the wall behind him was a sheet of crappy inspirational calligraphy—*Know Truth in God.*

"And how is being a priest working illegally?" I asked. "Do you need a work visa?"

"*Non*, nothing like that," he chuckled, stroking his smooth fore-head which swept back to a bald pate. What little remained of his gray hair was yellowed in places from nicotine. "Immigration permits me to work up to three days a week."

"Only three days a week?"

"Funny you do not know your own country's laws."

"I'm sorry, Father. My specialty is violent crime."

"*Tiens, intéressant*... Well, I am a priest of the Nouveau Port-Royal denomination. From France. In our sect, we work. Proselytizing is not considered work, not the kind Immigration means. *Alors*, I work to support this church. Or as you might put it, I get my hands dirty in the secular world. I go out among the people. Such is our way."

The Runt, my partner that day, occupied a ratty settee, notebook on his lap, watching intently. Père Guignard rose, folded his arms, and walked past him to throw open the window to a grand vista of an air conditioning unit groaning on the wall of the neighboring house. Plenty of secular dirt to be had just standing there.

He shut the window again and returned with questions. "Have they been found guilty? Can I go to them in prison?"

"Guilty only of dumping a corpse. What comes next is for the court to decide."

"I work at the warehouse company myself, through the introduction of one of my parishioners. I could not just walk in, could I? Me, a *Européen* and a priest? I keep stock records. Log incoming and outgoing shipments into the computer, write up waybills and invoices, for three years now."

"And what's your relationship with them?"

"Those boys work the night shift. They sweep the warehouses and do the rounds, sometimes come here for a meal and conversation."

"They're members of your parish?"

He grinned with an exaggerated shake of the head. "*Mais non,* they are Buddhist. *Théravadistes.* How shall I put it? They hold their monks to be living saints. Which might not be such a bad thing, to be held in such high regard, *eh?*" He then assumed a sterner look and leaned forward. "This is an open-door church, people are free to come and go. If asked, I will talk religion. If not, I say nothing. People can relax here as they like."

"So in other words, they're work acquaintances."

"*Exactement.* But on that day, I left early. Saturdays I work until three. They arrive later. The boss checks in very rarely, golf is his main business."

"So why did you come along with them to the police?"

"Because we are associates. And they confessed to me. Tran showed up right after I left apparently. The four of them talked and he gave them box lunches. They said he looked *misérable.* When he went off saying he had something to do, the three boys finished eating and began their cleaning."

"Wait a minute. So all of you knew this Chen, or Chan, or Tran?"

"*Bien sûr,* he was a *catholique Vietnamien,* of the congregation."

"Okay, then what was he doing at the warehouses?"

"I do not know. Maybe he worked there at one time? He was the one who introduced us for our jobs there." The priest shrugged like a Riviera croupier. "*Alors,* the three boys cleaned the warehouses. All three warehouses. By the time they finished and had a smoke, Tran still had not returned, so they locked up and went home. The next day was Sunday. When the three of them went to open up on Sunday night, there was Tran, frozen to death inside. That is the story."

"The Burmese work Sundays too?"

"*Non*, Sunday is their day off. Unless, how shall I say it discreetly, they run short of money over the weekend."

"Stealing from the stock!" came the Runt's voice from behind the priest. "Is that how it goes?"

Guignard seemed flustered by his accusing manner. I was even put off myself.

"Please let's not call them thieves. Just ask the boss. There is clearance stock, meat and other imports waiting for disposal. It is permitted to take a little."

The third-generation head of the small but established ware-housing company later denied his generosity. A denial staged for his customers, from what I could tell. He never said anything of the kind, he asserted, those darkies just helped themselves to a free meal. The frozen meat was mostly US military provisions, which probably made him nervous about any hint of theft.

"So they opened the freezer on Sunday night to get some meat."

According to the priest, Tran was on his back and frozen in place, with a scrap of plastic caught about his ankles. The three Kachin testimonies confirmed this. He must have run around desperately calling for help, slipped on some plastic, and banged his head. Either that or he'd been drinking and stumbled, then passed out in the cold. Whatever the scenario, he froze face up on the floor and when the boys tried to lift him, they tore his clothes and the skin off his hands where they stuck to the permafrost.

"And what was *he* doing in the warehouse?" I pressed on.

The parishioner was an honest man, but the sheep had strayed. "I guess Tran went to get meat. He ran a hamburger shop, after all." Nodding slowly, he added, "And the warehouse had a trolley for hauling meat."

"The door wouldn't open from inside?" the Runt butted in. "Warehouses are supposed to have safety equipment."

"The warehouse is quite old, I doubt it is up to code."

"Didn't he have a mobile?" I tried to salvage the line of inquiry. The coroner's report already stated that they found no such device among his effects.

"*Hélas*, I do not remember."

"Strange for someone who runs a 24-hour restaurant not to have a phone, don't you think?"

By way of reply, the priest extracted a business card from a lacquer stationery box on the table:

Kaput Bar and Grill
Chen Bin-long
OWNER/OPERATOR

Aside from the shop address and telephone number, the card listed no contacts.

"I was thinking to hold the funeral here, but he had no friends. And his sister and her husband aren't in Japan now."

"Ever hear the name Billy Lou?"

"*Non*, I cannot say I have. We do not see many *Américains* here." Père Guignard went to his desk for cigarettes. Neither Gauloises nor Gitanes, just a familiar blue can of unfiltered Hopes. "Mind if I smoke?" he said as he lit up.

"Where did his sister live?" I asked.

"*Aucune idée*, no one ever told me, but somewhere in Yokosuka. What country he came from or if that was even his real name was of no consequence. Tran came here to rest, that is all." The priest did, however, know the sister's married name: a Madame Lê.

"Will those boys go to prison here in Japan?" he asked with some concern.

"Who knows? It's not my call."

"They broke the law, they must of course accept their punishment. But their country is a military dictatorship. If deported, they will be tortured or killed."

"Were they activists or involved in any opposition movement?"

"All three were students kicked out of university."

"Hmm, hard to tell what the judge will say. I have no idea what to expect."

"Deportation is no joke. The Japanese *gouvernement* must know. If it comes to that, I will fight. This is serious."

"Don't worry yourself on that account," said the Runt, "this country's not like that." A big bulk when seated, he screened off half the room when he stood up. He leaned over and whispered in my ear, "What say we cuff him?"

I pulled away in surprise. "What for?"

"He works full-time at the warehouses, doesn't he?"

"We don't haul people in for that."

"Otherwise we'll have to get him to come in voluntarily to get his deposition. This chalkface isn't going to understand the procedures."

The priest protested calmly: "Why did you not arrest me in the first place? Because I am a priest? Because I am white? If I had been neither, you would have taken me in right away, *n'est-ce pas?*"

"Not so," I said. "My association with the police isn't as straightforward as your relations with God. There's no piety in our profession."

My idiot partner didn't get it, he just thudded back down onto the settee.

Anyway, I pulled out the forms and did my duty with a mechanical pencil.

8

Back at Investigations, the accidental-death-and-disposal-of-corpse line was already pegged solid. One senior officer didn't even show for the final meeting. With so many other investigations to juggle in First Division, who could be bothered to think twice about an open-and-shut case like this? There was no way to open the warehouse from the inside. The victim had become unconscious, which was why he hadn't called for help. The scar on the back of his head proved it: a mild concussion would surely be fatal at minus 30°C. Even supposing he'd come to and tried to use a mobile, the connection from inside the freezer would have been bad, and the odds of mechanical failure at sub-zero were high.

Most of the evidence did point to an accident, but the only real certainty was that three immigrants had disposed of the body and thrown his phone and wallet in the sea beyond retrieval. Still, before the meeting dragged to its foregone conclusion I had to propose that we re-examine the homicide line, namely with regard to a certain American pilot and his shady Taiwanese employer. Predictably, my tired colleagues pretended not to hear me.

Afterwards, Section Chief Komine lectured me about breaking rank in the presence of higher authority. He was furious. "Next time you pull a stunt like that, can you at least tell us beforehand!" Why was he so edgy? It wasn't simply that he didn't want to take on any more thankless work. Maybe, like Sato said, he was feeling the heat from above, pressuring him not to do what could be left undone. Do nothing and you don't fuck up.

*

Back home in Yokohama, I saw Billy four times in the course of three weeks—at the Karlingchen Hofbräu, naturally, during off hours. He always came alone, like me.

"You never married?" he asked. I forget which time, we were both sloshed.

"Nah," I said, "how about you?"

"I only go for ones that aren't the marrying kind. Any woman who'd try to snare herself a non-marrying man's got to have something going on."

I nodded.

"There was this Korean chick at an A-sign bar on Dong Khoi. From what I heard, those bar girls came over with the Korean troops, then switched to ARVN officers in hopes of starting up a local business. But their real dream was to hook up with a GI, someone with lots of green." His eyes went distant, or was he just looking at the bottles on the shelf? I waited for him to continue.

"The girl I liked was always out on the lanai drinking tea or crocheting something. Rarely left the house, like she had no money worries in the world."

"But you didn't marry her."

"'Course not. Let wild flowers grow wild. Japanese see a flower, first thing they want is to pick it and put it in a vase. Like that makes it prettier or last longer."

Hilda mixed new drinks for us. That day she wore a short apron over a pink polo shirt like she'd been busing tables at an Anna Miller's pie kitchen franchise.

"How did a carrier pilot know so much about what went on in town?" I asked, fresh cocktail in hand.

"Do I look like the kind of chump who'd stay put on board ship?"

I opened my mouth to say something, then thought I'd better just take a drink.

"Hey, I like you," said Billy out of nowhere, with a slap on the back. "We're goof-off kings, us two. Both got jobs, but here we are drinking from midday."

I drank to that. Now that the investigation had wound down I had a fair stretch of time off, though of course I didn't mention it— as if he were listening anyway.

Almost anything could start Billy talking about the old days in Saigon. He was a sump of odd information. The Americans had four PXs around the city, as he recalled, but the Air Force PX—Macy's Saigon—was known for its lax security. Built on the river, so you could load right into your boat. "In the day, the PX wasn't just a military store, it was more like Duty Free or an Expo pavilion. A window on the world."

"As seen from Hollywood," I ventured.

He dodged my comment. "I was dead set on cornering the PX black market. Girls sold themselves for exchange privileges. MPs would rather be strung up from a tree than forfeit their clout at the PX. In staking out the turf for goods, first thing they'd find themselves a mark, a woman with a serious jones for material things. Then they'd muscle in—get the girl and the goods in one go. There wasn't an honest soul in Saigon at the time. Everything was on the block, from cigarettes to cement, antibiotics to bombs. And dollars weren't the only currency either. Ration cards and five-day holiday packages to Wanchai were plenty popular, too . . . Nah, we were all in it together, everyone in the same racket." He shook his head like a teacher assigned to a class of dimwits.

The way he talked about the chaotic fall of Saigon, it was the stuff of legend, hard to tell what was real and what was newsreels: people clutching their valuables, scrambling for a place on any ship or plane going overseas, some even willing to kick out their own parents to grab their seats. Those scenes of the last choppers to leave saw his "Nam" vanish from the map.

Maybe because he never saw action on the ground, his stories had a certain distance to them. No cheerful exploits, no poignancy.

The battlefield he saw on flyovers from an offshore flight deck was a backgammon board.

"Was your carrier the *Midway*?" I decided to ask.

Billy shook his head again. He knew what I was getting at, what brought him here to these parts. "No, the *JFK* wasn't based in Yokosuka. But whenever I got leave, I'd fly into Yokota and make straight for the Tokyo nightlife. Why'd you ask?"

"Well, I thought you were a regular at Kaput." Something still stuck in my craw about Tran. As far as I was concerned, the case was still open, though up to that moment it had somehow slipped my mind.

"I still got friends on base in Yokosuka," Billy said. "Whenever I came through I'd stop by the bar . . ." He paused to work on his drink, then started talking about "crop-duster F-4s" and "dead-in-the-air Phantoms." Only talk of planes seemed to arouse any emotion in him, and I didn't feel like steering the conversation back on course.

That day Billy left early, saying he had some business to take care of, though not before Hilda handed him a paper cup with a plastic lid.

"Here, take this," she said. "The sun still high."

"*Gracias por la copa del estribo*," he told her with a little bow. "That's 'Thanks for one-for-the-road.'"

The gruff old lady's gesture surprised me, but then Billy had a way of bringing out the unexpected in people.

9

It was late Thursday afternoon. The summer rainy season wasn't over, although it scarcely even drizzled and people were worried about water shortages. At sundown, I canned the air con and opened the window, then camped in front of the TV with a beer. The Giants were in top position coming up to the All-Star Game, with forty-eight wins and thirty-three losses, a five-game lead over second place.

I had nine beers in the fridge, the plan being to pop one each inning, but after only two points scored in the first there was zero movement from the time I tuned in. Three-up three-downs on both sides for the most part. By the bottom of the fifth I was tired of beer and moved on to gin and tonic.

There was a knock on the door. I knew who it was without even peering through the peephole.

"Pretty half-assed security," said Billy. "Only one door between the street and here, and it was wide open."

The entrance to my apartment house stays unlocked until 11 p.m. No lobby to speak of, no concierge office either.

"Mind if I come in?" he asked, taking off his shoes. Today he wore the same linen suit and a clean white shirt, but there were bags under his eyes and he looked pale.

"How did you find me?" I asked. My address wasn't printed on the card I gave him, was it?

"I once saw you head in here and you got a mailbox downstairs. Not too many people with your last name. You always park illegally by my office."

"Not always. Only when I come home late. The lot is a long hike."

"No sweat, I didn't come to lecture you." He sat down on the sofa by the window and looked out. Not that there was anything much to see but the cheapest *fugu* restaurant in Yokohama. They hang out their dried blowfish-skin lanterns even in summer, but not once in the five years I'd lived here had I gone in.

Billy's eyes were fixed outside like a sailor watching harbor lights from out at sea. "Listen, Futamura. I got a favor to ask. Think you could move your car?"

"Oh, so now you're moonlighting as a traffic cop?"

"Sorry, I'm not in a joking mood today." He folded his hands between his knees and hunched down, breathing listlessly.

I excavated a bottle of Glenlivet from the back of the cupboard, broke the seal, and poured him a generous slosh. He drank it down in one go, then stared at the empty glass.

"Just this once," he asked, "could you drive me to Yokota?"

"I'd like to hear some kind of reason why. The trains are still running."

"I got cargo."

"I'll lend you the taxi fare. I've already had five or six gins."

"Money I got. But there's a lot to haul, too much for a regular car."

True, a VW Golf holds a lot more than it looks, but certainly not as much as a Range Rover. "What happened to your car?" I asked.

"Circumstances. That's why I came to you."

Ice rattled in his empty glass. He gazed out at the *fugu* restaurant again.

"You've got stuff to haul. That's your reason? This is your friend asking, what's going on?"

"I got to make a night flight. They say there's a front moving in." He spoke to the window. "I need somebody to see me off."

I dumped my drink in the kitchen sink. Billy looked up as if startled by the splash.

"I'm making coffee," I said. "If you haven't changed your mind by the time I get some caffeine in my system, I'll go fetch the car."

I drank two cups extra-strong. Billy poured himself another scotch, but just sat on the sofa watching the ice melt without raising it to his lips. Then, after downing nearly a pitcher of water, showering, and rubbing enough Tiger Balm on my neck to blitz my eyeballs, we set out walking to the car.

Billy's Parklane Terrace "office" must have been a swanky foreigners' residence before the canal was paved over into a concrete slab "park." The weathered stone walls were now shot with cracks and the revolving glass door looked decrepit, but the interior had been refurbished and they'd installed the latest electronic entry-lock system. There was imported furniture in the lobby and even a fancy reception desk.

I'd left my car on a street nearby. The tow truck never patrols these parts after 8 p.m. Billy had me drive halfway around the building to the opposite side and stop by the underground garage. He then got out and walked down the ramp, but the shutter wouldn't budge, so he let himself in through a side-door service entrance. There was no sign of him for almost ten minutes. I was beginning to worry when the door pushed open and he emerged hauling two extra-large, navy-blue Globe-Trotter suitcases. I folded down the back seat so he could load them, but he ran off saying there was one more.

As soon as the service door closed, a uniformed night watchman came sniffing around the perimeter of the building. He stopped and stood watching from a distance, eyes glinting in the mercury light. He didn't jot down my license number, but was clearly committing the car to memory. I could tell from his bearing he was an ex-cop.

Five minutes after the guard went away, Billy came out again, this time with a beige Globe-Trotter. No, all these would never have fitted in the trunk of a taxi.

"That's the lot," he said, climbing in.

We had to do another half circle around the building to get onto the return street. As we came up to the main entrance, there was the watchman out in front. He gave us a suspicious look as we hummed past.

I drove the kilometer back alongside the concrete park and nosed onto the expressway ramp. For a while there was little other traffic.

"Y'know, I think I may have got you in a heap of shit," Billy said as we hit the first bottleneck.

"I don't know what you're mixed up in, but so long as you're not a terrorist, the police here won't steamroller you."

He sent a tense look my way. "There you're wrong, Futamura."

"Oh really. I'm wrong. And you're the expert to tell me that?"

That shut him up. I held my tongue for a while too. The highway got broader, tall trees whizzed by on either side, city lights glowed straight ahead.

"Sorry. If it makes you feel better, we can turn back," he said.

I raised my voice. "Don't let's stop in the middle of what we started. Better we didn't do anything to begin with."

"Don't get mad."

"I'm not mad. Yet. But I will be if you keep saying you're sorry."

He shut up again. Past Sagamihara the route turned dark. Factory-grim restaurants and garish outlet stores loomed up, then fell away behind us. Had something happened tonight? I didn't bother to ask; I was sure. In spite of which, I had no hesitation about driving him. Didn't make much sense, even to me.

"Don't worry," I said. "I didn't especially want to turn in yet tonight anyway. I'd just been thinking about maybe stepping out somewhere."

We bypassed Hachioji, crossed the Tama River, and hung a left at a confusing intersection. For one fleeting moment, just as the over-pass angled up alongside Haijima Station, I caught a glimpse of the American airbase. The runway was hidden in the trees. Save for the hurricane fencing, the vast shadowy expanse dotted with rows of drab structures might have been a failed suburban development.

We drove straight along the fence for ages, until the Customs and Immigration checkpoints came into view on the left and Billy told me to stop. By the time I pulled over on the shoulder and set the handbrake, he was speed-dialing on his phone, the LED display tinting his face a sickly green.

"Yo, it's me. Everything tight?" He'd slipped into flyboy talk.

The Immigration checkpoint was dark, but even during daylight hours there are no regular officers on duty. They only man the port of entry if the US military first request it. During the Vietnam War, loads of GIs enjoyed a free pass to go play in Tokyo. Some of them never returned. Even now, Immigration and Customs officers generally don't have much say in GI comings and goings. They fly in from Hawaii or the continental US or off aircraft carriers with their face for a passport.

"We're outside the main gate. Yeah, gotcha. Can do," Billy was saying, then clicked off. "Turn this thing around, we need to enter through Gate 5."

I backtracked about a kilometer to where he indicated, then turned left to find a brightly lit gate area where a blue-uniformed Japanese attendant and a foreign junior officer stood waiting. Billy rolled down his window and the officer waved us through. We didn't even have to slow down.

We drove between squat housing blocks right out onto the airfield. And again as instructed, I swung left and paralleled the flight line past a large hangar.

"Over there," Billy said. "Pull up to the next hangar."

He got out as soon as we stopped, but just loitered there without touching the luggage.

"Should anything happen, you don't need to cover for me," he said.

"Tell me one thing first, though, does all this have anything to do with Chen?"

"Not directly." His face soured. "You a cop, Futamura?"

It took me a few seconds to find any words. "A drinking buddy."

He gave a big nod and slapped me on the elbow. "You had me worried, for your sake. Why're you so concerned about Chen? Next time we meet, I'll tell you all I know."

"But you're leaving Japan."

"This here's not Japan."

Now that he mentioned it, on base here *I* was the foreigner. "So when's this 'next time'?"

He pulled back his shirt cuff to look at an oversized watch. "Ninety-nine hours. That's another four days and three hours."

"Counting from when?"

"From right now."

"Are you allowed to take off at this hour?"

"Like I said, it's a night flight. Just can't fire up fighter afterburners, anything loud that might disturb the locals." Billy raised a finger for emphasis. "I'm coming back, I got my reasons." Then, rummaging in his pocket, he produced a hundred-dollar bill, which he promptly tore in two and handed me half of. "I swear on Ben Franklin, the Stars and Stripes, and the Red Baron. Believe me."

"I don't believe drunks. Too many drinkers make friends every night. The more friends they collect, the less any friendship means anymore."

"You're beginning to sound like the big guy up there."

Did he mean God or Richthofen?

A Ford Bronco cruised up from the taxiway and slowed to a stop twenty meters behind us. Not an official military vehicle, a regular Y-permit plate. A tall man got out. It was too dark to make out his face. He approached our car and opened the hatchback without a word.

I stayed put in the driver's seat, with half a hundred-dollar bill in my hand, while Billy helped unload the suitcases onto a trolley. After the man disappeared into the gloom, Billy returned to the front seat and I got out to stretch my legs. Deep in the dark I could hear steps halt in front of the hangar, then a heavy door slide open. All of a sudden the tarmac around me went bright as day and the slim silhouette of a low-wing, two-engine aircraft came into view. A private minijet with five windows that could carry maybe a dozen people. Its sharp stork beak swept back into fine black-and-gold stripes down the streamlined fuselage and up the tail fin to the rudder.

I turned to Billy. "Is this going to be dangerous?"

"Flying small aircraft over the open sea is never *not* dangerous. We just don't freeze or sweat as much as Lindberg anymore."

By now, the man had folded up his trolley and stowed it away in the back of the Bronco, a safe distance from the plane. Billy walked over and stuck his head in the car window to receive some papers, then quickly filled in a few details and headed toward the plane. That much booze in him and he was still steady on his feet.

"Don't think I'm doing this for Yang's sake," he shouted as he grabbed the foredoor to pull down the gangway and climbed onto the first step. "This babe here's why I go to all this trouble. You might forget me, but you'll always remember the way she sings."

A thrum of rotor torque, and Billy's babe flew off, circled twice overhead, flashed the wingtip navigation lights three times, then slipped into a seam in the night sky.

I ran into nothing but red lights on the way home. As if someone were trying to make me regret what I'd done.

10

Arriving in Yokohama, I parked in my lot. Monthly rates were a bargain in that depressed strip of real estate backing onto Chinatown, but it meant I had to walk a good half kilometer to my apartment. I was almost there when I felt the pull of some strange depression. I could either poke around for somewhere to drink, or go home. I opted for the latter.

I showered and turned on the TV A blonde detective in a bikini fired off fifteen shots from a six-cylinder revolver and jiggled ecstatically. I went to grab a beer, but decided to have a scotch and hit the sack instead. Drinking it straight amplified the whir of the kitchen fan. I usually leave it on or the sink smells by morning. Do American detectives make enough to hire housekeepers?

My glass was half empty. While contemplating whether to go get some ice for a second round to blank out thoughts of the bikinied gunslinger and Billy's destination and the kitchen fan and my skimpy salary, I fell asleep.

I woke with a start. My head hurt. I thought I was dreaming, but no, there was a telephone receiver in my hand.

"Police here," was all I could say. "Business hours are nine to five." And I hung up. The clock read six-thirty. My whole body was drenched in sweat.

Almost immediately the phone rang again. "Don't hang up, Futamura! It's me," shouted Komine, my boss. "Get down here right now. Or do I have to come for you?"

I lurched out of bed. "Here *where?*"

"A couple of minutes away, the park in front of Parklane Terrace. There's something dribbling water with a ledge in front of it," he added.

"That's a fountain and a bench. Just sit tight and I'll be right there."

I threw on some clothes and headed out the door to find Komine perched stiffly on the designated bench, though he'd loosened his tie and lined his collar with a handkerchief. The heat was fierce for so early in the morning.

"You sure know how to make a nuisance of yourself," he growled. "And I'm not your old man come to pick up after you either." He stood up but didn't even reach my shoulder. "Where'd you leave your car, Futamura?"

"In a lot. What's it to you?"

He took a neatly folded slip of paper from his agenda. Written in a precise hand were the make, model, and color of my car, along with the license number. "This yours?"

"Yeah, that's the one."

"You sure now? Remember your license plate, do you?"

I almost felt sorry for the guy. "If it was the watchman at that condo over there who reported me, then you've got me. The lot is far away, so sometimes I park around here."

"I suspected as much. My wife is always getting towed like that. But giving a lift to a key figure in a murder case, that's not playing ball. Especially you don't ferry him away from the scene, out of local jurisdiction."

"What 'scene'? You mean Billy's office?"

"Billy who?" he asked, raising his eyebrows. "The guy you said was involved with the Yokosuka freezing case?"

The very same, I told him.

He clenched his fist to stifle an outburst. "So you and this guy hauled his things somewhere?"

I proceeded to relate the previous evening's events from beginning to end. Came clean about everything save for Billy's promise to return after ninety-nine hours and the torn hundred-dollar bill. Nor did I tell him about the warning light that throbbed in my gut from the moment I saw that watchman, either.

"Can you ID her?" Komine said, handing me a picture of a woman's body crammed into a waterlogged Louis Vuitton steamer trunk. The space around the corpse was peppered with what seemed to be plastic pellets.

Dead women generally look either very young or ancient. She, however, was an exception to the rule. Flattish nose, broad forehead, she could have been anywhere from her twenties to fifties. Her white blouse was stained blood-red, but the wound was covered with a Post-it.

Why wasn't I the least surprised? I guess as soon as I realized my friend was in some kind of trouble I must have known a bona fide murder was on the cards. He'd just kept the secret stashed somewhere in his socks the whole time. Until now.

"Stabbed?" I asked.

"Undetermined as yet."

"This shiny stuff ice?"

"I'll do the questioning here. You recognize her?"

"Never seen her before."

A sudden shaft of morning sun broke through the clouds, bathing the trees in a summer glow. The rainy season seemed to have blown over.

"Your pal's car a Y-license Range Rover?"

"You tell me."

He stood up and pulled a small photo from his pocket—a video printout showing Billy getting out of a green Range Rover in a garage. "This your Billy?"

"It is. And is that surveillance-camera footage?"

"We're tracing the owner through US military channels. Know which condo unit he visited in the building?"

No idea, I told him, nor did I understand what this was all about.

"The guy doesn't rent there," Komine said, "but we found a remote control to open the garage door in the car. That's our only direct lead tying him to the condo. He parked in a visitor space. Residents are supposed to sign in with the super, but some don't bother. The garage sees a lot of traffic, half the spaces are contracted out."

"And you found the trunk with the body in that car?" I asked.

Bingo, nodded Komine.

"He told me he had an office in the building. I thought he dragged the luggage out from there."

"What kind of luggage exactly?"

I gave him a detailed description of the three suitcases. He didn't take notes, he already had his surveillance images.

"He lives on Motomachi, a place called Palm Brothers House." Now Komine took out his agenda and began writing. Seems they hadn't sussed out Billy's address. "Tell me, how'd you know there was a corpse in the car?"

"Water. A steady stream leaking from the luggage compartment."

Water? He offered no explanation. He merely gritted his teeth and held himself in check until finally his irritation burst. "Just how much did you have to drink?"

"Three or four cans of beer, maybe four or five gin and tonics."

"You fucking idiot!" he yelled for the first time. If we hadn't been in public, he'd have come at me with clenched fists. "Now you listen, don't breathe a word about this to anyone. You know damn well that's DUI Inadvertently aiding and abetting a suspect is just plain stupid. But drunk driving is an outright crime."

Then just as suddenly he stopped. I read his face. He'd already come to a decision.

"You're grounded," he said. "Stay put until further word."

As if I had a mind to go anywhere.

"Watch out who you hook up with, like I didn't warn you a thousand times! And not just women, I mean everyone. You're a detective, remember?"

To which I dutifully responded, "Okay, I acted like an amateur. I apologize for that, but that's as far as it goes. I'm a tax-paying adult of twenty years' standing, but whatever dirt my friends want to get into isn't my responsibility."

"Jackass. Now crawl back in your hole! And don't go out poking around on your own, understood? You write up a full report. In detail—only leave out the alcohol."

That was the morning of Thursday, July 20. From then on everyone stayed away from me. Not once did the phone ring, no one asked me to deliver any report or came by to pick one up. I held off on writing but nobody even cared, so I guess I knew where I stood. Colleagues on the force I had, but not a single friend. Had my only "pal" suckered me into helping him pull off a crime before flying off into the blue?

Come Sunday night, four days of drinking hadn't helped. Beer long since gone, at least I'd had the good sense to stock up on gin and a dozen bottles of tonic water, but now I'd run out of ice. Eventually I dozed off on the sofa until almost 4 a.m., but my head went on autopilot and began counting the hours all over again. Four full days since Billy's plane had taken off, four complete cycles of twenty-four hours and then some. The promised ninety-nine hours had passed. What was I waiting for? I just lay there, marking time.

11

It was almost midday when next I saw light. I dreamed the room was full of cats with bells around their necks, only it was the phone again. Komine was on the line, telling me to report to Headquarters at twelve-thirty. "And be sure to wear a tie," he added.

I took out my linen summer suit and hung it by the window, had a quick shower, and was out of the apartment by just past noon. I could have walked there in time, but I didn't want to get my shirt all sweaty, so I hailed a taxi.

The Kanagawa Prefectural Police Department stands on the waterfront site of the old Mitsubishi warehouses. No place to build a police headquarters. Hidden away on a side street far from the nearest train station, it backs onto a canal known for the occasional dead body, just opposite the quay where they staged all those brawling shootouts for "Tokyo Drifter" flicks.

Komine was standing beside the entrance. He walked over the moment he saw me, grabbed my elbow like it was a mug handle, and set off across the boulevard toward the Kannai end of Chinatown.

"Plan to reopen the Chen case?" I asked to his back. "Now that Billy's name has come up on this other murder, it might make sense to square it with the frozen guy."

"Chen or Chan or Chink, you can just pack it away," he snapped.

We came to a restaurant with a dark wooden fence, hemmed in between a disco and a Korean pub. I followed my boss up the stepping stones to the sliding door, where a waitress in a tasteful kimono conducted us to a spacious back room.

Captain Tanabe, Chief of Criminal Investigations, sat on the tatami waiting for us. "Sorry for the sudden call," he said, sitting up. "There, have a seat . . . make yourself comfortable." His gesture was addressed to me, not Komine. He sat cross-legged on a cushion, though his posture was anything but casual from the waist up. Nor did the knot in his necktie or the pupils behind his tinted glasses show any slack. "At ease, at ease. Don't mind me," he said, looking me in the eye.

"Sorry for all the trouble, sir," Komine put in.

"You go apologizing before him, what's *he* supposed to do?" The Chief stared at me again, his mouth in an inverted smile.

A bentwood lunch tray with saké had been set out for him, though his cup was still face down and he hadn't even touched the starter.

"Please let us know when you wish to be served," said the waitress, replacing his lukewarm carafe of saké with a hot one. The papered door slid shut behind her.

"Listen, I didn't summon you for a report. I already got the lowdown from Komine here," he said, glancing at the door. "We obtained follow-up intel on your American through outside channels. Unofficially, mind you, we've pretty much pinned down his destination and flight path. Only there's the US–Japan Status of Forces Agreement, and if we make an issue of this—well, you can see the complications." He gave me a dirty look. "Hell, we haven't even cracked the suspect's identity. A joker who goes in and out of US bases free as he pleases? Can't be. They're jerking us around."

He paused, eyes bulging behind his glasses, then cleared his throat and spoke again. "Plenty of folks out there just waiting to catch the Director on some mistake, but that's not going to happen."

He nodded to himself and Komine followed suit. The Director General of Prefectural Headquarters, appointed the year before last, was not popular, though both the media and halls of government had him earmarked to be Chief of the Tokyo Metropolitan Police Department before too long.

"So where do we stand? The American is gone. We have a body, but can't even tell if we've got us a goddamn case." He reached for his saké cup. Komine poured.

I knew I should say something. "I'm aware of the gravity of what I did," I told him.

"Aware or not isn't the point." He spoke across a darting glance from Komine, whose folded arms and tight lips seemed to be offering a silent bit of advice. "Habeas corpus notwithstanding, what you did is nothing special, though we're not about to let you off with just an apology. A friend asks you to give him a lift in the middle of the night, so you let a felon escape? Nobody does that. And even if someone did, who'd want to be his friend? I know I sure wouldn't."

Komine forced a laugh and nodded in agreement. The Chief twisted around in his seat to grab a large envelope from behind him, pulled out a photograph, and slid it over to me. It was the windshield of my car, taken from a height above the road, showing me and Billy through the glass in scrupulous detail. A moment captured by speed-trap camera, for some reason both of us were grinning like apes. Were we really so cheerful that night? I wished I could remember.

"The Director, well, you know how he is," chided the Chief. "Back in the Academy we were buddies, but he's up there now and I'm still here. You get what I'm saying."

"Get what?" I asked.

"Where I'm standing. My position."

"You appear to be sitting."

He laughed, then poured himself a cup of saké, though it failed to douse his unamused chuckles. "You brought along quite a comedian," he said to Komine. I sat up straight. "But in our line of work reputation is no joke. Nor can we neglect the company we keep. You should choose your friends more carefully. That much is understood, I trust." Any trace of a smile was erased in a single stroke. "Bad manners to keep the waitress waiting any longer, hmm?"

"Shall we go, then?" Komine cued me. "We're not very good at this kind of thing."

"Really?" said the Chief. "Well, I guess I'll just have to eat alone."

"Much obliged if you would, sir," Komine said with a bow, hands pulled back stiffly. "So, if you'll excuse us, we'll leave you in peace."

". . . to have my head on a platter for lunch," I muttered on the way out.

Komine shoved me hard down the hall. As I ducked out through the *noren* curtain, I heaved a sigh of relief.

"Take off from tomorrow," said Komine. "You'll be paid for the time being, got it?"

"What am I supposed to 'get'?"

"You're suspended until such time as you decide to resign."

"Me?" I asked in surprise.

"Who the hell else am I talking to!" he practically yelled. "Listen you, the Chief went out of his way to see us. Was that your idea of good behavior?"

"No one said a word about me quitting."

"Well, what did you expect? No one enjoys axing his own boys."

I started walking.

"Wait," Komine called out sharply.

I didn't. "If you're telling me to quit, then say so. It's your call. Tell me to write out my resignation and I'll do it." I kept walking.

For a long time, Komine followed right behind, but he didn't say "Wait" again.

12

A short item jumped out at me from the news-in-brief column of the morning paper: last Thursday before dawn, an unidentified jet had disappeared over Yushan, the tallest peak in central Taiwan. Local authorities tracking the aircraft surmised it was a "ghost flight," most likely a defector from mainland China piloting a military plane.

My coffee turned sour. Billy had flown off just past midnight on Thursday. They'd run the article right next to the obituaries. I started drinking before noon.

By late afternoon when the phone rang, I was sleeping off a liquid lunch. "My name is Orimasa," came a man's voice. "A mutual acquaintance asked me to ring you up." Deep and smooth, a perfect FM announcer voice for introducing Harry Connick Jr. I almost mistook it for a recording. "By rights, given your present circumstances, I shouldn't impose, but do you think you could spare a moment sometime soon?"

Suspended from the force, I had enough time to wholesale. But when I hesitated, the man quickly suggested a movie theater. "There's a small arthouse cinema not far from you. The lobby's inconspicuous, nothing unnatural about talking there. You can always say we met by chance. They don't mind you going to the movies, do they?" He seemed to know all about me, not only my grounded status but also where I lived. That alone got my attention.

We agreed to meet forty minutes later, in time for the four o'clock show at Teatro Zero in the back alleys of Isezakicho—what used to be the bad side of town, jokingly known as the "Demoralized Zone." No one calls it that anymore; the massage parlors and iffy clubs have all moved out front and center onto the main street. Not much neon there now, it gets very quiet after dark.

I climbed the broad, steep steps to the theater entrance, above a coupon-redemption center, and peered inside. Sitting on a sofa was a big sturdy-looking man, somehow familiar, wearing a silk double-breasted suit and dress shirt with the collar unbuttoned.

The clothes horse stood up the minute he saw me. "Excuse me . . . Mr. Futamura?" said the deep smooth voice. I looked in disbelief at the owner of those vocal chords, so ill matched with that flashy getup. He held out a card:

Yasuichi Orimasa

Producer

9–4 Oimatsucho, Nishi, Yokohama

When he bowed, with his two feet neatly aligned, I could see an old Lino Ventura poster on the wall behind him. Compared to Orimasa, the gangland actor looked like a friendly railway attendant.

"Nice address," I said. "That condo on top of Noge Hill? Is the whole place yours?"

"Just the fourth floor. There are only four units. We've got the sea to the east, but what with all the reclamation work down by the water, you can't see the morning sun, let alone the bay."

"You a pilot, too?" I asked, noting the chronograph watch on his wrist, a Lindberg commemorative Breitling.

"Gift from a friend. From a long way back."

"And that friend, is he alive and well?"

His manner changed. He said, "Let's drop the third-degree. It's been a decade since I walked, and in all that time not once have I had any run-ins with the police." He followed this by presenting me with a pearl-gray business card:

Arrow Planning Associates
Yasuichi Orimasa, CEO
6 Shimbashi, Minato, Tokyo

That's when I remembered. This Orimasa was the wise guy who'd made a ritual *yakuza* pledge to the previous boss of the ultra-rightist Kanto Shinseikai brotherhood, then on his mentor's death went clean and turned movie producer. He'd made his name doing a film about an actual armed heist of twenty years ago, so realistic in every detail it raised suspicions he'd been the brains behind the robbery. But this only added to the publicity, making the movie a hit. He then went on to author a string of similar crime stories, which brought him further notice. A man of the times.

"So where's Billy?" I asked again.

"How should I know?"

"You're friends, aren't you?"

"I've got nothing to hide, unlike you." He stared. I stared back and counted to three.

Slowly Orimasa brought out a smile. "Late last Wednesday, or maybe it was already Thursday"—he'd dispensed with the velvet voice—"I got a phone call from Billy. Said he forgot something at your place, could I go get it? Who is this person, I ask. Just somebody he met in a bar, that's all. Well, I don't go for that. I do a little digging and what do I find? A plainclothes cop. I couldn't believe it."

"That's funny. He was with me the whole time till the plane took off."

"He called from the cockpit." Orimasa gave me a knowing look, then sighed. "Like he couldn't be bothered to tell whoever-the-hell had my stuff to return it? There's an envelope he said he left at your place. He's a genius at losing stuff."

Billy had been sitting on the sofa the whole time that night. I'd sat and stretched out on it how many times since, even napped there. I didn't recall seeing any envelope lying around. "Well, maybe it's in my car," I told him, "but Investigations clamped it, and by now they've probably taken it to pieces."

Orimasa went dogfaced, his eyes narrowed to wary folds. He was trying to play cool.

"What's in the envelope? Nothing incriminating, I trust."

"A snapshot," he said. "A memento."

"Well, no use getting sentimental over a picture unless Billy gets himself back here. How else are you supposed to return it to him?"

"I'd take it to him. We had a date to play golf in Hawaii." The man was a lousy liar, but I didn't pursue it. He changed the subject. "Did you read the morning paper? Some 'ghost flight' over Taiwan? Billy said he was headed for Taipei. The timing and heading match."

"You think he crashed? If so, why come collect a keepsake photo?"

"I prefer to believe he's alive." He stopped and shook his head. "Call me a soft touch."

"Billy was in some kind of trouble. Probably pressured into going on the run."

Orimasa gritted his teeth, then laughed. "You mean the woman who got killed? Billy wouldn't crash his plane for that. He might have ditched it somewhere, though."

I was getting confused. I hadn't considered that angle. Ditch the plane and save his skin?

"Do you think he killed her?"

"I know nothing about the woman, but I'd swear up and down that's not his doing. Come what may, our boy's just a little too smart for that."

A murmur came from the theater hall, followed by the sound of movement.

"About the plane," I said. "There's plenty of runways around, lots of places to set down and escape."

"But nowhere you can land without someone knowing. The Civil Aviation Authority sees everything that lands on US bases."

Orimasa was a sleight-of-hand artist drawing attention to an empty cup, always one step ahead of me. I wasn't about to quibble.

Four doors opened and moviegoers ambled out looking bewildered. All nine of them.

I promised to search my apartment one more time. He stood up and excused himself, saying he'd stay to watch the films. "I've been wanting to see them."

Which was my intention as well. So the two of us sat, a few seats apart, through a French classic double-bill. There was no one else in the theater, but we didn't say a word. And when I dozed off at some point during the second feature, Orimasa disappeared.

13

The next morning, while washing the dishes that had piled up in the sink, I heard angry voices below, followed by some dull thuds. Solid punches by the sound of it.

Instinctively I moved to the door. Down in the entrance hall I found a man in a tracksuit—a sushi chef who lives on the ground floor—straddling a T-shirted young punk with a gangland tattoo on his close-cropped scalp. Not your ordinary morning scene. The kid was knocked flat and pleading, "I give up, I give up," but before the cook could stop pounding him, a patrol car pulled up with its siren off.

"Here, officer. Over here," the cook called out, only to find himself prized away in an armlock, shouting, "What're ya doing? He's the thief!"

"Maybe, but you'd better come too. We need to get the story," he was told.

The punk still lay sprawled on the floor, his nostrils bleeding. "My nose, I think it's busted," he complained to the cop. Seems even burglars can claim damages for broken body parts.

The door at the far end of the hall now opened and out came the sushi chef's wife, who launched into a rant the moment she saw me. "He's a mail thief I thought he was delivering handbills but no he was messing up the mailboxes you're a detective do something."

I told her I'd call Isezaki Precinct. Back in my apartment, I tried to think of a sympathetic ear at the station, but couldn't come up with anybody. Meanwhile, the cop escorted both brawlers to the local police box, then sent the sushi chef home with a commendation. The tattooed kid, a total stranger to our building, was found to have a sharpened screwdriver on his person, but the police just gave him a lecture to avoid filing a report.

In the end, I didn't do anything either, thanks to which the mess got squared away before noon. Mrs. Sushi thanked me as I left to get lunch. Never mind what Sato the demon detective would have done, this is how proper policemen handle things.

After lunch I took a bath, put on a clean shirt, and sat by the window. The day was stinking hot. I was wondering whether to stay in with a cool one from the fridge or go out for a drink when the phone rang. It was Yamato down in Yokosuka.

"Sorry it's taken so long, but I got a few things just come to my attention." He sounded as salty as ever, but there was a spring in his voice. I held the receiver and searched for pen and paper. "So hey, about that case happened near your place, the Parklane Terrace thing—you know, whatshisface Billy? Well, his 'sociate, some businessman named Ackerman, lives there in apartment 504. Seems like the police ain't wise to it yet."

I raised my voice. "You sure?" They'd mobilized dozens of investigators, how could they not have figured out where in that one building Billy went? Yamato knew not only the apartment but even the telephone number. I jotted it down on an electricity bill.

"The guy's residence?"

"Office is what I heard. Prob'ly import-export. Not real solid, but that's what I got."

"Where do I send the gratuity?"

He told me to save it for the next shoeshine, then hung up.

My hand was on the phone when it rang again. This time it was Komine.

"You're in luck," he said. "They found the plane, crashed in the mountains. Tough luck for your friend, but you're off the hook."

"Did they identify his remains?" My own voice drifted off, but the phone kept jabbering.

"Yeah, the fuselage was blown to bits, but they did recover the corpse. Unofficial word from USAF sources confirms it's the same aircraft that took off from Yokota. Before long, we'll get a full dossier on the guy. He had a military service record, after all. But anyway, it's over. A dead suspect's no use to anybody."

"But the case isn't finished. There's still the dead woman."

"Investigations is working on it. But that's got nothing to do with you." Komine cleared his throat, then assumed a more confidential tone. I took it as a sign of reconciliation. "How about Matsuda Precinct? Or would you rather stay under me?"

The place he mentioned was way up in the hills not far from Mount Fuji. "Hey, I could ride around on a tractor with police plates," I said. "Can I mail in my resignation?"

Komine went silent, then whispered, "What did you just say?"

"I'll write out my resignation."

"What're you talking about? You're a police lieutenant. A grade-five civil servant. These days, even Tokyo University graduates are glad to get a town-hall job out in the sticks. You're impossible. Please, don't make this any more complicated." I could still hear him speaking as I hung up.

I stepped out to buy some stationery to write my resignation on. Then I strolled over toward Yokohama Park to a diner across from the Bank of Japan for hashed beef and a beer. I had time. Time for anything.

As the sun started to sink, I got a call to come pick up my car, so I walked to Isezaki Precinct and signed for it. Nothing worth mentioning had been confiscated. I searched, scoured everywhere, but of course there was no envelope.

Back home, I retraced Billy's movements that evening. I soon found myself tidying up, which led to a full-scale housecleaning.

Down on my hands and knees, I spied an unfamiliar shape collecting dust beneath the sofa. It was wedged under a pile of old newspapers, nowhere you'd leave anything by mistake. Unless you'd wanted to stash it in a safe place and then promptly forgot it. The envelope was addressed in cursive felt pen to *Mr. Orimasa*, and printed along the bottom edge was a Chinese-sounding company name: Nanyang Perpetual Holdings, Ltd., located at 4 Honcho, Naka, Yokohama, close by the Prefectural Museum. It was unsealed.

Inside was an old black-and-white photograph, foxed and partly faded, probably taken with a tripod. Five men were posed in bright sunlight outside the portico of a stately villa. All held glasses in their hands, mostly smiling. One man, a Caucasian in his twenties, wore short-sleeved US Navy officer's summer whites. He was squinting into the light, with thin, prissy-looking lips. Another man, mid-thirties, also Caucasian and in full dress-white Navy uniform, puffed a cigar. Three stars showed on his epaulets and there were rows of ribbons pinned on his chest. Next to him stood a man with a pronounced forehead and white mandarin-collar shirt. In his forties maybe? Shoulder-length hair, temperamental mug and beak nose. Probably Chinese. Right beside him was a short fellow, clearly Indochinese—big square forehead, sharp cheekbones, broad nose. He wore an aloha shirt, his face scrunched up in a grin. Only one man was seated, front and center in a wicker chair. On the elderly side, dressed in a linen suit and tie, he seemed to be the linchpin connecting the other four. His dark skin and upturned nose marked him as Indochinese as well. His eyes, deep in their sockets, looked serious. And on closer inspection, he may have been missing his right ear.

The photo was poorly composed. The right side had obviously been trimmed away, leaving the five men well to the left of center in the frame. Judging from the rest of it, there might have been one or two more people in the shot. The columns of the colonial villa in the background rose from a riotous growth of tropical plants. On a table beside the seated gentleman was a buffet of dishes and drinks, all the makings of a garden party.

What was this doing under my sofa? Given that Billy knew where he'd left it, why would he not tell Orimasa exactly where? Or had Orimasa been shooting in the dark, hoping I'd find it for him?

I changed and headed out to the nearest Kinko's. The staffer who did the scan must have thought I was nuts, asking if he could tell when the picture was taken. "No way, man. Old tech's not so user-friendly."

Back at the apartment, I laid the photo on the table and considered what to do. Well, Orimasa's name *was* on the envelope, no reason to blow him off. It was getting late. I got hold of him at home. When I reported that I had my car back, he practically crooned in that mellow voice. "And?"

I told him I'd found the photo and would mail it to him tomorrow. Better yet, he said, he'd send a bike courier for it right away. Before he could hang up, I thought I'd play it safe and change locations. He knew my address and phone number. What else must he have known about me?

"I'm eating out tonight. Let's do the pickup at the blowfish place across the way."

The shop was a couple of steps down from street level. The ceiling hung pretty low too, but the interior was remarkably clean. The only blowfish to be had until winter was on the sign. I ordered grilled salmon instead.

The courier came quickly for the envelope. Which started the shop owner talking about the mail thief in my building. He'd had an earful from Mrs. Sushi. I passed up on an after-dinner drink, paid, and returned to the apartment. My mailbox was overflowing. The newspaper boy delivers to the door, so I hadn't checked it in days. In among all the fliers, dodgy "pink" ads, and utility bills was an airmail envelope, the sender identified as "The Red Baron." It had to be from Billy. The elevator was taking forever to arrive, so I ran up the stairs and tore open the letter. The message was short and easy to read in block script.

I'M IN SAN FRANCISCO. SORRY I CAN'T KEEP OUR APPOINTMENT, BUT STUFF CAME UP. SO I DECIDED TO WRITE WHAT YOU'D BEEN WANTING TO KNOW.

MY EDUCATED GUESS IS CHEN'S DEATH WAS NO ACCIDENT. IT WAS SUICIDE. HE RAN UP SOME SERIOUS BUSINESS LOSSES AND YANG WAS PUTTING THE SQUEEZE ON HIM. I EVEN HEARD HIM SAY HOW DYING WAS THE ONLY WAY OUT. I DON'T KNOW IF YOU'RE INVOLVED WITH YANG IN ANY WAY, BUT BETTER WATCH YOUR BACK.

I'VE HAD MY BAD LOSSES TOO, THOUGH I NEVER CROSSED YANG. I DID IT TO MYSELF, FUCKED UP MY OWN LIFE. ALL THE TROUBLE I LEFT BEHIND IN THAT BUILDING IS MY OWN FAULT, BUT I AIM TO MAKE IT RIGHT. USE YOUR HALF OF THAT HUNDRED BILL AND HAVE YOURSELF SOME PAPA DOBLES AT BRUNHILDA'S ON ME.

YOUR FRIEND, BILLY (the sloppy signature, however, was almost illegible)

That was it, nothing concrete whatsoever. More of a farewell note, a farewell to his life up to now.

The envelope was postmarked Friday, July 21. He'd flown off at midnight July 19 or just into the twentieth. Supposing he'd posted it Friday noon, that made almost thirty-six hours later. No, wait, San Francisco was over the dateline. I dialed the international opera-tor to check: sixteen hours' time difference. So Billy had to have been alive a good fifty-two hours after takeoff.

Say he refueled in Hawaii or Midway or wherever, San Francisco was just over half a day away in that little plane of his. If on the other hand he'd bailed out over the mountains of Taiwan and boarded a passenger jet in Taipei, it wasn't inconceivable for him to have reached the West Coast by Friday. Assuming he survived, of course.

I examined the postmark with a magnifying glass. The outer ring was stamped USAF APO 93272. No mention of San Francisco or anywhere. Probably mailed from a base or some other US facility. Clearly, Billy was alive through Friday, a full day after the crash.

I went to the fridge for ice, made a gin and tonic, and stood there taking in Billy's words one more time. Before mixing another round, I pulled my afternoon letter of resignation out of the desk drawer and tore it up. The scraps fluttered into the wastebasket. I filed Billy's note away in the drawer instead, then grabbed the pile of newspapers I'd set aside, a pair of scissors and my glass. Every paper had something about the body in the Parklane Terrace garage or the minijet that disappeared over Taiwan. Slowly I proceeded to sip and clip. For once, time was on my side. Time and nothing else.

14

It was a clear September afternoon. Quick brushstrokes of cloud whisked the high blue sky, the air outside was crisp and dry. I sat smoking near the wide-open window.

How long did I have to keep this damned window open? Shelves crammed floor to ceiling with books and folders, the stale mold of old paper in here was suffocating. Despite which the place was drafty. I could just imagine it in winter.

At the end of July, it dawned on someone upstairs at Headquarters that I had librarian qualifications. Back in my school days, I'd been given a bookkeeping certificate as a kind of booby prize. Thanks to which, I didn't have to ride a tractor around the foothills of Mount Fuji after all.

Komine had lectured me, dead seriously: "Turn over a new leaf and use your qualifications to make a difference there on the job." Not that he even knew where the Police Archives was.

My new workplace turned out to be a rat's nest of rooms in a decommissioned tax bureau on a back street in Hanasakicho. The building had stood derelict for years, the main entrance boarded up and stairwells piled high with cartons of office supplies. There was only me and two trolls from the Kanagawa Department of Culture. Between the three of us, we had seven rooms full of unopened boxes to sort through, so we could spend days on end without staring at each other's faces. We never saw a shadow of the supervisor from Police Administration who was supposedly in charge.

On the first day, we were informed that this project got started when the Kanagawa government agreed to budget a police plan to digitize potentially useful material from the massive backlog of files and reports—in exchange for which, the authorities in their wisdom proposed that an unspecified portion of the records would be made public sometime in the future. Fine, so there was no rush. Before anything else, we decided to bone up on our computing. Yet a month later, far from learning the basics, we still didn't have networked computers.

It was a Monday. The Giants had clinched the league pennant the previous night. At two in the afternoon, I had grabbed a sports tabloid and ducked out of our makeshift office for a cigarette break by the window in the largest room while reading the paper from front to back. A Japanese woman athlete had raced for Olympic gold, but otherwise there wasn't much I'd consider news.

For want of anything better to do, I rang up the number Yamato had given me for Billy's friend at the Parklane Terrace. My daily routine of late. I always got the answering machine and never left a message. What did I have to say to Jason Co., Ltd.? The company checked out to be a wholesale firm for imported clothes, accessories, and decorator items, registered to a Christopher Ackerman, whose residence was listed as the same apartment, 504.

Once again, he wasn't in. This time, however, there was no recording, only a sudden beep before the line cut off. Maybe the machine was full of messages and on the blink. I'd put down the receiver and turned away when the phone rang.

"Call on line one," shouted one of the trolls, without bothering to screen the caller.

"Hello, Sato here," announced the extension as soon as I punched in. "You have a Lieutenant Eiji Futamura there? Formerly in Homicide?"

"Speaking," I replied to the familiar voice of the ex-demon detective. "Don't tell me you've got a case for me."

"Well, not a case exactly, but I *do* have a favor to ask."

"I'm in the middle of work."

"Yeah, we know what kind of work."

"So where do I have to go?" I asked.

He mentioned the name of a bar in Yokosuka. "Appreciate it, much obliged," he said, sounding strangely old-fogeyish.

Returning to the office, I found only one of the trolls, dozing over the open pages of Kafu Nagai's *Miscellaneous Diaries*. The other had written "Gone to Prefectural HQ—then home" on the blackboard. Following suit, I was just chalking up "Gone to Police HQ—then home" when again the phone rang.

"It's me, Tomoda," said the voice of an NHK journalist friend of mine. Now a news stringer at their Yokohama studios, he'd started out as a crime reporter around the same time I made First Division.

"Can't talk. Summoned to Yokosuka."

"Your buddies in blue are probably tapping the line anyway. I'll meet you at Yokohama Station."

"I'm in a hurry, I'm going by car."

"If you're in a hurry, it's faster by train. Today's the twenty-fifth. Payday. The roads will be jammed."

I hung up without bothering to answer.

The upper level of the first-class Green Car on the Yokosuka line was almost empty. As soon as the train door closed, an old lady climbed up to the compartment and, pressing a hand over the silk neckline of her kimono as she caught her breath, stepped out of her neatly aligned sandals and sat down with her legs tucked primly beneath her.

Slowly the train started to move and pick up speed. Once out of the station, sunlight came flooding through the window.

"You're too honest for a detective."

I turned to find Tomoda blinking at me with those beady little eyes of his, a smirk on his compact features. He swiveled the next seat around to face mine, put his mini-camcorder bag down beside him, and wiped his forehead. "I had a hunch you'd use this line, so I kept watch at the transfer gate."

"I might've taken the Keikyu instead."

"Hardly anyone takes it down from this direction."

My head nodded of its own accord.

"But first-class Green Car? Who'd have guessed. It'll never pass on a policeman's budget."

"I'm paying my own fare. This isn't official business. I can't talk."

"Well, then it'll be an unofficial conversation." He pulled two fax pages out of an NHK envelope and handed them to me. "This morning, in a Taipei paper."

The first fax was a front page clipping, the picture smudged beyond recognition. The second was a translation. One sentence was highlighted in pink: the crashed jet was registered at San Jose Airport to a local company, ostensibly owned by a central member of the Kuomintang, the Taiwanese Nationalist Party.

"It's only now the Taiwanese authorities came out with the information." He lowered his voice, as if letting me in on some dark family secret. "You think I don't know why you were booted out of First Division?"

I smelled vinegar. The old lady had spread a handkerchief on her lap and was sampling a lunchbox of mackerel sushi from a station kiosk.

"Why I was booted out? Since when was it in the news?"

"I don't have many friends and I don't want to lose the few I've got. But there wasn't any protocol or Press Club hush-up to keep me from covering the story," he confided. "It's no secret that you drove a murder suspect to Yokota airbase, he flew off, and the plane was smashed to bits in the mountains of Taiwan. But the thing is, we still have no verifiable ID on the pilot. The man you drove to Yokota is a non-person, the incident as such never happened."

"What do you mean it never happened?"

"I mean the US Air Force now says no plane took off from Yokota that night. And if the official word is no such flight existed, our Japanese aviation authorities are stuck, literally up in the air. US personnel come and go via Yokota all the time. It's a legal loophole, but they do it quite openly. Spies are one thing, but sometimes even officers transferred to other tours of duty come through just to see their girlfriends."

He pulled out another slip of paper. "That's not all. The license plate on his Range Rover was registered to a Navy captain, totally the wrong guy. He and his family shipped out to San Diego last March, with the car on the bill of lading of personal effects sent back to the States. So why was that license number still cruising around over here?"

"Two similar cars?"

"Different makes, one number per car," said Tomoda, pushing the paper at me. "Then there's his Palm Brothers House apartment. Leased to a nonexistent guarantor, a ghost company. How come an import company that went bust ages ago is paying the rent every month?"

"So what are you getting at?"

"There is no Billy. Letting a nobody escape is no reason for a detective to take the rap. If anything, there's something suspicious about police fingering a ghost suspect. Anyway, since your Prefectural Police aren't about to go picking a fight with the Americans, you're in the clear. So you can return to the fold in First Division."

"Hold on," I said, handing back the paper together with the faxes. "I gave a friend a lift. I kind of figured he was mixed up in some nasty business. On top of which, I'd been drinking the whole evening. And I still drove him. I'm not ashamed of it in the least. A person like me shouldn't be a detective."

He sighed and shook his head, then fixed his eyes on me. "There's stuff the police don't know. Chinatown stuff. About a Taiwanese politician. A certain Li Szi-cheng, ninety-something, gray eminence in the Kuomintang. Well, his right-hand man by the name of Yang—more his arms and legs, actually—is based in San Francisco, but he's got a Yokohama office. He was just here in Yokohama from June to the end of July. Seems he flew in on a private jet." He paused, his eyes alert with nervous energy.

I didn't say anything.

He pulled out his notebook and flipped it open. "Yang Yun-shi. Shady character, the Foreign Crime Squad has been watching him for years. Departed from Narita for Taipei on July 27, but the odd thing is there's no record of him ever arriving here. No stamp in his passport, nothing. Immigration gave him a hard time apparently."

"Amazing. NHK doesn't waste taxpayers' money," I said.

The old lady had just finished her lunch. She bowed and said her thanks to no one in particular, then carefully folded up the box in its original wrapper, tied the strings, and placed it beneath her seat.

Girlish laughter floated up from the lower compartment. Tomoda jerked his head around. "At the end of July, rumor at the Club was you'd volunteered to leave the force. It sounded like something you'd do."

"I thought about it, but after forty it's not easy to find a new job."

"So no regrets? As it is, the bastards figure they've sealed your lips."

"Who's they? If you mean the guys upstairs at Headquarters, all they want me to shut up about is the drunk driving."

His expression went hard. "You don't get it, do you, Futamura?" he said sharply. "You're such a babe in the woods. William Bonney? That's Billy the Kid. Billy Lou Bonney is a fiction."

I gave him what must have been a pathetic-looking frown. He nodded as if he couldn't bear to watch. "Here, read this." He handed over yet another sheet of paper from the same envelope. "It should make you happy, at least your friend's not dead."

"Fiction or true, it wouldn't save me now."

"Fine. Just read it anyway. I'll be in touch."

The train slowed into the Kita-Kamakura approach. Railway crossing bells clanged past the window. Tomoda stood up and reached across to get his camera bag.

"A story to cover?"

"A pretext. I'm going to take a little walk, have some soba, then go home."

"That's the life."

"Just getting old." He headed down from the upper level before the train pulled to a complete stop.

"How wonderful to be young!" the old woman turned to exclaim. Was she talking to me or Tomoda, or maybe to no one at all? "Let me tell you, Kamakura's the place for soba."

The door opened below and the drone of cicadas invaded the car.

15

Trains used to run from the outskirts of Yokosuka down to the old pre-war naval port, right where Tran died in that cold-storage warehouse. The harbor is nearby but there's not a hint of the sea anywhere, only rusty sheds overgrown with weeds. You have to burrow through a succession of tunnels before any warships come into view.

Yokosuka Station still exuded that same drab old end-of-the-line decay. Painted and repainted in flat gray, the original Taisho-era wooden structure now looked more like a Quonset, but a brand-new condominium high-rise overshadowed the tracks. Anyone oblivious to the surroundings might go for an ocean-view pad here within seconds of the station, particularly commuters to Tokyo.

Walking from the station via the waterfront park toward Shioiri crossing, I saw a thick round cloud hovering directly above the American base that sprawled out on the far shore. Only that one odd cloud, otherwise the whole sky was impossibly blue. I watched its shadow slowly devour the base dockyard, then sat myself down on a sidewalk bench to read Tomoda's printout. It proved to be a summary of a Hong Kong newspaper article from two months ago, a little after the fateful night.

Secret flight raises suspicions / Pilot escapes midair, possibly lost control before crash / Recovered engine shows no irregularities, though missing rear door indicates emergency escape / Pilot identity still unclear, strong winds over Taiwan but otherwise optimum weather conditions that night / Chinese sources cite

*indications of underlying rift between military intelligence and
CIA or other US government counterparts*

My back felt burning hot from sitting in bright sunlight. I crumpled up the paper, tossed it in a wastebasket, and headed in the direction of the Shioiri railway underpass. Just this side of it was Sato's bar, literally a hole in the wall—one of three wartime bomb shelters carved out of a cliff face, the only one still accessible. I rattled open the sliding door to find an elderly woman at a far table stroking a Siamese cat. But before she could look up, a voice called out, "Futamura? Up here."

A ladder-steep staircase by the restroom led to a narrow landing.

"Didn't think there'd be an upstairs," I said.

Sato greeted me from a low table, one leg outstretched across two thin cushions. "Back in the Vietnam War days, most bars like this had upstairs rooms for the working girls and their customers. For a little grind with your drink." He poured me some beer and offered me a plate of edamame, which were surprisingly tasty. "Sorry to drag you out like this. I really ought to have gone up to see you."

"Not to worry, I've got time to spare. Time enough to index all the characters in *The Brothers Karamazov*."

He closed his eyes and rubbed what passed for a chin. "I've got a favor to ask. It's private, kind of pains me to mention." He placed both hands on the table. To bow his head, I thought, but no, he thrust out his chest and looked right at me. "I'd like you to find someone. An old hostess friend of mine. She's been missing for over a month now. Her family came to beg me, kind soul that I am."

"Did they report it?"

"No, but I made inquiries about accidents and pending cases, and checked listings of unidentified bodies. I really ought to do it all myself, but with this damn leg of mine . . ." He trailed off, pointing to the stiff limb thrust out on the tatami mat.

"She's probably seventy-two or seventy-three this year. Used to run a little *akachochin* right around here. She has a daughter—an adopted daughter, a violinist."

"Anyone I might know?"

"Ever hear of Aileen Hsu? Plays classical, but draws big enough crowds to fill a stadium."

"Yeah, I know the name. She won some big competition as a teenager, right? I thought her folks were Chinese-American."

"Well, yes and no, it's a bit complicated. I don't know what her family registry says now, but for a fact this *mama-san*—Reiko's her name, Reiko Hiraoka—she's the girl's foster mother, the one who brought her up. I was a regular at Reiko's for ages, from when I was still a patrolman. I pulled all kinds of strings to get the girl into good schools."

As soon as I emptied my glass, Sato topped it up and ordered another bottle from below. Now I remembered, he wasn't much of a drinker. His glass was still two-thirds full and the beer was flat.

"You worried about the press?"

"Hell no," he said with surprising vigor. "Suzu's not hiding her origins. She sometimes even gets her mom up on stage at curtain calls."

"Suzu?"

"Her nickname. Aileen is actually Hai-ling—Ocean Bell in Chinese—and 'bell' is *suzu* in Japanese, right?"

"Any other relatives? You said 'family' asked you."

"To the best of my knowledge, she's got no one else. No husband. Had a kid, but lost him in an accident decades ago."

I sighed. "A seventy-year-old spinster with a musician daughter, what makes you so anxious about her whereabouts?"

"Sorry about this. But I need your help, Futamura," he said, gripping the edge of the low table and bowing for the first time.

"Haven't said I'll take it on yet."

"Hey, where's that beer?" he shouted downstairs as a distraction. "And the usual for me!" Then he turned back to me and pulled a piece of paper from an inner pocket of his jacket. Penciled under the heading REIKO HIRAOKA was a short bio:

Born 1928 near Yahata, N. Kyushu. Older brother killed in war.
Both parents died in Yahata firebombing. Remained unmarried.
According to her own information, employed briefly in
accounting at US Yokohama PX, then moved to Yokosuka
Honcho and worked in a nightclub.
In 1957 opened small teppanyaki place called Rei.
In 1975 adopted daughter (then 6 yrs old) Hai-ling Hiraoka.
In 1989 closed Rei, bought and moved into current condomin-
ium: Shonan Pacific Court 301, 1-31 Nagai, Yokosuka.

"Worked at a bar in Yokosuka Honcho? That's Dobuita." I couldn't hide my surprise. Everybody knows the kind of work they did there in the Fifties.

"Sure, it was a cabaret for GI johns, but she wasn't a *pan-pan*. And she wasn't someone's mistress either, she didn't come by her child like that." He told me this flat out. "Like I said, she had a child in the mid-Fifties. A boy named Yuichi. Don't know who the father was, but he wasn't American, I'm pretty sure."

There were footsteps, then hands reached up to the edge of the landing and pushed a tray with a large bottle of beer and a bowl of sliced beef into view. Sato promptly picked up his chopsticks and scraped them together several times before taking a first bite. After the third mouthful, he stopped to bring out a photocopied map and snapshot from an envelope. "A photo of Reiko and a plan of her neighborhood."

I held the photo up close. A woman of maybe thirty was standing behind a counter holding long cooking chopsticks, a smile on her prominent features. A face that called for makeup the minute she got out of bed. She wore her hair up in a traditional bun and a full-sleeved kitchen apron over her kimono. Two customers sat in the foreground, both men in their twenties. One had on a parka with a fur collar, the other a tired-looking suit. It took me a while to realize the parka man was a younger Sato.

"The guy in the suit, is that Oba?" I asked.

"Does he look like Douglas MacArthur? Back during the student protests against the US–Japan Security Treaty, our desks were side by side in Investigations at Yokosuka." He laid down his chopsticks in a glow of reminiscence. "Those were good times. Nobody gave a shit if you smoked or drank saké by the mugful right in the office."

"So does Oba know about this, now that he's Station Chief?"

"Whoa now. We're not thinking there was something funny going on between me and Reiko, are we?" He gave me a loaded look as he polished off the last of the beef. "I wrote the telephone number on the map. Give Suzu a call, she should answer."

"Like I told you, I didn't say I'd take the job."

"Just hear what she has to say. Set her mind at rest a bit before her next concert. You know, the day before yesterday, the papers were talking about some 'priceless instrument' she's got."

"A Stradivarius?"

"What's that? Sounds like a fancy car."

There was nothing to do but take the map and photo. Sato placed his chopsticks on the table and said, "Sorry to burden you with this, Futamura. I owe you."

I descended the ladder stairs backwards. The woman was peeling garlic at the counter and didn't even look up when I thanked her. "Do you remember a place near here called Rei?" I asked.

"Used to be the next one along," she finally acknowledged. "You tell your friend Sato there, I hate customers who don't drink, just as much as I hate cops."

I went out to the street. The cliff face on either side was shored up with cement. I could barely make out where other bomb shelter bars had been. A red train raced out of the tunnel on the cliff overhead. Express runs seldom stop at Shioiri these days.

16

I called the number jotted on the map from a phone booth by the station.

A bright, clear voice picked up immediately. "Hello? Hiraoka residence." Her accent wasn't foreign at all. Maybe the intonation was a little unclear, but if you nitpick about that then schoolkids nowadays don't speak Japanese either.

"My name's Futamura. Mr. Sato asked me to look into your mother's disappearance."

"I was expecting your call. Are you at the bus stop?"

"I'm still in Yokosuka."

"Shall I come meet you? Or no, you should probably come here to check it out first."

Definitely. I now regretted not having come by car. The town of Nagai is located on the same Miura Peninsula as Yokosuka, but on the other side facing Sagami Bay. Buses were surprisingly frequent, but traffic was bad. They've been carving away at the Miura hills to lay in more and more housing tracts, but still only one country road leads across the middle, and that feeds right into a highway interchange. A recipe for congestion.

The sun was just setting in the sea as I got off the bus one stop before Nagai. I left the main thoroughfare and started down a shoreline lane along a ditch. A succession of short trees punctuated the distance. On the seaward side of the ditch was a rustic beach park, complete with fishing shacks and landed boats.

Before long a residential hotel came into view. The walls were painted pastel pink, and through the glass-and-steel front door, beyond the concierge desk, I could make out a courtyard and pool. It must have taken some doing to move up from a makeshift eatery ticky-tacked into an old bomb shelter to a layout like this.

I pressed the call button for unit 301. At the buzz, I gave my name and the autolock opened. As instructed, I took the elevator to the third floor and found Aileen Hsu standing at the end of the hall. She had to be over thirty, but looked easily five years younger in those loose cotton shorts and black tank top. There wasn't a hint of a stage presence, and yet I sensed a glimmer of something even in the dim corridor.

"Mr. Futamura?" She eyed me anxiously and said, "I'm Hai-ling Hiraoka, but please call me Aileen." I handed her a homemade name card with my home address on it. "Uncle Sato told me you're a homicide detective, so I was a little apprehensive." There was a half-smile on her thin lips, wrinkling her upturned nose.

The apartment door opened into a hallway with a bath and toilet recessed off to one side. A further door ahead led to a sizable living room whose two outer walls were framed floor-to-ceiling by sliding glass doors, beyond which a wraparound veranda looked out at the sea. There was nothing else but a kitchen and a bedroom, nowhere as expensively furnished as the outside suggested.

"You must be thirsty. Care for a drink?" Aileen asked.

"Well, just a glass. Maybe not beer, though."

She went to a cabinet for a bottle of cognac which she took into the kitchen, then switched on a spotlight above the pass-through counter and set out two glasses with ice. I walked over and sat on a stool.

"When did you first discover your mother was missing?"

"A month ago—no, wait." She came out from behind the counter to unzip an enameled leather backpack on an armchair and take out a bulging Filofax. She leafed through it as she sat down next to me. "Let's see, when a September concert got canceled, my manager booked a few rush engagements in Japan. Five concerts at four venues over two weeks, kind of like a working holiday. Well, at the end of July I thought I'd tell Mom about it."

"By phone?"

She nodded. "But oddly there was no answer. This would have been seven in the morning Japan time, no way she wouldn't be home. I had a bad feeling about it, so I tried her mobile and got an 'out of range or turned off' recording. That's when I really started to worry." She looked down at her diary. "This was on the twenty-seventh. I kept calling every day after that, but got no answer on either phone. I was beginning to panic. So first thing in August, I asked my agent over here to drop by to see what was up—and word came back that the apartment seemed in order but there was no sign of Mom. Even the concierge said there was nothing amiss. Well, my hands were tied. I was busy with recording, contractual obligations and things."

"Did they find her wallet and keys?"

"No, and I looked through all her clothes too. Nothing in any pocket, no car keys or mobile phone either." Apparently, after moving here her mother had taken her driving test because getting around was so inconvenient. The car was still in the basement garage.

"Well, let's assume this wasn't a kidnapping. She went out on her own."

"But the strange thing is, she left her purse, the one she always carries." Aileen went to the bedroom and produced a black leather handbag, cosmetics and handkerchief still inside—but no wallet.

"Nothing else missing?"

"The Gucci carryall I gave her is gone. She never took it out shopping, she said it was too good to use. She kept important things in it, and always put it away in the bottom dresser drawer."

"Valuables?"

"Stuff like the deed to this place. Silly, isn't it? But that's her. Well, now it's gone."

"And she was living alone for how long?"

"About ten years or so. Right after I went to London, she closed the shop and moved here."

"Where did she live while she still had the place in Shioiri?"

"Right nearby, an apartment just down the hill. She said she'd been living there for twenty years by the time I was adopted." There was a note of anguish in her voice, which she doused with a swallow of her drink. Then she disappeared into the bedroom and returned with a battered cookie tin. Pressed inside were layer upon layer of papers, all neatly folded like ironed napkins.

She quickly dug through the stack. "I know exactly what's where. Nothing's changed since I was living with her," she said. At the bottom of the tin were two bank passbooks: one recorded monthly debits for utilities and condo dues, along with the occasional withdrawal of a few thousand yen; in addition to national annuity income, there were regular deposits of seventy or eighty thousand from an Anzai Corporation, as well as four or five deposits of forty or fifty thousand from a Sumiko Nakazato. Aileen Hsu's three wire transfers over the last ten months brought in unquestionably the highest sums, amounting to more than two million yen, yet each time the entire amount was transferred to some other unspecified account. The last entry was on July 11.

The other bankbook, dating from six years back, showed only savings deposits, five hundred to seven hundred thousand yen three or four times a year. The last three times corresponded to transfer dates in the other bankbook. These occasional fixed savings deposits had by now accrued some twenty million yen.

"All these, are they your contributions?" I asked.

"Yes, from the time I began to make money from my music," she said, reaching across the counter to show me the cover of the bankbook. The account was under the name of Hai-ling Hiraoka. "She saved it all, completely untouched. I had no idea until recently."

"You pronounce your name 'Aileen'?"

"Mom always read the Chinese characters in Japanese—Misuzu."

"So then who's this Sumiko Nakazato?" I asked.

"A lady who used to live nearby," she replied. "Mom sometimes did sewing for her, so those must be the payments." She headed for the bedroom again and returned with a bundle of postcards. About two dozen were summer greeting cards, mostly mail-outs from places where she shopped. Three, however, were addressed to her personally.

One postcard with a picture of a flowering gourd vine read *Thanks for the lovely dress—Sumiko.* The return address was 1-13 Honcho, Yokosuka, not far from Dobuita. Another, a post office readymade, was inscribed *Hang in there this summer!—Yoshiko* and signed Yoshiko Anzai beside the stamped corporate logo of Anzai Corporation, 5-12-33 Namamugi, Tsurumi, Yokohama. The third was a promotional card for a wedding hall, with the name Takashi Kishimura signed in the margin. No job title, which struck me as odd.

I copied down the names and addresses while Aileen filed away the bankbooks in the tin. The lid wouldn't close properly, so she had to bang it shut. Which would no doubt upset the owner, if she ever returned to see it.

"I hope you don't treat your violin like that," I said. "Incidentally, did you check with the bank whether any money has been withdrawn?"

"Why? Her bankbooks and ATM card are all here."

"Tomorrow I suggest you go to the bank and have them updated."

"Updated? Can't you do that for me maybe?"

"Protection of privacy, et cetera. If you insist, you'll have to write me a waiver."

"How about I just waive the waiver?"

We both laughed and emptied our glasses.

After she had topped them up we moved to the sofa in front of the television. Among a stack of newspapers and magazines on the glass coffee table I noticed a Japanese edition of *Newsweek* with Aileen on the cover. Inside was a feature article entitled "The Ten Most Promising Performers in the World" and photos of her as a celebratory soloist at last year's Lucerne Festival. The headline read: AILEEN HSU'S VIOLIN COOS LIKE A DOVE, SOARS LIKE AN EAGLE.

There was also an issue of the tabloid *Zoom*, whose color pages were a burlesque of paparazzi snaps and topless girls. Opening it to an earmarked page, she showed me a picture of a child in a white apron playing a violin—herself age four. "They reproduced it from a UK weekly. I did the interview on a previous visit to Japan without knowing what kind of magazine it was. After that, I hired myself a good Japanese agent."

"The picture's from before you came to Japan?"

She nodded. "A few snapshots and a violin were all I brought with me. Mom says they were my last link with Vietnam."

"Vietnam? But aren't you Chinese?"

"Born in Vietnam, so probably Chinese-Vietnamese."

I glanced at her long legs and sipped my cognac.

"I remember someone taking me to a ship and boarding. Before that it's all a little hazy. I have vague memories of the house where I was born, but can't seem to recall what my father and mother looked like. Mom tells me I was rescued by a Christian group, so I guess that makes me a war orphan."

"But the violin you brought with you was yours?"

"Who knows? It wasn't a child-size instrument, maybe someone's family keepsake. Anyway, Mom started me on violin lessons as soon as I got here. Apparently I could play a bit already. She made up this story how I'd come with a Stradivarius—typical of her, though obviously she thought I had something worth investing in."

"And did your mother object to you going to London?"

"On the contrary," she said with a smile. "She'd been determined to put me through music school, but I beat her to it and got recommended for the Yamaha Master Class. At that point, Mom handed me all this money—much more than her annual income, for sure.

The overseas scholarship helped, but without that I'd never have been able to go to Juilliard. No, when I signed with Decca and moved to London, Mom was thrilled." She leaned forward, glass in hand. I caught a faint scent of cologne from her neck.

I thought of the crappy little eatery half-buried in a bomb shelter. How much income could you make in a hole like that? Not the kind of money Aileen was talking about, but I let it drop.

"Your Japanese is excellent for someone born in Vietnam," I told her.

"Well, I have a good ear. And big ones too. See?" She brushed her hair back and showed them for a second.

When I got ready to leave, saying I'd start the next day by seeing the people who sent those cards, she quickly stood up. "There's one more thing." She led me to the bedroom—Japanese-style, eight tatami mats in size, furnished with a rug and a low bed. "*That*," was all she said, pointing toward a corner of the ceiling.

She walked over and stood on tiptoe to tap high up on the tea-green wall above a knickknack shelf. "You know about these things. Isn't that a bullet?" Her tone was like someone showing a soy sauce stain to the dry cleaners.

I touched a finger to the slight indentation right below the transom. Sure enough, embedded there was a small metal cylinder, just under a centimeter in diameter. I stretched up to take a better look. "Certainly does seem to be a handgun round."

"I thought so," said Aileen with a little sigh.

"In London, is it common for bullets to be fired in bedrooms?"

"Not that I'm aware of."

"Well in Japan, this alone makes it a case for criminal investigation."

"And the police are here already."

"I'm not 'the police.' I'm just one cop. And even that's not too sure anymore."

"Sorry," she said without moving her head.

I could hear a motorboat putt-putting across the harbor. Picking up the floor lamp, I shone it on the mark in the wall. If the buried metal was in fact a bullet, it would have had to be fired from a very low angle, by someone crouching at the foot of the bed.

I moved the bed to search underneath, but there was no casing anywhere. With her permission, I went and looked through the kitchen drawers for an ice pick, then proceeded to excavate the bullethole. The plaster broke easily and a small lump fell into my waiting handkerchief. I held up the bullet to the lamp. It was largely intact, probably a 9 mm. No visible deformation or rifling grooves, though the surface was dark with rust. I hardly noticed when Aileen nosed in beside me for a closer look.

I wrapped up the evidence and slipped it in my pocket. "Did you tell your Uncle Sato about this?"

"No, I only noticed a while ago."

I angled the lamp around the perimeter of the ceiling, only to stop a meter away from the bullethole. The panel framing the knick-knack shelf had slipped out of position, and the wood bore telltale marks. Climbing up on a dresser stool to check where the shelf projected from the wall, I detected some scrapes on the crosspiece as well. "I'd like to examine the room by daylight, if you don't mind."

"Of course. I have a spare key I can lend you."

"No, I need you to be present here. This may take a thorough search."

"I don't mind, I trust you." She extracted a set of keys from her backpack, removed one from the ring, and handed it to me. "I'm at a hotel in Tokyo near work, but I'll stay on in Japan through mid-October."

She wrote down her mobile phone number for me. I told her I didn't have a mobile, but she merely shrugged. "I'm heading back to the hotel tonight. Shall I drop you off?"

"That's okay. It's out of your way."

"I enjoy driving. Music's not the only thing I'm good at." She grinned as she slipped on a knit jacket and shouldered the backpack.

Her violin wasn't the only thing that soared like an eagle, either. Aileen drove a black five-gear manual Alfa Romeo 145. It didn't take eighteen minutes from the moment we set off to arrive at the Bandobashi exit, a stone's throw from my apartment. The other cars seemed to be standing still.

Only later, when I calculated the average speed needed to cover a map distance of thirty-five kilometers, did I remember that I was a cop—and that she had been drinking. She didn't even decelerate down the whole length of the off-ramp, the lights of Yokohama shimmering like dizzy flies on carrion.

Finally she slowed onto the access road running alongside the concrete park and stopped at the first traffic light. It soon turned green, but we didn't budge. She gripped the steering wheel, then bit her lip as tears came. I pulled out a tissue and put it on her lap. Her voice broke as she thanked me, dabbing clumsily at her eyes. "Sorry, sometimes I get like this. It goes way back."

A car drove up behind, flashing its high beams to get us to move, then swerved past, honking. She slowly accelerated. "I just remembered when I first went to New York by myself, I told Mom I was losing my home again. And now, ten years later, it's maybe the third time."

I didn't know what to say. I just looked straight ahead as we picked up speed.

"Didn't some poet once say 'Three times makes true'?"

I had no idea what she was talking about, what she kept hidden inside. I asked her to stop the car after the last intersection. Across the park I spotted my car where I had left it. Only a few lights were on in Parklane Terrace. A lot of units had become vacant after they opened the case.

I got out and said good night. She thanked me for agreeing to help. "Tell me—you're the professional—do we have a case with my mother?"

"Can't say. Maybe I'm not such a pro."

The Alfa Romeo revved and raced away like a sprinter kicking off. The taillights faded into the night air.

I didn't move. My eyes were on Parklane Terrace. I'd already worked out which fifth-floor window was Ackerman's, but it was dark. Only when a taxi approached and the driver showered me with abuse did I realize I was standing in the middle of the road.

17

The next day, I woke to a normal sort of morning. I couldn't say why, but it struck me while shaving—this had to be the most normal morning to come my way in ages.

A low pressure system was approaching. Layer on layer of heavy clouds draped the skyline, yet it wasn't particularly dark outside. I took my car out of the lot and drove to work, the first time I'd used the car to get there since the demotion.

On the way, I stopped at a bank and updated the passbooks from the day before. The Hai-Ling Hiraoka account had no outstanding transactions, but the other one added a few new lines. Mostly utility bills and condo dues, except for one entry: an ATM withdrawal of five hundred thousand in cash on July 19, leaving a balance of 43,221 yen. Never before had she withdrawn such a large amount at one time. I went up to a teller and asked whether they could identify the ATM from the recorded data. She tapped her keyboard and found out right away. It was the central Yokosuka branch.

Leaving the bank, I turned into a back street just past an off-track betting joint. The Police Archives was set back from the street with just enough space for a car. I moved the No Parking cones the trolls had placed out in front and parked. At the sound of the engine, the two of them came out and lined up to greet me like salt and pepper shakers.

"Gee, a foreign make," said one.

"Ah, the bachelor life," said the other.

I read the newspaper at my desk for half an hour, then headed to the stacks as usual and called Jason Co., Ltd. After four rings, an

English message in a man's voice kicked in, followed by the recording beep. Someone had reset the machine. I left my name, home phone number and a request to please call me back.

I smoked a cigarette by a window, then flipped open my agenda. Three names stared up at me—the three who sent greeting cards to Reiko Hiraoka. I had just begun looking up the addresses in a street atlas when the reporter Tomoda called.

He gave a loud "Yo!" like he was hauling up a big catch, before getting down to business. "I met Yang last night, through an intermediary. I seriously doubt you'll make much headway."

"Who's this intermediary?"

"A politician who seems to be cozy with Taiwan. Yang's a crony, one foot in America and another in Taipei. These last few years, he's been spearheading a big development project south of Saigon, reclaiming marshland to build an industrial park and high-rise office complex. I asked for an introduction to interview him about it."

"Sure you want to be peddling a story like that? Financial news isn't your field."

Tomoda chuckled. "He saw through it too, so I just cut straight to it. I asked him, did he know the pilot who crashed his plane was a suspect in a murder case? I half expected him to deny any involvement with the plane, but no."

"He admitted it?"

"Well, he admitted the plane belonged to his company, but the pilot was a hire from an American flight operator. Said he knew nothing about the guy himself."

Billy had told me Yang was an old comrade in arms. He'd made it seem his job wasn't just flying private planes for him, but I kept that to myself.

"He said it was the first he'd heard of the case. There'd been no contact from the police. Which checked out, strangely enough."

"And?"

"Seems he wanted to know lots of stuff. So I told him about

you, a close friend of the pilot. The one who drove him to Yokota that night. Very suspicious, this guy. I played up the mystery, and said Investigations was still sorting out leads. And Yang showed more than passing interest."

"So what did you hope to beat out of the bush?" I asked.

"I wasn't expecting much, but small game's fine by me."

"Did you ask Billy's real name? If he hired him, he must have seen his pilot's license."

"It's Billy. Billy Lou Bonney, according to the US Federal Aviation Authority."

I wheezed out what probably sounded like a snigger. "So you're saying that's his real name?"

"Who knows with American families," he hedged, before steering the briefing back on course. "The Kuomintang lost the election this past March, right? Since then Yang has shifted his Asian base of operations to Japan. You know that nouveau-ugly gold money box monstrosity on the corner of Bashamichi? Nanyang Perpetual Holdings—that's our man's company."

I didn't respond. That was the addressee on the envelope Billy left under my sofa.

"There's a whole lot of shit piling up, so you just be careful," said Tomoda.

"What exactly are you getting at?"

"Up until recently, Taiwan's been a Kuomintang one-party dicta-torship. The national coffers were the party's coffers, far more so than the Liberal Democratic Party could lay claim to here in Japan. Yang has a reputation for operating on funds from untold sources and this Vietnam project of his is no exception. But with the new administration making a clean sweep of Kuomintang corruption, the man's fortunes in Taiwan now hang in the balance. Meanwhile, the Kuomintang is cutting off loose ends, disowning anyone who might be a liability. It's got Yang jumpy as hell. Instead of birds coming out of the bush, you might find yourself up against a tiger or a tank."

"Spoken like a true TV man. Climbing over others to get your scoop."

He pretended not to hear and asked me if I had an email address now that I was jobbing at the Archives. Email my ass, I told him, they haven't even hooked up our computers to a network yet. "Anyway, I can't stand any gadget smarter than a fridge and I already got a mailbox by the front door."

"You're a caveman. Least you can do is buy a mobile phone."

I hung up and ran out to my car. The map put the Anzai Corporation on the Tsurumi River in what remained of a fishing village, a hidden pocket in an industrial zone, no place for a corporate base. It didn't take ten minutes to come in sight of my landmark, the elevated trestle of a pre-war rail spur they'd built to ferry workers to dockside factories. I parked on the shoulder and walked across traffic into an alley lined with shops. A hand-painted sign read ANZAI CORPORATION above a glass door, but it was shut tight and dusty.

A little further on, the alley led to a parallel street where the houses backed right onto the Tsurumi River embankment. Recreational fishing skiffs crouched low on the water. I spied an old man mending his nets on a winched-up boat and asked him what he knew.

"Oh, y'mean Yoshiko's place," he said. "Anzai Corp ain't nothing but Yoshiko herself, not since her husband died. And she ain't been open for a while either." He told me where she lived without my even asking. It was the next street over.

I found a scraped plywood door with an oval ceramic ANZAI nameplate. I knocked and got no answer, but in a little while the door opened. A hunched woman showed her face, her features hollowed by age.

I held out my card. She flinched at the word "Police" in my job title before even reading the remaining "Archives." And when I said I was looking for Reiko Hiraoka at her daughter's request, she glanced left and right down the alley, muttering "Can't talk here," and invited me in.

The narrow room had a small cooking area tucked under sharply pitched stairs, but no dining table I could see. The floorboards were piled high with clothes neatly folded in clear plastic bags down the entire length of either wall.

"What's this now? Did something happen to Reiko?"

"She hasn't been home since late July, no contact at all."

The old woman shook her head, saying she didn't have a clue. She only saw Reiko a couple of times a year. Hardly even talked by phone unless something urgent came up. When was the last time they met? At the beginning of the rainy season, she and another friend met her in Kamakura to go flower-viewing at a temple there. Then that afternoon, they'd driven in Reiko's car to Hayama Hydrangea Park.

"Did she drive a lot?" My question seemed to catch her off guard.

She gave me a blank look. "Reiko? Well sure, she used it for work. Good driver, too. Just think, she got her license well past sixty."

"Work? What kind of work?"

She grabbed a bag from a pile at hand and showed me an aloha shirt with a hula girl print and coconut shell buttons. I thought I recognized the tag.

"Genuine vintage articles like that must fetch quite a price," I said.

"Who said anything about vintage?" She stopped herself. "Mister, these are just repro. They retail for under ten thousand yen."

"Could've fooled me. Her daughter did say she's good with her hands."

"That she is. Her work's popular with everyone. All the more reason not to run a shoddy shop. 'Course there were times back when . . . Here, take a look at this." She took a bag from another pile and handed it to me—a polo shirt with a crocodile logo on the front, virtually indistinguishable from the brand-name originals. Whole stacks of them. "First it was Korea undercut us, now China. The way they mass-produce is just criminal, got us small-timers at their mercy."

"So Mrs. Hiraoka did the sewing and you the selling? I take it you've known each other a long time."

"Uh-huh, I'm from Yokosuka too. My man was a base employee, practically middle management. Should've plugged away at that job, but no, we had big ideas. Went and opened a boutique in Yokohama—and just look at me now. I've known Reiko since then, her being so good at sewing. Made all her son's clothes too."

"Shame about him," I said.

"A real tragedy. Such a fine boy. Raised in that dump and never once got mixed up in any trouble. Everyone liked Yu. If that hadn't happened, how old'd he be now? Poor kid, had his whole future ahead of him."

"It was an accident, right?"

"Yes, a car accident, somewhere in Mexico. Dropped out of high school and off he went. Saved up all on his own. In those days kids couldn't travel to America without a guarantor, but he arranged that himself." She gazed up at a corner of the ceiling and counted on her fingers. "Twenty years is it now? Thirty? From the time she got pregnant with the boy, she saved up and opened that little place of hers."

"You know who the father was?"

"She never said a word, not even to me. Oh, there were rumors, might've been this customer or that, and back then what customers did she have but GIs? I tell you, Reiko was in a bad way. Losing her only son, it can make a person crazy." She blew her nose loudly. "But, hey, things turned out okay after all. It wasn't till she took in Suzu she finally picked up the pieces. And then Suzu getting to be so successful. I mean big time. Nothing wrong with enjoying a little good fortune, is there? But no, Reiko was her old stubborn self. Nice condo, but she lived on the cheap even more than before, still jobbing as a seamstress . . ." With a big sigh, she laid the shirt bag on her lap.

"And nobody looks after her?"

She let out a cackle. "What d'you think? Who'd look after a woman her age? And living in a condo?"

I got up to go, then on second thought I asked her about the friend who went with them to Kamakura.

"Sure, you mean Sumi?"

"Would that be Sumiko Nakazato, from Yokosuka?"

"Oh, you know her? Yeah, she was a clever one, did alright for herself. Husband was a tailor, made clothes for the Americans for years. Bought property too, on a main street where they own a big building by now."

The old woman didn't, however, know any Takashi Kishimura or his Yokohama wedding hall. All she wanted to talk about was that "moneybags Sumi."

"Why am I so poor? Why've I been dealt such a bad hand? Back in the day, we could get all the liquor and canned goods we ever wanted."

I kept quiet and stared up at the peeling plywood ceiling.

18

From where I stood by the floor-length tempered glass window, the gold roof of the Kwan Tai Miao Taoist temple was right below my feet. Beyond it spread the bustle of Chinatown under low sweeping clouds.

The ten-story wedding palace was the tallest thing around. Red granite and marble throughout, there were see-through elevators twinkling with mini-lights that boosted newlyweds skyward to a top-floor restaurant where a celebrated chef served up his signature California cuisine. Rumor had it even Chinese locals came to sample "alligator fajita spring rolls with avocado remoulade."

The manager of the restaurant was Takashi Kishimura. Tall, slender, middle-aged, the man wore his crumpled looks like a morning suit from a bargain tuxedo outlet. When I told him my business, a troubled look came over his face and he led me to a bar counter at the far end of the premises.

"I owe a lot to Mrs. Hiraoka from when I was in high school," he told me quietly. "I got in trouble and, well . . . if she hadn't put in a word with a detective named Sato to get me off with a private settlement, I wouldn't be here doing this today."

That said, he hadn't seen Reiko Hiraoka in almost twenty years, not since his father died and he'd left Yokosuka. They'd exchanged season's greetings without fail and he knew about her closing shop from a change of address notice, but hadn't realized "that little girl of hers" was Aileen Hsu the violinist until he saw her picture in the papers just recently. He spoke with hospitality industry ease, but kept glancing down at my name card. He'd probably had more than his share of unpleasant encounters with cops.

"Were you in the same school year as Mrs. Hiraoka's son?" I asked.

"Me and Yuichi were together straight through from elementary school. Which is why it came as a real shock when he died."

"In a traffic accident, right?"

"Yeah, hitched a ride that crashed. That was a big deal in those days, going abroad with little or no money. Especially us kids born near the base there in Yokosuka, we had this thing about America." He turned away with narrowed eyes, looking much older than his years.

A waitress brought some coffee. The restaurant may have served California cuisine, but the demitasse was dark Italian.

"Wasn't far from where he crossed over into Mexico. Right after I heard he died, I got a postcard from him saying he was traveling south of the border. And that was it."

"When was that, you remember?"

"Spring of my junior year in high school," he said, then paused to think. "He quit school in our sophomore year, made secret arrangements, then just left. During summer vacation. I came up to see him off here in Yokohama, he'd booked passage on a freighter. Yu died the following year . . . But Vietnam was where he really wanted to go."

"Vietnam?" I blurted out, disoriented.

"He told me before he left. He wanted to bone up on his English and enlist at eighteen. But then all that happened."

"Did his mother know?"

"Of course not," he said with a grin. "He made me promise to keep quiet about it. A green card, that's what he was after."

Out of nowhere Billy came to mind. How old was he anyway? The Vietnam War ended in 1975. Two or three years before that the US withdrew all its troops except for military advisors. Even if he volunteered at eighteen, he'd have been twenty-four or twenty-five by the time he trained and saw combat as a fighter pilot. Say he was in his late twenties in 1973, that would put him well past fifty now.

Could Billy really be that old? Somehow all those times with him seemed far off, like half-remembered dreams.

I got up. Kishimura looked at me and apologized for not being much help. "Mrs. Hiraoka, you figure she'll be alright . . . ?" He trailed off, frowning.

"Why, something bothering you?"

"No, nothing really, it's just . . . I got a phone call in June. I'd read about her daughter in the paper, so, well, I wrote her a postcard by way of congratulations. Which must have made her nostalgic, and she called me up. Naturally the talk turned to Yuichi—and she starts crying. Crying so hard she can't even talk over the phone. I mean what was I supposed to do . . ."

"When in June?"

"Middle of the month, was it? First call in twenty years, but till I heard your news I didn't think about it one way or the other. Now it does seem a bit strange."

"The conversation?"

"No, the fact that she called. And even more, crying, to me. She wasn't that kind of person at all—but then she's older now too. What do I know?"

I said my thanks and got in the elevator. The bubble plunged down its clear tube into the tumult of Chinatown. The polychrome Taoist temple was hidden behind dirty tin roofs, a sweating cook was flipping a wok in a back alley window as I passed.

Stepping out on the main street, I quickly gave up on lunch in Chinatown and headed against the flow toward where I'd left my car. The whole place was swarming with schoolkids from the suburbs and old folks with backpacks. Even the side streets were crowded with people queuing at cheap chop suey kitchens or milling about with blank smiles like onlookers at a neighborhood fire. No wonder some of the locals preferred overblown California fare.

*

My beat-up Golf looked out of place by the fancy new carport at Kagacho Precinct.

"Hey!" called a young detective, a face no one ever asked for an opinion at meetings. "You can't park here. You're no longer in Investigations."

I glared back at the startled underling. "I'm lending it to the Chief for the day. You got a problem with that, tell it to him. And don't forget to wash behind your ears." With that parting shot, I walked around to the back of the building to the Forensics Lab.

There I called up from reception to ask Notomi out to lunch. He didn't have time to eat, but if it was urgent he'd be right down. That suited me fine. A minute later he walked straight out of the elevator to a vending machine in the hall, bought two bottles of iced tea, and ushered me over to a bench.

"I'm afraid there's not much I can tell you. The boys haven't come up with anything new on the Parklane Terrace case," he said, handing me a drink. Chubby build and round face, he was the classmate everyone had in elementary school.

"I didn't come for that." I produced the bullet from Reiko Hiraoka's bedroom and handed it over. "Can you tell me the daddy to this baby? Also if possible the DOB."

He slipped the bullet in his pocket. There wasn't time to give him the excuse I'd prepared, but maybe he hadn't heard I'd been axed from Investigations.

"Recently I came across this great website," Notomi said, "an American gun homepage. Our info doesn't even rate. It's got thousands of charts of firearm and bullet data, you can even run searches. I might give it a whirl."

He saw me out to the street, then asked as we were parting, "That Vietnamese who froze to death in Yokosuka, weren't you the investigator involved?"

"Something come up?"

"The mud from the fingernails of the corpse, I analyzed it. The manager of a diner with mud under his nails, that doesn't figure. Well, I checked and there was cadmium in the mud. That and poly-chlorobiphenyl."

"And what does that mean?"

"Polluted soil. Maybe you've heard of PCB? The testing took so long it wasn't toxic anymore, but still."

"Mud polluted with chemicals."

He nodded, eyes shining. I thanked him, then added, "That bullet, it didn't come from a body. Rest assured."

"Oh no? Shucks." He was visibly disappointed.

19

I drove back to my interim workplace, then walked to a shop on Noge Avenue famous for its *tanmen* soup noodles. Every last customer was having *tanmen*, so I ordered the cheaper *sanmamen* instead, ate one mouthful, and hated myself.

The rest of the afternoon I spent reading in the stacks. The next thing I knew, the trolls had gone and it was a quarter to five. Time to wipe the blackboard, notify the guard, and go to my car. An uneventful day until, walking home from my rented parking space to my apartment building, I noticed someone hovering by a lamp-post across the way. A young dude in a double-breasted suit, no tie. As soon as he saw my face he turned away and put a phone to his ear. Something about it made me jumpy. I heard an engine rev and a big black Chevy van turned the corner.

Footsteps came running this way from the opposite direction. I stopped in my tracks and swung around to see a big bruiser of a man closing in from behind.

The black van pulled to a halt, blocking my way to the left. The door opened and an older man wearing a tie and gold-rimmed glasses leaned out. He wasn't Japanese. "We got things to discuss. Get in."

The bruiser poked me in the back, while the young dude blocked off my right.

"My name is Wang. Please come with us, we not keep you long."

There were people around in the street. That blowfish restaurant was preparing to open. If I raised a commotion, I could make a break for it.

"Yang Yun-shi wish to talk, he waiting for you," I was told emphatically.

The bruiser poked me in the back again. I climbed in. Wang barked something in Chinese and the driver pulled away, leaving the other two there on the spot.

"Sorry for late introduction," said Wang, handing me a Nanyang Perpetual Holdings card, with his name in a big brushstroke font, though no job title.

Wang then got on his mobile and spoke at length in businesslike tones. Meanwhile, the van drove through the Chinatown East Gate, under an expressway, over a canal and up to the Yamate Bluff, where a big tourist bus blocked the narrow street at the top of the hill. The driver, a suit of another color, fumed.

Just beyond the old Foreign Cemetery, we turned right down a parkway of transplanted Victorian villas, bringing us up to a homely two-story building. The brass plaque on the door read YOKOHAMA AMERICAN CLUB.

The entrance check was stricter than at a police station. The driver remained in the car. By then the other two had caught up in their Mercedes, but neither of them got out.

Wang led me inside. Sure enough, the place was packed with Americans. They had a fitness center, restaurant, banquet hall, even a smoking lounge, though apparently it wasn't an old-school men's club—I saw women and children too. Descending two floors by elevator, things got quieter. An events calendar posted at the head of the corridor listed a busy schedule of performances and lunch gatherings. "Cocktails with Richard Parr, Resident Fellow at the AEI Policy Research Institute" was fully booked at a thousand dollars a pop.

I was shown to a room with a large window looking out through the trees to the harbor. Lights winked across the misty skyline, buildings staircased the steep green hillside. Eating steak at an eight-seater dining table with his back to the scenery sat an elderly gent, looking like a Sunday squire in his velveteen jacket and silk pocket square. He slowly put down his knife and fork and looked up.

Mid-sixties, balding, Yang Yun-shi's small head was framed with long strands of silver hair. This was the long-haired man with Chinese features in Billy's photo, no mistaking that stern mouth. "Do have a seat," he said in fluent Japanese. "Mr. Futamura, wasn't it? I trust my man, the pilot, hasn't put you through too much." His beak of a nose pointed straight at me, then snuffled with laughter. His face, however, wasn't smiling at all.

"Care for some dinner?" Wang promptly produced a menu. The offerings included three beef entrées, spare ribs, chicken, lobster and three kinds of hamburger.

"No thanks. I had a big lunch."

Yang laughed again. "What is it with you Japanese? A person only has eighty-five thousand meals in a lifetime. Here's a chance for a good one."

"Where did you learn your excellent Japanese?"

"I was born here. After the war, right up until university, I lived here in Yokohama. Granted, I'm an American now, on paper at least."

"Which explains how you can use this place for an office. Must make for nice relations with the US Forces."

"You seem to have the wrong impression. This is a social club. It has no special connection with the US military. Don't go thinking we enjoy legal immunity either. The police can set foot here whenever they want to." His skin was glossy smooth like a hardboiled egg, his expression was sharp. "I like my steak with no frills. Is there anywhere else these days a man can eat plain and simple fare like this in peace?" he said defensively while dousing the last fries on his plate with ketchup. He picked one up to nibble and Wang moved in to fill his glass with Cheval Blanc.

"I'm nothing like who you think I am," Yang said, then muttered, "Let me show you something . . ." He motioned to Wang, who opened an attaché case and brought out a small bottle half-filled with what looked like granulated sugar. "Here's what I've been importing lately. White sand. I sell the stuff to local governments all over Japan."

"Special sand of some sort?"

He laughed through his nose. "Ordinary sand, from the South Pacific. As you must know, sixty percent of Japan's coastline is filled in with concrete and tetrapod blocks, and the currents wash away whatever's left, so they have to make artificial beaches. Japan hardly has any white sand beaches, right? If you're going to all that trouble, you might as well make them beautiful, as a kindness."

At a look from his boss, Wang brought me a glass and filled it with wine.

"Go on, drink up. You're no longer a cop, are you?" Yang said.

"No longer a detective."

He took up his steak knife. "You do know, don't you, where Billy is right now?"

"Up there somewhere, no?"

"Up where? Is he really dumb enough to try to play dead and forfeit his future? And you don't have so many years to spare yourself." Eyes fixed on me, he slowly stirred the steak juice and ketchup on his plate with the knife. "It's not like you fellows to simply drop me and Billy out of the investigation. As soon as I heard about the affair, I briefed my lawyers and waited, but no one came knocking. Which rather threw me off."

What was he getting at? Obviously Tomoda had painted me larger than life. "I know an NHK reporter came sniffing around. Would you rather we didn't keep him quiet?"

"Maybe it's *you* who should be kept quiet," he joked, taking a sip of wine. "I think you can guess the reason why I called you here. It's about the cargo."

The only way to hide my surprise was to cast about for my cigarettes and ask if I could smoke.

"Of course." Yang shrugged and waited patiently for me to light up before opening his mouth again. "You took the suitcases to Yokota. What then?"

"How could you know about that? Were you there?"

"Where do you mean?"

"Parklane Terrace. Number 504. The police still haven't figured out which apartment."

"You think I'd go anywhere near that place? The building's no business of mine. I have no idea what his car was doing there or how the dead woman is involved. Let's not confuse that case with my concerns. I was in Hakone that whole day for a little get-together, then I stayed over for golf with a client the following day."

"Was that the best advice your lawyers could give you?"

Yang returned to the subject without a twinge. "Listen, all I know is he made off with my cargo. That and he wasn't on board the jet, not in any way, shape, or form."

"Well, it burned up."

"Indeed, but let's not get sloppy about this. Something burns, it leaves carbon. They've recovered seventy percent of the remains from the crash site, but not a shred of those suitcases in any of it."

"All I did was drive him to Yokota. Any more about the baggage, you'd have to ask an American in a Ford Bronco, the one who unloaded my car."

"What did he look like? You remember his license plate?"

"White guy, tall, regular build. I didn't see his face, let alone the number."

What about the color of the car, Yang insisted, or any other features? He also wanted to know the size and number of the suitcases, but I had stayed in the driver's seat and didn't lend a hand with either loading or unloading. I wasn't lying.

"I sincerely hope not," he said with emphasis, "for your own sake. If what you say is true, you were taken for a ride. The man defected and ran off with our goods." He lowered his gaze and finished the last of his wine. "I'm not in the habit of indulging fools. As I see it, you're implicated, an accomplice. I have to hold you responsible."

"Sounds pretty unreasonable to me."

"You think I'm threatening you? No, nothing like that. I have a two-way proposal—you decide what's better. If you want to leave now you're free to go, but whatever happens I'll still hold you responsible."

"And what's the alternative?" I asked calmly.

"If you're really not involved, then make an effort to convince me. You have to prove those suitcases were on board that plane, or else see that they're returned to me. You're good at finding things, aren't you? Then again, if you know Billy's whereabouts, that would also be good enough."

"That's hardly what I'd call a fair bargain."

Yang made no comment. He wasn't inclined to listen to others' views.

"You stand to gain by this. I don't know how much Billy paid you for what, but it doesn't matter. I can pay you much more."

I stared him in the face. He'd assumed from the outset I wasn't an honest cop. Not that I was too sure myself either. But accepting or refusing dirty money to sell out a friend, that was different.

"Sure," I said. "I've no idea of Billy's whereabouts or where those suitcases got to, but I'm in. Only first I'd like to seal the deal."

He gave a satisfied nod. "How much?" he asked.

"Champagne?"

"Dom Perignon rosé, perhaps . . . and caviar?"

Wang went over to an intercom in a corner of the room and placed the order.

"Since we're shaking hands, maybe I can also get you to tell me about Chen," I said.

"You mean Tran. Chen was his Chinese name. Didn't he die in an accident?" Yang answered off the cuff. "I met him ages ago in Vietnam. After the Liberation, when he fled to Hong Kong, I looked out for him. Similarly when Hong Kong reverted to China, I was the one brought him here. In spite of which, he made problems, it was always one thing or another. As if I needed someone to skim off company funds." He shook his head, wrinkles on his egg-smooth brow.

I remembered something Billy wrote in his letter. *Tran's death was suicide. He ran up some serious business losses and Yang was putting the squeeze on him.*

"It seems Tran drifted into some dubious dealings. What about it?"

"I was the detective on that case."

"You don't say. What a coincidence, I didn't know," he said, then asked Wang something in Chinese.

The latter chuckled briefly and gave a quick response.

"I'm told he ran a bar somewhere down Yokosuka way," Yang said. "With a woman possibly? A needy woman is more trouble than she's worth." Something about his suave delivery bothered me. I was about to inquire further when there was a knock on the door and a waiter brought in a champagne cooler and a plate of hors d'oeuvres.

Wang filled and passed us two glasses. A faint currant scent complemented the fine flavor, but couldn't compete with the lingering smell of the fries.

"You have any grounds for saying Billy's alive?" I asked after my first sip.

"Well, you seem to think so." He never failed to return my serve. "No baggage was found in the downed plane, so the person with the baggage can't have been on board. A natural deduction, surely?"

"Was there gold, maybe, in those suitcases?"

"Gold is not one of my interests," he said, turning sideways in his chair. Night had fallen in the window behind him. The park below was a blotch of shadow, making the streetlamps stand out even more brightly behind. Beyond the docks and silhouetted buildings the background fused into Tokyo's purple glow. "It's a question of trust," he rephrased it. "The missing goods may give certain parties cause to question me, unless I do something about it. Doubt is undesirable. It's a personal thing, not really a vital concern."

I wouldn't have thought a figure like Yang would care one way or another about contracting an agreement with me over champagne, but anyhow, as soon as we'd finished the bottle he gave me his mobile phone number and sent me on my way. That same van was waiting at the entrance. Same driver, same two characters sitting in the back. The bruiser slid open the car door from inside. Not wanting to have them staring at the back of my head, I took the furthest rear seat and sank into the leatherette, trying to ignore my empty stomach.

Why had Yang waited two months until today? Tomoda's visit probably prompted him, but that was only yesterday, which made today's reception seem a little too well prepared. Yang knew about me right after the event, but maybe me being police made him wary enough to simply watch my movements. His whole spiel told me as much.

The van sped along the one-way street on the far side of the park from my apartment. "Let me off here," I said.

The younger guy relayed an order to the driver and we eased to a stop. The heavy stared at me in a meatheaded way, letting the other one get up and open the door. I had one foot on the step when, sensing a lump of muscle lurking behind me, I dodged away at an angle as a misplaced goodbye kick flew out in midair and the kicker flew with it. I left him on the tarmac clutching his leg, said my thanks to the younger one, and hurried off across the park.

My street was a cold stretch of darkness, the unlit apartment building edged darker than the sky. I glanced back. The night I drove Billy, there must have been car traffic and people milling about until nine. But tonight it was just me and a scrum of drunk company men who turned the corner as I went up to my place.

20

Without bothering to change, I took the photo out of my desk drawer. The man standing against the colonnade was definitely Yang, no mistaking that beak of a nose. His hairstyle wasn't much different either, only the hairline had receded and the mane gone gray. I took a closer look at the younger of the two Indochinese with a magnifying glass. His chin was cocked up in a grin so all I could make out was the shape of his cheekbones and nostrils. Maybe it was Tran, but I only knew him by the postmortem photos.

After a drink for better focus, I soon fell asleep, forgetting to eat, then woke up before dawn feeling ravenous. So I headed out early and walked to Isezakicho where I found a 24-hour joint for grilled fish, a meat-and-tofu casserole, and a double helping of rice. Then I strolled along the canal-bottom expressway to the Police Archives.

Properly fed, I did without my usual smoke and phone calls to Jason Co., Ltd. and had a good long laze in the stacks.

I'd been asked to write a report on the Billy business. So I did just that. I came clean about everything that happened that night except for the drinking and the torn hundred-dollar bill. Everything I'd heard first-hand from Yang about him being the owner of the aircraft and Billy his hired pilot. Also about Yang's readiness to submit to an investigation, which Headquarters never seemed to have carried out. No wonder Tomoda thought something was fishy.

I picked up a pencil and tapped Tomoda's number with the eraser end. "A van came for me out of nowhere. Valet service coming and going."

"Fast work, even for the Chinaman," he chuckled. "Where'd you meet?"

"The American Club. He's not only quick on the uptake, he's a steak-and-potato Chinaman."

"Hey, the French love McDonald's."

"His name still hasn't come up at Investigations."

"Didn't you hear? They phased out the whole thing. Some decision from high up." I recalled my strange interview with Chief of Investigations Tanabe. "Maybe Yang's under investigation by an external team?"

I had no answers. Tanabe had cited the US–Japan Status of Forces Agreement. Were other factors at play, something besides the usual in-fighting at the Department? I tried a different tack. "The day before yesterday you said something about there not being any US flight record for Billy's plane."

"Uh-huh. Inside the chain link fence anything goes. No records, nothing."

"How about outside? There's all of Japanese airspace above. Once a plane leaves Yokota, don't our air traffic controllers keep track?" Still fishing, I took out my notebook and flipped through the pages. "Well then, what about this? There's a company called Arrow Planning Associates in Shimbashi. The CEO, Yasuichi Orimasa, lives at Nogeyama in Yokohama."

"Yeah, I know. The *yakuza* turned producer, right? Well-known guy."

"Well, there's some connection between him and Billy. Don't know how close, but that night, Billy called him from the plane."

"Hey, slow down. It's my turn to ask questions . . ." As he started to speak again I clicked him off and, with the same hand, punched the Yokosuka number for Sumiko Nakazato, the third person who'd sent a greeting card to Aileen's mother. An older man's gravel voice answered, "Anchor Apparel."

I told him my business.

"Wife's out. Said she wouldn't be back today."

"Would you mind if I came by tomorrow?"

The husband seemed to know Reiko Hiraoka and said he'd make sure they were in the shop in the afternoon. I thanked him and hung up.

There was nothing else I could think of doing. I probably ought to have gone back and given the Hiraoka condo a thorough once-over, but my heart sank at the prospect of heading down to Yokosuka two days in a row.

When I showed my face in the office the two trolls had already left on their lunch break at a quarter to twelve.

All at once, telephone extensions on all four office desks started bleating. I counted seven rings before picking up. It was Orimasa.

"Finally got hold of you . . ."—the voice was breaking up—". . . in my car, under the tracks . . . wanted to say thanks, maybe lunch?"

No need, I answered, but he pressed on, how about now? He'd just left the house and was driving nearby. I had no reason to say no.

Five minutes later the phones rang again and I stepped out to find a pearl-tone Cadillac DeVille blocking traffic. Bronzed glass windows obscured the interior and a whiff of real leather beckoned the moment the door opened. I plunged into a deep-crimson calf-skin bucket seat.

"You see the dealership sticker on this baby? They don't sell to *yakuza*. Guess it paid to go straight," Orimasa said as he stepped on the gas. Again today he had on an expensive double-breasted suit and tie.

"*Yakuza* these days don't drive cars like this," I offered.

"Probably not, but *this* is an automobile . . . Are you from Yokohama?"

"Uh-huh, born not far from here."

He nodded his approval. "Okay then, let's eat at the top of the town."

The Cadillac nosed under the train trestles at Sakuragicho Station toward the Bay. Navigating the landfill zone beneath the high-rises, we pulled to a stop in the underground garage of the tallest building in Yokohama.

A private elevator soared straight to the seventy-first floor, where a thick frosted door engraved with Diamond Spa was opened by a doorman who conducted us across what looked like a hotel lobby to a reception desk, and a flash of a card saw us through.

"Great. I've got an appointment here an hour from now," Orimasa said.

A floor-length panel of glass skirted the dark blue carpeted corridor overlooking an indoor pool one floor below. Men were wading and exercising. Not one was actually swimming. We passed some in bathrobes, mostly overweight white guys. Or no, on second glance, half of them were Japanese with similar complexions and paunches. Walking through to the dining area, I recognized someone under a chandelier. "Let's go somewhere else," I said. "That's my Section Chief."

Orimasa laughed and led me via another corridor to a much less formal place. A café, he said, handing me a menu, though they served lunch specials too. Paper napkins and no tablecloth, but the windows gave a sweeping view of the entire Yokohama waterfront save for a red lighthouse beyond the tall suspension bridge at the mouth of the Bay.

We had each polished off a beer by the time the food arrived. I waited until we'd nearly finished eating before speaking up. "I met Yang yesterday. He's in that photo, isn't he?"

Orimasa looked up and fingered the scar on his lip, but he didn't complain about me having taken a peek at the picture.

"Who *is* Billy?" I went on. "You must know his real name."

"It's Billy. Billy Lou Bonney. Says so in his passport." They'd met as young bucks in Saigon over twenty years ago, he told me. Orimasa had snuck into Vietnam from Manila to buy amphetamines and took advantage of the confusion to turn a tidy profit, he claimed unapologetically. "A prescription-perfect situation. Wherever America fights its wars, there's going to be drugs. Suppliers over-produce and prices collapse. Me, I wanted to buy cheap and make a killing. I was just a kid, wild and foolish. Check out my next movie for the inside story."

I stopped listening as a cop. What else could I do?

"We'd rendezvous at a bar on Dong Khoi. We were regulars. Sometimes we'd get so wasted we'd wind up sleeping in a *sanpan* on the river. I tell you, there's no better drinking buddy than Billy. Every night was a blast."

"Must've been good fun."

"Not only that, despite appearances he was quite a hero, too. He saved my life. And not just mine, some others' as well. Hard to believe, I know."

"Not really. Even a loser sometimes does the right thing."

He smiled, but then seemed to run out of humor and ordered himself a scotch.

"A quarter of a century ago, that was. Didn't see him for ages, then we met up again these last few years. I don't know much about anything in-between." His Laphroaig on the rocks came and he drank half in one go.

I ordered a cognac. I could go straight home afterwards and there'd be no problem. I only regretted not having chalked "Gone home" on the office blackboard.

"Where were you back then," he asked, "toward the end of the Vietnam War, when the Americans were pulling out and Saigon was going to pieces?"

"In university, playing baseball."

"A jock? You don't seem the type."

"Not surprising. Never was much of a team player. Hated wearing the same helmet as everyone else."

Orimasa lapped up the last of his drink and called for another. "Back in those days he went by the name of Gilly or Guillermo Kano."

I spread a napkin on my lap and quietly jotted it down.

"Said his father was a Peruvian-Japanese immigrant. Mother was ethnic Chinese by the name of Law. In Hispanic countries, you take the combined surnames of both parents. Like García Márquez, so Guillermo Kano-Law. When he got citizenship after his discharge, he changed his Latino name, and Guillermo became William or Bill."

"Wait a minute. What about the Bonney part?"

"Some kind of joke, maybe? It wasn't difficult to change legally, no more than Guillermo to William. There must be plenty of ways to do it in America."

"I heard he was born in Alameda. And he lived in San Diego and Long Beach."

Orimasa gazed outside, pale sunlight lingering in his eyes.

I went on, "Didn't he say anything about naval training, how the Navy made a man out of him? Both cities are famous for their Navy bases."

His refill arrived. This time he drank more slowly.

"So where is Billy?" I asked.

"Let's not go there."

"But didn't you say there isn't a better drinking buddy? Or did you mean *wasn't*?"

"You sound like a TV detective. I just don't want to write him off as dead and gone. Call me a sap."

"I got a letter from Billy, posted on Friday. The plane crashed on Thursday. It said he was in San Francisco. Even if that was a lie, there was one whole day between the time of death and the postmark."

Orimasa made a bored face and nudged his chin at me. "What about it? What did he write?"

"When he left Yokota, he said he'd be back within ninety-nine hours. So he apologized for not keeping his word."

"Just a trick, he's slippery. And if he does return, you better watch your back . . . I bet it was APO postmarked. Sometimes they're not franked at all, it's hit or miss. All letters from Far East US military installations get funneled through San Francisco, then go out by regular mail to the rest of the world from there. Friday's the date it got to San Francisco, but I'll bet it was mailed on-base in Yokota before he took off."

"But why? Are you saying it was deliberate?"

He frowned. "Sorry to say so, but ..." His smooth deep voice made it all the more aggravating. "Maybe he felt he had to fool you to get away. Whatever, the truth is the plane crashed and that letter's his last testament. That's about the size of it."

I had to think. The note was in English. Handwritten, but not scribbled, the letters neatly aligned. His only chance would've been to write standing up, on the hood of that Ford Bronco. No, I shook my head, it was impossible.

"I know how you feel," said Orimasa. Then suddenly he looked over my shoulder and raised his hand toward a presence behind me.

His appointment had a moustache and round glasses. Orimasa introduced us as he held out his card:

Tsunetoshi Inamoto
Assistant Editor-in-Chief
Zoom Magazine

"Mr. Futamura, I believe you know Mr. Bonney?" he said, taking a seat. "I'd been asking Mr. Orimasa for an introduction to him."

"Oh? I wouldn't think he was magazine material."

"Nothing like that. Actually—should I be saying this?—there's a connection with one of Mr. Orimasa's novels we published, which is going to be made into a film."

". . . co-written by my friend here. Between the two of us, the book's like a three-legged race."

"I'm honored you would say so." Inamoto was grinning from ear to ear. "The story involves Billy, too. Hence the introduction. Interesting character, I'll say that. And fun to go out drinking with."

"You know about the crash?"

"Crash? What crash?" he asked, grin still glued in place.

I glanced at Orimasa, who quickly assured Inamoto it was a "minor complication." Then to me, "Now if you'll excuse us, he and I have business to discuss."

He stood up to encourage me to leave and even steered me to the corridor. "I don't want the media in on this," he told me quietly. "Not just magazines but movie people either. Lately I'm just a cog in the machine. The least little thing and there goes the whole deal."

"You mean, if word got out about this Billy trouble, it'd mess up the movie?"

"Sorry, but I got to insist." He gave me a sudden solid handshake.

Back home, I took out Billy's airmail letter first thing and examined it under the lamp. Sure enough, there was a round franking stamp on the back of the envelope, but I couldn't decipher a date among the string of letters around the edge.

I rang up a woman I'd met on a previous case, who worked at the US Naval Air Facility in Atsugi. She was able to confirm the story: all mail posted on base, even letters to Japanese addresses, were channeled to the APO sorting center in San Francisco, then went out worldwide via regular mail. The military mail sack to San Francisco was faster than conventional carriers, but after that it was ordinary airmail.

"So, sure," she said, "the postmark's probably a day or two later than the day it was mailed."

I sat on the carpet for a long time holding Billy's letter in my hand. I'd lost all proof he was alive. Even supposing, as Orimasa suggested, he'd used me to make a getaway, what was the point of the note? Why dash something off on the hood of a car after making a promise? Why bother making a promise in the first place? Or if not then, when and where the hell could he have written this letter?

21

Anchor Apparel Ltd. was right across from the main gate of Yokosuka Navy base on Route 16, a proverbial stone's throw from a police box and Naval MP guard post. Which made this the safest address in town despite backing onto Dobuita Street. The shop window displayed various eye-catching leisure wear items under a sign boasting WORLD'S NUMBER ONE ORDER-MADE ALOHA SHIRTS.

Half the place consisted of a raised tatami-mat work area where a sinewy old tailor looked up from his sewing machine as soon as I entered. He turned to shout "Sumiko!" then had me know he used to do bespoke suits. And had quite a reputation too, his wife came in to say. "He hates alohas, but they're so popular."

Sumiko Nakazoto was on the chubby side, maybe a little older than the proprietress of Anzai Corp. "Yoshiko called me," she said, wiping her hands on the back of her apron before offering me a cushion. "Honestly, where could Reiko have got to?" She cocked her head to one side. "I mean it's just so odd, her not answering the phone and all."

"She have any work pending?"

"If she did I'd have gone to her condo myself. This being the end of summer, aloha season, and all these Americans coming in by the shipload."

"Did Mrs. Hiraoka make most of the shirts?"

"No, only the real fancy ones. Specialty numbers, the kind made from antique fabric, they can go for amazing prices. Reiko does repros, she's real skilled."

"So the last time you saw her would've been when you went to Kamakura?"

Sumiko gave it some thought, hand pressed to her cheek as if taking her temperature, then shook her head. "No, it was two months ago, middle of July, I guess. I saw her one evening right near here, but she got in a car before I could say hello."

"Her car?"

"No—which was, well, surprising. But there was no mistaking it, her car's a bright red station wagon."

"She means a hatchback," her husband interjected. "Second-hand company car, red paint job, bought cheap from a local dealer."

"I know *that*," she waved away his comment. "That's why I'm sure. This one was completely different."

"What're you talking about? That wasn't Reiko Hiraoka. I saw the woman myself. Why on earth would she go for a drive in something like that?"

"Was too. I've got the better distance vision."

"What kind of car was it?" I put in.

"A minivan," said the husband, no longer at his sewing machine. "Painted in—what's it called?—like a tank."

"Camouflage?"

"Yeah, like in the Gulf War."

"Where did you see it?"

Sumiko fought to get a word in. "Right nearby. We were walking along the Central Station shopping street, you and me. Remember? That's when that funny-looking car pulled up and Reiko got in. On a side street by the Seiyu store."

"Impossible. No way would she be getting into a guy's car like that."

"So the driver was a man?"

"Yeah. Short, scruffy-looking character," he said. "And the car was a—what's the make?—one of them four-wheel drives, a Suzuki WagonR."

"Oh c'mon, you hardly saw him, and from behind at that," scoffed Sumiko.

"Any idea of the exact date?"

"The nineteenth probably. Anyway before the twentieth. From the twentieth I'm tied up making payments, no time to be mooning about with the wife here."

"Really, is that any way to talk in front of others?"

The husband huffed and muttered something about police investigators homing in on small details. Yoshiko Anzai must have mentioned my police background when she called.

Anyone going from Yokosuka to the condo in Nagai might drive by the Seiyu grocery chain store, then head off past the Central Station. I turned the corner at Seiyu and drove dead slow looking for a place to park, until I saw—straight ahead—the local bank, the Yokosuka Central Branch where Reiko Hiraoka had her accounts. I stopped and checked the sign. Here was the ATM where she withdrew five hundred thousand yen on July 19. My mouth went dry. I should have had Mr. Nakazato draw a sketch of the man he saw, the "scruffy-looking character" in the camouflaged wheels. So much for my detective know-how.

Pulling out onto the bus route, it took a good hour to reach the Hayashi roundabout in slow-moving traffic, but beyond that I passed only a few cars in the opposite lane, until suddenly I could smell the sea. Last time I didn't even notice. Was the tide different that day? Trees swayed their branches in the salty breeze as if waving handkerchiefs. I parked under a great big green nose rag.

When I opened the electronic front door lock with the key I'd borrowed, an old man checking the mailboxes turned around in alarm. Pale and thin, he wore a four-button gray tunic somewhere between a uniform and a suit. "Visiting someone?" he asked. He let me know he was the superintendent, adding by way of justification, "Residents don't like gettin' fliers from those massage parlor places. Some even complain about pizza handbills."

"Most of them here only on Sundays?"

"That was the idea. Supposed to be 'weekend accommodation' so I'd have the rest of the week free. Not on your life. Nothin' but old folks with too much time on their hands." He glanced at me in recognition. "Say, aren't you the guy come to see about Mrs. Hiraoka in 301? Daughter told me. Police, right?"

"Yeah, but this isn't police business, it's a private matter," I clarified. "The last time you saw Mrs. Hiraoka, you know when that was?"

He had me wait by the reception counter and went into his office, a plain six-mat tatami room. Scooping up a stack of printed papers from a low plywood table and tossing them into a cardboard box in the corner, he pulled out a collegiate notebook from underneath. "Can't tell you exactly," he said, flipping through the pages. "End of July was when I was asked to stop the newspaper delivery. That's near as I know."

"Asked by whom?"

"The daughter. She called and I told her the papers were pilin' up, so she got me to have 'em stopped. Then in August, this fellow came by on the daughter's behalf and we opened the unit, but wasn't anything specially out of place."

"She have any friends among others here at the condo?"

"Well, folks here all say hello. But hardly anybody even uses the pool—just sometimes in summer, family relations come barging in with kids." He laughed. "Some folks rarely show at all, they just let it all go to waste."

"Did anyone else have access to Mrs. Hiraoka's unit?"

"No, not a soul. She got very few deliveries. Still she couldn't've just disappeared. The lady was an adult, she wouldn't do anything foolish."

"Adults do foolish things, too. And things do sometimes get nasty."

The super lowered his voice to a whisper as if turning down a volume knob. "Think it might've been loan debts?"

"You got any reason to think so?"

"N-no. Just wondering 'cause you asked." And he hurriedly shut his notebook.

I took the elevator up to the third floor. Opening the door to 301 with the second borrowed key, I put on cotton gloves and went through every drawer in the living room and kitchen. The woman was a real neatnik. Everything was in its proper place, nothing but writing supplies in the desk, only dishes in the cupboard. After sifting through it all, one crucial fact came to light: there wasn't a single account ledger or address book in the place. Had someone walked off with them? That would be the natural conclusion.

The only notebook I found had a Miffy bunny on the cover. The entries were scribbled and loop-de-looped every which way, and in the margins were cartoon figures of starry-eyed girls with kitty-kat ears and gingham aprons. Probably something of Aileen's from when she was a child.

Naturally I didn't turn the whole apartment upside down. A quick peek in her closet was enough to discourage me. More of a jigsaw puzzle or Lego barricade, boxes large and small were wedged in so tight you couldn't poke in a finger. Pull one out and they'd all come tumbling down, but even before that you'd have to loosen them somewhere or nothing would budge. Probably there was a set order to disassembling it.

This wasn't my first closet like this. I'd had challenging encounters in other spinsters' apartments, and experience told me the contents of the boxes would be ribbons and string and wrapping paper and fabric remnants and folded empty bags.

I opened a small cabinet at the base of the shoe rack in the entryway. Just as I thought, inside were cord-tied bundles of old magazines. No newspapers. I went back to the kitchen, then to the bedroom, opening this and that. Finally I found the missing newspapers neatly stacked behind a recessed panel under the sink.

On the very top of the papers was the July 18 evening edition. Was it her habit to fold them up before going to bed?

I went out to the sofa and checked the few newspapers squared up on the glass coffee table. There were four of them, from the July 20 morning to the July 21 evening editions. Someone had been here till then. Only the ones for the nineteenth were missing. Something wasn't right, but what? I just stood there thumbing through the magazines on the table, then went back to the bedroom and pulled off the coverlet. A lump on the bed I'd noticed last time proved to be a crumpled pair of women's pajamas, about the only sign of a real, live resident in the place.

A small reading lamp and ashtray sat on a bedside table with no room for much else. No cigarette butts, though the ashtray was indelibly stained from tar. A cordless extension phone occupied a lower shelf. I picked up the handset and pushed REDIAL. The entire five-number memory queue had been erased. Just to be sure I tried the main landline, but all dial records had been deleted from it as well.

Something still bothered me, something wasn't here. I opened the wardrobe and went through the clothes, what few there were. The pockets had been picked clean, there wasn't one speck of lint. Below the dresses and blouses on hangers were two chests: a largish footlocker densely packed with sweaters and underwear, and a Korean lacquered-wood *tansu*, a bit scuffed but probably the only furniture of any value. This antique held various aloha shirt supplies and notions, as well as a sewing machine in a double-door upper compartment. In a tiny lower drawer was a Nissan car key tethered to another funny little key—maybe spares of some sort. I pocketed them both and left.

The elevator went only as far as the ground floor; there were no stairs from the lobby to the garage. You had to detour outside the building and down a slope to a tiled gateway barred by an aluminum shutter. It wasn't locked, so I cranked it up.

An irate voice assailed me from behind. "Hey, you there! You come around here before?" An old man in a green polo shirt stood scowling at me.

"And while we're at it, who might you be?"

"Shimazaki, from 204," he said, pushing up his bottle-thick glasses. "What's *your* business here?"

I gave him my name and said I was an acquaintance of Reiko Hiraoka.

"Mrs. Hiraoka, you say? Guess that's alright then." His expression relaxed a bit.

"Anything the matter?"

"Well, only that some strange people have been traipsing through a whole lot lately. A bunch of rowdies they were, too. Why, just last month I saw three or four Americans partying in the pool. Black and white guys together, GIs they were. The rules are, guests of residents get free use of the pool, so I guess we got it coming, but . . ."

"And the super doesn't do anything?"

"He's useless, he is, pathetic. Can't even clean either, just bumbles about. And what's with the lights on in that vacant ground floor unit? Downright spooky."

"Maybe it was a realtor showing the place?"

"Late at night? I ask you."

"When was this?"

"Let's see, middle of July maybe? Those foreigners making the racket was in late July. I'm pretty sure—I had my grandkids visiting at the time." The old man said he wanted to take up the issue with the homeowners' association, but few of the other residents showed any interest. On that score Reiko Hiraoka was more conscientious. "How is Mrs. Hiraoka? Haven't seen her around lately."

I told him she was away on a long trip.

"To London?" he asked, so I nodded vaguely. "The daughter was always inviting her, but she hates flying. What's with that? When she was a lot younger, she flew to Hawaii in a Navy cargo plane and got in a heap of trouble, she said."

Now this was news. A woman telling that story around Yokosuka was as good as admitting what she did for a living as a girl.

"Nothing fancy or phony about her, she's the real thing." The old man smiled and bowed, then walked away, bent over in an arthritic slouch. I waited until he was out of sight before pushing up the shutter the rest of the way and heading inside.

The garage was bigger than it looked from the entrance. On either side were rows of two-level parking lifts, four cages of five pallets each, all about half full. I didn't have to search for her car, it was the only domestic compact. Otherwise there were half a dozen Mercedes and economy BMWs, the rest mostly hulking SUVs.

Reiko Hiraoka's red Nissan Sunny perched on the upper pallet of the furthest cage at the back. The funny little tethered key worked the lift. I lowered the car, unlocked the driver's seat door, and the first thing I saw were footprints. Muddy blurred outlines that stood out in bold against the well-scrubbed gray floor mat.

The battery still had juice in it. I took the car out of the dark garage, careful not to step on the footprints, and parked on the street in the sun where I could examine the interior. A woman's wallet and summer cardigan lay tossed on the passenger seat.

I had a bad feeling. Reluctantly, I emptied out the contents of the wallet—about thirty thousand yen in currency, plus various smoothed and tidied receipts. The credit cards and driver's license in their separate slots belonged to Reiko Hiraoka. She'd probably just grabbed whatever and flown out the door without a handbag. She must have been in just as much a rush when she came back.

The cardigan had two pockets. I leaned over to search them when I spied something shiny in between the passenger seat and gear shift console. From down in the crack I pulled out a silver mobile phone with a black leather strap. It wouldn't switch on, the battery was dead. I wrapped the thing in a handkerchief and slipped it in my jacket. One cardigan pocket yielded a memo jotted on a scrap of newspaper:

Tran Kaput Route 16 behind bakery

A fuse burned in my head. Out of nowhere, Reiko Hiraoka's July 19 and my July 19 crossed wires and shorted. On her busy July 19, she drove this car to meet the scruffy character, switched to his camouflage wheels and withdrew five hundred thousand yen from the bank, then hurried home in a panic. On my July 19, I'd watched the Giants on TV, got interrupted by Billy showing up, then saw him vanish into the sky. Both scenarios tied in neatly with the names Tran and Kaput.

22

I left the car at the curb and went back to the condo. The sun was still high, cutting dark shadows at the overhanging ledge of each unit. From far off came the sound of traffic on the main road.

There was no sign of the superintendent, only a plastic ON PATROL placard sitting on the office counter. I leaned over to take a look inside. The low table was now piled with more bundles of printed material. If I strained my eyes I could just make out the words *Important Survey on Residents' Quality of Life*, probably a mailout from the management to the homeowners.

A short passage at the far end of the elevator hall led to the court-yard. I opened the glass door and stepped out onto a faux-terracotta patio. A juniper hedge shielded the kidney-shaped pool from prying eyes. Still, even here at the back of the building, away from all the sea-facing verandas, a rowdy late-night group might well disturb the residents.

Just then a dog barked on the other side of the hedge, echoed by some guy growling, "Get down, dammit! Scram!"

A wallop made the dog whine, followed by a shout: "Go! Gagarin!" Suddenly a scruffy shape came flying over the hedge and raised a column of spray in the pool. As the water stilled, the dog paddled its short legs over to the side and tried twice to climb out before finally succeeding. Long tongue flapping, a gray-and-black mongrel of a bull terrier stood there shivering on the drenched patio.

I retraced my steps back through the lobby, around the side of the building, and out to the street. I heard deep throbbing music with a boom bass line I could feel in my gut. It sounded like a pachinko parlor on wheels. A General Motors pickup truck rolled by. The chrome gleamed, the body was painted eyesore yellow. The man in the driver's seat turned toward me in passing, but I couldn't read his face through the bronzed window glass.

Walking further I came to the juniper hedge. It was taller than I thought, too high for a person to throw that dog over unless maybe from the back of a pickup. The area behind the condo was residential, mostly two-story woodframe apartments built to resemble single-family homes. There were commercial awnings and *noren* shop curtains on some of the buildings, even a sign for a newspaper delivery service. Chickens pecked at the ground beneath the eaves of a small-time contractor's office amidst a jumble of plumbing supplies. I didn't see a soul anywhere.

I heard a rustling. Under the low branches, the pool cosmonaut was groveling through a gap in the hedge.

"Here, boy," called a cool voice from behind. A slim woman with shopping bags in both hands was giving me the once-over. Gagarin plodded toward her feet.

"That your dog?" I asked.

"Why? He bother you?" The woman was in her late thirties and seemed tired, eyes squinting against the glare.

"Just now, he dive-bombed the swimming pool in there."

Her face clouded over. She crouched down and petted it. "Ooh, you poor thing. Got all wet, did you? How did that happen?"

"Somebody threw him in." I couldn't help noticing there was a glint of blood by her feet. She wore mules, but her feet weren't cut anywhere I could see.

The woman noticed it too. "Ye-ow, whose blood is that?"

"Is your dog a fighter?"

"Not at all. He's a softie, this one."

Her hand flinched and the dog slipped away under the Sunny.

"Hey, isn't that Mrs. Hiraoka's car?" she said, more to herself than me.

"You a friend of hers?"

"I should have introduced myself, sorry. My name's Ukita, from right nearby."

"And I'm Futamura, Eiji Futamura. Mrs. Hiraoka's daughter asked me to run the engine so the battery doesn't go down."

"Her daughter? Then you must be in music."

"Not music, more like cultural affairs. Sent by City Hall."

"Mm, that so?" She tilted her head. "I've been worried, haven't seen her for ages."

I refrained from comment. Meanwhile she walked over to the car and crouched down to look for the dog.

"Have you known Mrs. Hiraoka a long time?"

"My father runs that place." She pointed to a *noren*-curtained doorway hung with a paper lantern advertising "Izakaya Cuisine." Gagarin surfaced by the shop and gave a short bark. "More like home cooking," she said, smiling at the dog. "Dad used to be a fisherman, but stuff happened and he got landed. Mrs. Hiraoka was a godsend."

"She did catering?"

"No, she was just a good customer. Sometimes for dinner, when she wanted company." Still smiling, she fingered her collar with half-closed eyes. "She came in not so long ago for sashimi."

"Oh? When was that?"

"In June, on her way home from shopping. Carrying lots of drinks and groceries, like she was having some people over."

"What date in June, you remember?"

"Well, a look at the receipts would tell—is it important?"

"No, not really. I was just wondering."

The dog barked again and she responded with an I'm-coming wave.

"By the way, is there a customer of yours who drives a yellow pickup?"

She stopped and turned toward me. "No, but I've seen the truck around a lot lately. Bright yellow, right?"

With a quick goodbye, she disappeared into the *izakaya*, but the dog stayed put in the street watching me. The woman had introduced herself only as Ukita. Like Billy said, Japanese never give you their full names. She hadn't told me Gagarin's real name either.

23

The setting sun gilded the rear-view mirror as I eased down the exit ramp to Yokosuka. I hung a U-turn at the light by the Navy base, doubled back to the bakery, and left the car at the corner while I took a look around. The alleyway was surprisingly unchanged. The shop sign and neon were still in place, though the heap of cardboard boxes where Billy sat crooning that first night had largely been cleared away to reveal a big trash bin marked KAPUT. In it was some food waste—pear cores and banana skins, still half fresh.

When had Reiko Hiraoka written that *Kaput Route 16 behind bakery* memo? On July 19? Or on some other day with no connection to Billy and me?

I tried the doorknob, but of course it was locked. Stupidly, I even knocked, as if anyone would answer. The power company had already turned off the electric meter.

That's when I heard someone shouting, "Hey! You wanna move your crate? You're blocking my kitchen door!" The man from the bakery was standing guard at the head of the alley. Then he recognized me. "I've seen you before. Police, right?"

"People park here often?"

"A lot fewer since the incident, but yeah," he said. Different kinds of cars, but no camouflaged WagonR or red Nissan Sunny, apparently. "Sometimes I think somebody's been poking around, going in and out."

"Who manages the property?"

"Some real estate company up in Yokohama. Your police buddies did their plastic wrap, but that's it. What's the story?"

I moved my car a few meters up the street and walked to Dobuita. It was too early for Yori to be at the club yet. One of the girls rinsing glasses while watching the Olympics on TV called her home phone and mobile for me, but she didn't pick up. She'd been like this lately, the girl shrugged. "Mama's gone head over heels."

No matter how often I heard Yori called "Mama" it still bothered me. I beat a quick retreat and kept walking as night and rain began to fall together. The dark tarmac glistened, yet the sky to the west was still strangely sunlit.

The rain didn't stop the following day, thanks to which water somehow seeped onto the Archives' floors, and boxes of papers were getting soaked. There was nowhere to move things except the corridors and stairs.

We stacked boxes to near ceiling height, reducing the corridors and stairwell landings to barely half their width. As the windows got covered up, the place grew gloomier than ever. It was close to 4 p.m. when we finished moving stuff. The two trolls helped straight through without a break; they even seemed to think it was fun.

With the wet floors now stripped bare and only occasional drips to be heard, I decided to ring up a contact at the City University Medical Department who supposedly did the forensic report on the knifed body found at Parklane Terrace in July. Luckily he was in his cubicle.

"I thought you'd never ask," Kakei laughed. Then, lowering his voice, he said Forensics were sworn to secrecy, but no one could stop him from having dinner with an old friend. "And if someone's treating, the talk comes easier."

We decided on a meeting place and I hung up. While I was thinking what to do next, the phone rang. It was Tomoda, who apparently had tried to get through to me earlier, and begged me to go buy a mobile. "There's simply no excuse. If it didn't count as bribery, I'd give you one myself."

"I've got a snapshot of Yang together with a few other people," I told him. "Can I trust you to find out who else is in the picture without asking questions?"

"You're not expecting much, are you?"

"If you can identify everyone, I'll tell you where and how I came by it."

"Reminds me of when my old man said he'd buy me a bike if I scored 100 in math."

"And did he?"

"I got 98 and he shortchanged me with a model kit." He said he'd send a courier for the photo. "Be at your place in an hour and a half for the handoff."

I returned to the apartment to shower and the bike came right on the dot. Then I put on a suit just back from the cleaners and stepped out.

The rain began to let up at dusk. Silent as mist, it merged into the night. I walked to Chinatown without an umbrella. The restaurant was off a side street past the Kwan Tai Miao temple, down an even smaller alley.

Kakei was already there, nibbling Chinese pickles along with his beer. Big and solid, but those old-fashioned Harold Lloyd glasses on that round face made him look like a kid. "In August, I met with one of your young staffers, the one everybody calls the Runt," he said, waving his chopsticks. "You know what he said? He said the Department made a human sacrifice of you. Ancient proverb, 'Punish one, warn a hundred.'"

"Meaning what?"

"What with all the funny business in the force, they had to put on a show of screwing someone who bucked the system."

"Well, they're going about it ass backwards. Keep shoving the system down our throats, we lose all drive. Take initiative away from the cop on the street, solving crimes goes way down. Plain and simple common sense."

"I'm not the one who said it, he did. He was worried."

"Since when did the Runt ever worry about anybody?"

A braised pig trotter arrived at the table. He deftly stripped the meat off the bone with his chopsticks, then had another go at his beer. "They're crooked—cushy, corporate, and corrupt the lot of them. Your frozen stiff down in Yokosuka's a prime example. First Dr. Kito has a go, and it's a drowning. Where the hell do you get a drowned man with the skin peeled off his back?"

I nodded and called out my order to the proprietress, who was busy watching synchronized swimming on TV Kakei eyed me quizzically, then addressed the trotter with his chopsticks again.

"So then that old-school detective takes a stab at it and the stiff gets farmed out to my classroom. Know what one of your colleagues said? He complained how the old duffer was making extra work for the Precinct. That's the reality of your organization."

He wriggled his head in dismay. "Stop me if you've heard this, but the weird thing is, the guy gets locked in a freezer but shows no sign of trying to escape. Normally you'd see scrapes and bruises on the arms and legs. And, as a rule, if you're freezing to death, you curl up, you don't lie flat on the floor."

"So where does that leave us?"

"Let's say, for argument's sake, someone punches you in the liver and you pass out. Or maybe you've been drugged unconscious. Frozen and thawed, four days later, there won't be any trace. That much I can tell you."

My food came—red cooked oxtail and a shot of *lao chiew*—while Kakei ordered another beer and some pork shank noodles.

"So you think it was homicide?"

"Well, we don't usually do CT scans or screen for drugs. On top of which, the stiff was already thawed for four days." He sipped his new beer and gave me a go-ahead gesture with his glass. "Your turn now. What was it you wanted to ask?"

"About the corpse they found in the garage at Parklane Terrace. You cut open the woman, right?"

"Dare I say it? . . . Isn't this why you quit Headquarters? To clear your friend of the accusations?"

"That night I was driving under the influence. For which I got booted out of Investigations. No recourse. But that still leaves a lot to explain. I just want to get my head around this, for my own sake. Whether or not he killed her, regardless."

Kakei heaved a sigh. "Same difference. Either way, you're out."

His order arrived, the noodles and pork served separately. Taking a chopstick in either hand, he proceeded to dissect the second pig's leg.

"Don't you ever get tired of that?" I asked.

"Tastes different. This one's simmered in soy." He switched both chopsticks to his right hand, holding the bowl with his left to slurp the noodles, slick with jellied pork fat. "The evidence showed cause of death: single knife thrust. Either the assailant was very practiced or very lucky. The blade slipped under the breastbone without hitting any other bones and went right through her liver. Instantaneous organ failure." He lifted the pork shank at the foot end. "If it's not well-cooked, this part is inedible."

I asked how old she was. The papers only mentioned a middle-aged woman and it was hard to guess from the photo the Section Chief showed me. Kakei thought probably thirty to forty.

"You sure? No possibility she was older?"

"Why would you think so?"

"There's a seventy-something woman who's disappeared. I found a memo linking her to this other case."

Kakei put down his chopsticks. "Individual age differences can be big, but no, she couldn't have been over sixty. That and the fact that she had no BCG vaccination scar. Nine-and-nine-tenths odds she wasn't Japanese."

My nod must have looked disappointed, because in consolation he added, "The woman had a bomb in her head, shrapnel from a grenade or artillery shell. There was an old surgical scar above her right ear, so we took an X-ray. Didn't see any connection to the cause of death, but it made me curious, so I opened her up and out it came. They probably weren't able to extract it from such a touch-and-go place." Kakei picked up the pork shank in his hand and sucked the whole length clean. Every last drop of the noodle soup was also gone.

"Think it disabled her?"

"I doubt it. People can go on living unaffected even with foreign matter lodged in their brain. You've heard those tales of samurai who lived for years with an arrow through the forehead." He tossed away the bone and gave a deep belch of satisfaction. Then, rubbing his belly, he stole a bite of my oxtail, before offering me one last comment. "Very likely she had bad headaches. It was awfully close to the brain stem. She might not have been long for this world."

"A terminal case?"

"Without surgery. But removing the shrapnel would've taken incredible skill. David Copperfield magic." He chortled happily. It took a second before I realized he wasn't talking about the Dickens character.

24

After Kakei and I parted company at the head of the alley, I bought some lilies at a florist. The area was flush with gawking tourists not buying anything. I found an overlooked lane and cut across Chinatown to the ginkgo-lined boulevard out by Yamashita Park. A damp wind was blowing in from across the docks.

I'd seen a poster earlier for a concert Aileen was giving at Kenmin Hall, slapped with a SOLD OUT sticker. I arrived just at encore time. I told the doorman I was a friend of Aileen's, and while waiting I heard a long round of applause and a short sonata. A few minutes later I was shown into her dressing room.

She was wearing a thick cardigan over a black silk stage gown. I handed her the bouquet, which earned me a smile every bit as lovely. "First flowers this evening."

"Just a prop for gate-crashing."

Her smile widened and I apologized for showing up unannounced. "I don't want to take up your time, but there's something I have to tell you."

"If you don't mind hanging around a bit, I'll have all the time in the world." Without waiting for an answer, she grabbed the bouquet and her violin case and left the dressing room.

People from her agency had a minivan ready by the stage door. Aileen introduced each one by name, and all of them ignored me in turn. We drove a few hundred meters, before stopping at the service entrance to the Hotel New Grand, where the two of us got out and walked across the courtyard.

I waited in the stately lobby of the old wing while she went up to her room to change. Half the lights were off, which made the ceiling look twice as high. Generally unpopular since they built the boring new wing, this side of the hotel had class. Aileen came downstairs with fresh makeup and hair up in a loose bun, wearing a white cheongsam-collar shirt and a short leather jacket. At the reading desk where I was sitting she handed me an envelope. I knew without opening the flap it was money.

"Last time I completely forgot. You said 'at cost,' right? This should cover expenses."

It was a hundred thousand yen. "I can't accept this," I said. "It's against the law. I receive plenty of research expenses from the Prefecture."

"Really? I think I like Kanagawa Prefecture. They also paid half of tonight's concert fee." She laughed cheerfully. "Well then, let's have dinner on them. We'll glut ourselves."

I nodded and laughed, maybe a little too loud.

"What's so funny? I like the word 'glut.'"

We descended the broad stone steps of the front entrance and looped around behind the hotel the way we came. I was thinking of heading back to Chinatown, but Aileen said she'd been eating too much Chinese lately. The Karlingchen Hofbräu sign blurred yellow in the misty drizzle up ahead. Neither of us had umbrellas. I suggested we go there.

The partitioned dining area was already dark, but the old German woman recognized me and said she'd serve us dinner at the counter. Aileen ordered a few dishes. I said I'd already eaten, but she wouldn't hear of it.

"Now this is rare. You not drink?" asked Frau Hilda.

I settled for a scotch on the rocks.

Aileen ordered champagne, but the bar lady shrugged no-can-do by the glass. "Do we even have Sekt? How many years it is since I serve such thing?"

"Anything is fine, whatever you have," smiled Aileen, then turned to me. "You know, I don't even know your given name. Or how to read your card."

Once again, Billy's words came to mind. "The name's Eiji, *ei* as in 'forever' and *ji* as in the Buddha's smile."

"Sorry, I'm no good at reading kanji."

My drink arrived, but the champagne was not forthcoming. We had no way to make a toast.

"I went through the apartment," I told her.

"And? Did you find anything?"

I shook my head. "Those newspapers by the sofa, were they there like that when you first entered?"

"They may have been on the floor, but Mom hates things left lying around."

Okay, so Reiko tidies away the evening paper on the eighteenth. But someone has to be there until the evening paper was delivered on the twenty-first. *Someone* but not Reiko straightens things up, taking pains to leave no traces, even deleting the telephone call history. But somehow that someone didn't think of checking the Nissan Sunny in the garage.

"I did unearth a spare car key," I continued, "and in the car was her phone. Mind if I check her call log?"

"Of course, no need to ask."

"And you made your mother's bed, didn't you?"

"Y-yes"—she tripped over the word—"but how did you . . . ?"

"She's not the sort of person who just tosses off her pajamas and leaves, is she?"

"No, as you guessed, I made the bed."

"How about cigarettes? How often does she smoke?"

"She gave it up after she closed the shop."

"There was one ashtray in the apartment. No smoked ends, but it was dirty."

"Gee, you're like a real detective." She laughed slowly but her eyes were searching. "So what about it?"

This time I didn't answer. Just as she was about to say something, a portly cook appeared bearing two trays with four dishes—hot vinegared potato salad, Alsatian onion gratin soup, elephant ear-sized *Wiener Schnitzel*, and, for the finale, oven-baked *Spätzle* with pizza toppings. Aileen spooned a bit of potato salad onto a small plate for me, then began eating the rest of the food herself.

At long last the champagne arrived, a cheaper Taittinger. "Ach, I have to raid tomb to find this," Hilda said, uncorking the bottle with scarcely a sound.

We clinked glasses and she guzzled her champagne like beer, then pressed a hand to her chest. "Concerts are like marathons. You push your body to the max, burn up all those calories, and when it's over you're ravenous." She said this while cutting up the veal cutlet. In no time at all, the salad and noodles disappeared too. I wanted to applaud.

"I'd like to borrow a recent photo of your mother, if you have one," I said.

She opened her backpack, pulled out her bulging agenda, and extracted a snapshot of mother and daughter in matching polka-dot dresses. The Reiko Hiraoka in the photo was maybe fifty, with permed hair and heavy makeup. The daughter, not even ten, stood shyly to one side. If I hadn't seen the *Zoom* article, I would never have recognized the girl as Aileen.

"This is all I've got. I have plenty of other photos, but they're all in London."

"Wouldn't your mother have any?"

"I know she has an album squirreled away . . . somewhere. But she's never liked photos of herself. Any album of hers will be pictures of me." Then suddenly she turned and said, "No, wait, I think she may have a few snapshots in that can, you know, the cookie thing where she kept her passbooks."

She was obviously puzzled by my request, but didn't question my methods. Had she asked "Why now?" I wouldn't have had an answer.

If nothing else, I'd ruled out suicide. Sato had already run checks through police databases for possible matches, I wouldn't be able to do much more than him. Not in my present position. Nor could I just walk around with a photo asking people if they knew her. The bottom line was, I hadn't made much of an effort until that memo popped out of her cardigan pocket.

"You must be disappointed," I said. "I've been no help at all."

She shook her head. "That's not true. I've got no one else to go to. Other than Mom and Uncle Sato, who else in Japan can I call besides 110 or 119?"

Hilda came and poured some champagne. If I'd been paying attention, I would have noticed that Aileen's glass was empty. I really wasn't much use to her.

"Mom was hiding something," she went on, touching her flushed cheek and staring at a mirror behind the liquor shelf. "Not just recently—from a long time ago. When I was a child I was sure she was hiding the truth about my real parents from me. I was little, but I knew I shouldn't ask." The Aileen in the mirror spoke to her champagne glass. "One night when I was alone at her condo in Nagai, it occurred to me. What if maybe she was hiding all sorts of other things too, because of me? I just hoped she hadn't been keeping horrible skeletons to herself all this time."

Her glass was empty again. I lifted the bottle out of the cooler, but there was only a tiny bit left. Marathon runners need to replenish their fluids.

Hilda looked on from the far side of the counter. "What become of *der Trinker*? I stock fresh juice and he not come."

"He's probably plastered somewhere."

"You want I make you one special?" She raised my glass of melted ice, practically bullying me to drink.

I shook my head and ordered another of the same.

"What's this 'special'?" asked Aileen.

"A favorite cocktail of someone I knew, a regular here. A pilot who flew off into the blue. Drink one of his specials, you get the feeling you'll never come down either."

"We all need a lift sometime," said Aileen, nodding. "A little shot of redemption."

"A lesson from Sunday school?"

"No, I'm Buddhist, I guess. We had a Buddhist altar at home."

"Which home?" I found myself asking.

"Vietnam. Strange, isn't it? Of all the things to remember so clearly, just that. There was this big room with only a Buddhist altar in it."

I asked for the bill, but when I reached for my wallet Aileen brushed my hand away. She paid with the money in the envelope, told the lady to keep the change, and stood up to go. Frau Hilda was so astounded she forgot to say thanks.

We walked back the way we came. A fine rain was still coming down. Here and there plastic signs and glass windows and steel handrails all seemed to be sweating. Lights blinked far away.

"I wonder how your foster mother managed to adopt you?"

"Especially when she was so poor," admitted Aileen. "She just said she wanted a child. She lost a son, did you know?"

I nodded. Reiko Hiraoka must have registered with some humanitarian group, and they'd have reviewed her qualifications for adopting a foreign war orphan. More even than her low income bracket, her family status would have been the biggest obstacle. A single mother, never once married? No way could that have counted in her favor.

Aileen took my arm. "Like I said, I just remember bits and pieces," she confided. "A tall man led me by the hand to a ship. A big white passenger ship, with a pool on deck."

"Do you remember where you boarded or landed?"

"No, that's a blank. All I know is he wore a white uniform and cap, and he helped me up a steep gangway. I was hot and sweaty, so he gave me a handkerchief."

"You still have it?"

"No, Mom said I never had it to begin with. According to her, I arrived with only a violin case that was bigger than me." She giggled. "A Japanese nun brought me to Mom's place. I don't know why I believe all this, but I do . . . Now someone sends flowers to my concerts, enough to open a florist shop. Always two hundred roses."

"Every time, without fail?"

"No, not every time, but often enough, especially gala occasions. I nicknamed him Signor Duecento. If this were a manga, he'd turn out to be my ship's captain. Wouldn't that make a great story?" Collecting herself, she led me into the Hotel New Grand courtyard. The windows of the hotel bar under their red awnings illuminated the paving stones. I could see the barman at work inside.

"Care for a little more, in there?" she asked.

"I think I'll pass," I said, holding her back. "In its day, it used to be a grand old bar where you could get a superb martini, but greedy officials and speculators ruined it."

"Why would they do that?"

"The land belongs to the City of Yokohama."

"Hmm, how about we compromise and have them bring some drinks up to my room?"

Surprised, I started to turn away, but Aileen tugged me back. I felt something cold and soft on my mouth. Her cheeks glistened but it wasn't from the rain. Then she took the lapels of my jacket in both hands and leaned against me.

"I'm sorry," she said after a while. "I get this way at times. Especially at night, when someone's about to say goodbye. Stupid, isn't it?"

"No, but too bad there's no moonlight tonight."

She bumped my chest with her forehead. "Don't laugh. It's not like that."

"Maybe it's something to do with losing your real parents?"

"I wish I knew. It's just that now, whenever someone says even a brief goodbye, I feel like I'll never see them again. Not everyone, of course..."

I wished I could piece together that part of her past too, but there are things we're never meant to know.

25

The rain had already let up when I left the hotel. I walked alongside the park under the ginkgo trees while far across the bay a new day showed signs of dawning. I made it as far as the Silk Center, then gave in and hailed a passing cab.

By the time I got home and showered, I could hear newspapers being delivered and the sky outside was light. Saturdays and Sundays the Police Archives was closed. For the first time since my transfer this made me happy. Up to now I hadn't known what to do with my weekends.

I read through the paper and turned off the light before noticing I had a message on the answerphone. "It's me," came Yamato's rough voice, as if he were standing right in front of me. "You just can't be bothered, can ya? Get yourself a damn mobile, you're a friggin' nuisance."

Apparently he had tried calling the office any number of times. After lecturing me on the wonders of modern technology, he reported that he'd learned the mobile phone number of "Mister 504." In keeping with our cash-up-front relationship of long standing, he said he'd trust me to make good on this. Then as he was repeating the number, the recording cut off with a beep.

I went to sleep and woke up at ten, probably because I'd failed to close the curtains. Sunlight beamed through my eyelids, but I couldn't drag myself to the window. It was eleven before I finally got up.

There was nothing in the fridge. I made coffee and found a tin of sardines under the sink and had them drizzled with soy sauce on toast. Then, after getting dressed, I went to an electronics showroom near Chojamachi that had a huge range of mobile phones. Contract fees for some older models were down to three thousand yen. I signed up for one whose charger would also work for the phone from the Nissan Sunny.

Back at the apartment, I started charging the other mobile and made a few calls in the meantime. Chris Ackerman's mobile was set to voicemail. I left my number and asked him to return my call. Neither Yamato nor Tomoda picked up, but I left my new mobile number with them too. When I called Aileen's mobile I got a message recorded in Japanese and English. Her pronunciation was perfect in both.

Not needing to fully charge the battery, I switched on Reiko Hiraoka's mobile at the fifteen percent mark, but the address book was empty. I tried to make a call but the contract had expired. There were, however, a few entries in the call history—a total of seven incoming and outgoing, but only four different numbers. She hadn't used anything like the advertised folder capacity of dozens of conversations.

None of the numbers was Aileen's. I pulled out my notebook to compare, but there was no number saved for Yoshiko Anzai or Sumiko Nakazato or Takashi Kishimura. Just one Yokohama number, one for Yokosuka, and two 090 mobile numbers. Did she really have so few friends with phones? Or did she intentionally not save their numbers, then delete the call history? Either way she must have had her reasons.

Starting from the top I called the four recorded numbers. The Yokosuka one was "no longer in service." The Yokohama one was "access denied at the customer's request." Both mobile numbers were out of contract. All four in the call history were already history.

I then phoned Sato in Yokosuka and managed to find him at home. No self-respecting public servant would be caught dead working on Saturday.

"I want you to ID some telephone numbers," I said.

"Whoah there, how many years is it since I was on active duty?"

"Well, I've been relieved of active duty. I've got no one else to ask."

He grumbled, "It's not about asking or not. Since they passed anti-bugging legislation, everything phone-related has become a major hassle."

I ignored him and read them off, two at a time. "Those are the only four numbers in Mrs. Hiraoka's mobile call history."

"She left her mobile phone behind?"

"Along with her wallet and driver's license."

He went quiet, as if he'd disappeared from the other end of the line. Then came a sigh. Was he thinking what I was thinking?

"Just now I remembered something. Back in June. No wait, it was already July. She rang me out of the blue, to ask me to mediate in something. It involved calling some criminal type. Naturally I refused. I wouldn't do it even for Reiko."

"And what did she say to that?"

"Not much. She was a little disappointed maybe, but she knew where I stand."

"Do you remember the number?"

That was two months ago, Sato said, and he didn't even write it down.

After we hung up, I reopened her call history. The incoming ones were all repeats, calls from the same mobile phone on June 18 and 19. And the outgoing calls all concentrated on one day, June 17. Again I got a creepy feeling. Had she not used this phone from then on until she disappeared a month later?

It was after midnight on June 17 that I parked my car outside Kaput and came across the crazy pilot at the end of the alley. Then on the twentieth of the following month, he flew off leaving a woman's corpse behind.

Everything was getting so mixed up that when my mobile rang on the table, at first I picked up Reiko's phone by mistake and put it to my ear.

"Ackerman calling," came a high nasal voice, "Chris Ackerman. Who the hell is this?"

"My name's Futamura. Thanks for returning my call."

"Yeah, yeah, heard it a hundred times. So what do you want?"

I thought for a second and introduced myself as rehearsed. "I'm a detective with Kanagawa Police Foreign Crime Squad. There's a matter we'd like to discuss with you."

He claimed to know nothing relevant, but his voice betrayed a hint of anxiety.

"You don't stand to lose by this," I told him. "Frankly, we both have something to gain by cooperating. Are you with me? As you may know, there was a criminal incident in the underground garage of your building a few months back. I was the detective on the case."

Silence ensued, an unexpectedly long silence.

"I'll give you fifteen minutes. Can you come right away?"

Naturally, I agreed.

"Not to the office. You know the Washington Hotel, near my place? How about we meet in the upstairs lounge there?"

I grabbed the old photo Billy had left and dashed out the door.

The lounge was done up in captain's cabin decor from the Seventies, varnished cedar tongue-and-groove paneling and every possible knickknack a landlubber might imagine on a cruise ship. Once upon a craze these interiors were everywhere, but now they only existed in port cities like Yokohama and Kobe.

A large picture window took in a grand sweep of the avenue and its median park, dotted with tents the homeless had patched together out of blue plastic sheets and cardboard boxes. Ackerman had stationed himself on a broad banquette by the window and was drinking a martini. Lunchtime was not quite over, but there weren't many customers. I recognized him right away, even without his designated *Herald Tribune*. He was the young naval officer in the photo with Yang Yun-shi. I just stood there looking at him,

167

practically forgetting to sit down. I never expected someone like Yang to tell the truth, but who'd have thought he'd be such a blatant liar, saying he knew no one involved in the Parklane Terrace incident?

"Futamura?" He looked up, eyes as expressionless as one-yen coins. "Sit. Time is money."

I sat down and handed him a Police Archives name card. Ackerman ran his eyes over the English flipside and frowned.

"It's a cover," I said. "Our section works incognito."

He nodded and produced his own card from a Cartier wallet. "Jason Co., Ltd., as in Jason and the Argonauts, hero of the Greek myth of the Golden Fleece."

"Got something going with Brooks Brothers knitwear?" I quipped.

His face took on the first shade of an expression. His gaze sharpened and for a brief moment there was a hint of a smile. "Okay, what is it you want?"

"I believe you know a homicide suspect currently under investigation, a William Lou Bonney? Goes by 'Billy'?"

"I know no such person."

"How about 'Gilly' then? Or 'Guillermo Kano-Law'?"

He straightened up. I seemed to have hit the mark. "Alright. I see you're on familiar terms. In that case, I'll tell you. He's dead."

I stared hard at him. Meanwhile the waiter came over, and without shifting my eyes I ordered a coffee. "We've been keeping Yang under surveillance, but still haven't cracked your connection with the suspect."

"Oh, but I think you have. Shouldn't we all just write him off?"

"Billy owes you, and you want to make good on it before he screws up."

"He already screwed up. And even before that, you were screwed when you did him a favor. Anyone who'd give him the time of day is a fool. It's your own fault he owes you and now it's too late to collect on the debt."

"All they've found is the plane wreckage and a charred body. Our counterparts in Taiwan don't run DNA tests."

"So?"

"We want to contact Billy."

"Time's up."

I looked at my watch. "It's only been ten minutes."

"One minute with a fool is already too long." He shrugged and pointed a finger. "The exit's that way."

"You conspired with Billy to make off with Yang's goods, and Yang knows it."

He brightened up and shook out a laugh. "If that's the case, how come I'm sitting here breathing? Those commercial samples weren't much of a loss for Yang."

"Well then, how come Yang is so bent out of shape about finding Billy?"

"An honor thing, maybe? He promises goods delivered by plane on such and such a date, but the plane with the goods does a no-show. It can make a serious dent in his credibility. Face more than money. He's Chinese, for chrissake." Having said his piece, he summoned the waiter and asked for the bill. "Happy hour's over."

I threw my last ball. "I was there that night at Parklane Terrace. Billy took three cases of 'samples' from your office."

Ackerman didn't twitch an eyebrow. "So what?"

"Add the trunk with the dead body, that makes four containers. Three of which you are complicit in removing," I asserted.

That finally got a rise out of him, though only the slightest emotion teased the corners of his mouth. "I wouldn't know, I wasn't even in Japan at the time," he said. "If what you say is true, then Mr. Bonney must have made a pirate copy of my office key. I've hardly been here this whole past year. If you want to grill me down at the station, serve me the proper papers." He gave me a tight-lipped shrug and that was that. The waiter brought the bill along with my coffee. I picked up the tab and made to go.

Ackerman stopped me. "Listen, it's too bad about Billy's crash, but I want you to know I didn't hate the guy. So let me tell you one last thing. He wasn't the sort to ditch his beloved wings just to swipe some cargo. Anyway they found the cargo, only yesterday. Scattered about seven kilometers from the plane."

I looked at him in surprise. Not surprise that they'd found the stuff, but that he knew and would volunteer the information.

"After so long?"

"There's a range of 3,000-meter peaks down there. Some university mountaineering club found it by accident."

"That I didn't know. You seem to know Taiwan. Our people will appreciate this."

"So what was it he owed you? Money?"

For a moment, I didn't know what to answer. Finally I took in a breath and said, "A drink."

26

The expressway on-ramp was a short hop from the hotel. I made straight for Yokosuka. Not a cloud in the high blue sky, gentle sunlight filling the car interior. I thought of Aileen. Then as long-haul trucks increasingly filled the road, I focused more on my driving, until traffic jammed up before the Hino interchange, leaving me walled in by trucks.

Why had Ackerman met me? He himself said he had no time to spare for people of no consequence. And yet the man returned my call. He even admitted to befriending Billy and having dealings with Yang. Someone must have brought my name to his attention. Billy never really knew for sure I was a cop. Whereas Yang went out of his way to find out I'd been axed from Investigations because of the incident. And Ackerman hadn't made a fuss about my stupid job title. It all seemed so piecemeal.

The line of cars began to flow. I accelerated hard to clear the trucks. As I pulled out into the passing lane, a silverflake Camry a few cars back also moved out, honking loudly and nearly hitting the next car. In the rear-view mirror the driver looked to be a big white guy with gray hair and solid shoulders.

When I left Ackerman in the hotel lounge, there'd been a big guy standing inside the main lobby door, who then suddenly ran out across the park. Not that I could be sure it was the same person, but it made me nervous all the same.

I changed to an outer lane and reduced my speed. The Camry didn't try to pass. In the passenger seat was a short tanned Asian.

They reminded me of the duo who had a go at Billy and me on the Mabori coast road. General Custer and his brother.

The cars thinned out past Asahina, but the Camry was still behind me. So instead of the Yokosuka bypass I took surface roads to try to shake it off, skirting Shioiri Station and turning left toward Yokosuka Station for good measure. It was just the one Camry tailing me for sure. Your typical detective agency would use two cars.

The main avenue dead-ended at the station. I nosed into a lane that led under the bypass until I came to an unmanned parking lot. I stopped the car abruptly, got out, and walked back for a look. The Camry sat there blocking the street. Just past the entrance to the parking lot, where a delivery van driver sat looking out to sea while eating his lunch, was the Japanese Marine Self-Defense Force base.

I walked toward the Camry. The two men stared at me but didn't move. The gray-haired guy wore some event-freebie windbreaker over a white T-shirt. His sunburnt sidekick was in a cheap suit and print polo shirt. When they broke eye contact, I slipped past to the unlocked rear door, swung it open, and climbed in, keeping one leg out of the car.

The driver spread his hands wide on the steering wheel and gazed up at the car ceiling. The sidekick turned around slowly and gave me a phony grin. "Ben Tyson," he introduced himself. He didn't extend his hand. "And this is R.J. Owada."

The name made me take another look. At a second glance the big guy could pass for a foreign sumo wrestler.

"So, you're from Hawaii?"

"Iowa," said Owada. "The boss here's from Hawaii."

"So then you're both Americans?"

"First, what about you, mister?"

"I'm from the islands, like your boss."

"The hell you are."

"Hey, I don't know what your gripe is, but I didn't come to pick a fight."

"Good, let's see your hands. Making a scene won't do any of us much good."

The delivery man had finished his lunch and was watching us. I pulled my leg inside the car and shut the door. Almost simultaneously the Camry backed up and turned around to head north through town.

"Aren't you gonna ask where we're going?" teased Tyson.

"Any place that serves coffee would do fine."

"How about our place?"

"How about somewhere a little more public?"

"Our coffee is plenty good enough," he said, prompting chuckles from the duo.

We passed Yamato's shopping center. The shutters at his booth were down. A little further up Route 16, we turned right. A huge anchor drifted by on the left and before I knew it we were at the main gate of Yokosuka Navy base. Owada flashed a plastic-pouched ID at the Japanese security guard. He didn't even bother to brake. The seaman in the booth saw Tyson's face and saluted.

"You seem to be known in these parts, Lieutenant Tyson."

"Warrant Officer Tyson."

Immediately inside the gate, the well-tended greenery and rows of low buildings to either side looked more like some overseas college campus than a military installation. The car veered left around a grassy knoll and piers came into view to the right. The sea retreated behind boatsheds and warships. Navigating between warehouses and workshops, we came to a patch of woods and small houses. Not fancy by any means, just normal suburban American prefabs.

The car pulled up to one of the houses. A flagstone walkway meandered through a lawn where a rusty sprinkler flopped this way and that. The whitewashed front porch had collected years of grime. Tyson opened the door and invited me in. The grotto-dark interior was so super-chilled I could feel my sweat shrink.

All at once, Owada grabbed me by the wrist and neck and twisted me against a wall. His movements were quick and precise. Tyson frisked me, then, having determined I was clean, they backed off and turned on the lights. Now it was dizzyingly bright.

"Don't worry, I'm no terrorist," I said, to no response.

All the furniture in the living room was draped with white sheets. Two computers sat on the table in the big dining room adjacent, the floor a tangle of wires and telephone cords. On the pass-through kitchen counter were only junk food wrappers and aluminum TV dinner trays. Every window was storm shuttered and curtained. Owada drew some water from a clunky water cooler in the corner and proceeded to brew coffee. Tyson settled in on the sofa and offered me a chair. "Sorry, no smoking here. The landlords are sticklers."

"You both billeted here?"

"We'll ask the questions, okay?"

"Is Naval Intelligence so short of personnel? Or is this some top secret mission?"

"What's that supposed to mean?"

"What's a warrant officer doing snooping around outside the fence in plainclothes? And just look at these digs, this has got to be an undercover operation."

He cut me short. "You know a William Bonney? Where is he now?"

"Up in the air somewhere."

"Like he had that much fuel. What say we cut the chitchat and you just give us answers? This is strictly a military internal affair. It's not our job to tell you what to do or go poking into Japanese police business. Whatever illegal activities occur on your turf are not our concern, but this here isn't Japan, got it?"

"Hope you're not planning to avenge General Custer."

Tyson deflected my wisecrack with a flip of the hand. Owada brought coffee in paper cups.

"Wow, real American java," I gasped after the first sip.

"This ain't Seattle," Owada said.

"Let me set you straight on one thing," Tyson added. "We weren't tailing you personally. It was the car, OK? That car was recorded at Yokota late on the night of July 19."

Well, of course, every shopping arcade had surveillance cameras these days, why wouldn't they install them on American bases?

"So then you must know who I am."

"You're King Kamehameha, aren't you?" Owada said behind my back, dragging a dining room chair closer.

Tyson went on without a trace of a smile: "We compare notes with the Japanese police, but that doesn't oblige us in any way. No matter what we turn up on this case, it's not a joint effort."

"I'll say. You came this close to wasting me that night."

"We're military. We carry guns. So sue us."

"I assume you folks know Ackerman and Billy were working together?"

"Of course. From 1972, the two of them were employed in the same section in Saigon for close to a year."

I let it pass and asked, "Were they on an aircraft carrier?"

"We don't need to tell you."

"They still work together. That's why you were keeping watch on them, also how you spotted my car."

Tyson just stared, then fired back: "What were you hauling that night?"

"Three Globe-Trotter suitcases."

He kept his eyes on me while Owada brought up the rear with a deep breath. Apparently this struck them as odd.

"I had no hand in the loading or unloading. I didn't even get out of the car."

"And what did you get for it?"

"Nothing. I'm his friend. He wanted me to drive him late at night, why would I expect compensation?"

"Is that some kind of boy scout code?" asked Tyson, making the other chuckle.

"Did the cargo belong to you guys?" I asked in return.

"No comment."

"Whatever, Billy's dead," I said. "I was willing to believe to the very last that he was still alive, but just today I heard they'd found the remains of the cargo up in the mountains of Taiwan. If Billy had been planning to make off with it, he wouldn't have to crash the plane and fake his death, now would he?"

Tyson leaned forward. Owada walked over to the table, where I heard a computer booting up. "Where'd you get this information?"

"From Ackerman. The man wouldn't lie unless there was something in it for him."

Tyson clucked his tongue. "Why can't Honolulu get their shit together!"

Owada blocked my view of the screen with his broad back as he jockeyed the mouse. Then, leaving the desktop clean, he whispered something in Tyson's ear. Contrary to appearances, the hulk seemed more competent with a keyboard than a handgun.

"No announcement from the Taiwan authorities. Where in hell does Ackerman get his info?" said Tyson.

"From Yang, maybe?" I suggested off the cuff. "I bet you boys were aiming to confiscate Yang's cargo that night."

"Don't jump ahead of the questions."

"Your call, but four or five days ago, Yang did the same thing as you. He nabbed me and made various threats. He seemed to think Billy and me were in cahoots to pinch his goods."

"Enough already," said Tyson, hands spread to stop me. "We've never threatened you. We're trying to beef up an alliance. It's the Chinaman got no morals."

"China's the homeland of Confucian morals."

"What's between him and Ackerman? He's as far from moral as they come."

"I'd like to ask that myself, but I only just met him today . . . Back in Vietnam days, was he a pilot too?"

"A pilot? Like a fighter pilot?" he scoffed in a loud voice. "The man couldn't even fly a mail plane. During the war he was CID Squad Leader, Billy's boss."

"What's this CID?"

"Combined Investigative Department, a cross-affiliation of the US Fourth Army and its counterparts. He was a glorified snoop for Allied Forces administrative staff."

"So Billy wasn't a jet pilot?"

"Only after his discharge. He enrolled in flight school as a Vietnam vet on the GI Bill, kind of a deferred scholarship."

I bolstered my head with both hands, anything to relieve my confusion.

Tyson stood up, went over to the dining table, and dragged a filing case from underneath. Then, picking out a sheaf of photocopies, he flipped through the pages, nodding. "Enlisted December 1971. We pulled out of Nam in March 1973. That's just sixteen months. How's he supposed to make top gun and fly missions in such short order? According to our records, he got his license in Alameda four years after the war."

"Alameda," I parroted. Didn't Billy say he was born in Alameda? I could feel the blood throbbing under my scalp, a headache in the making. So he wasn't a fighter ace, he was just a dick like me.

The phone in the dining room rang, loud and cranky like an old-time bakelite job. Owada picked it up and answered, "Aye-aye, sir," twice before giving Tyson a go-ahead look. The latter now confronted me. "It's time you gave us your real name and address. And while you're at it, a guarantee not to squeal about what happened here today. Do that for us and we'll drive you wherever you like."

"No comment," I said.

He shrugged. "Too bad. Out with your wallet and phone."

I didn't budge. Nor did he. "Don't want to have to use muscle, not just yet."

Owada tapped me on the shoulder. I twisted away and stood up. The two of them tensed as I slowly pulled out my wallet and phone.

Tyson extracted my driver's license and handed it to Owada. He didn't examine the rest of the contents before returning the wallet to me.

"What did they steal from the Navy?" I asked.

Tyson snickered. Was I so far off the mark? "Like a *yakuza* wouldn't know."

"*Yakuza*?" I repeated, incredulous. "I take it you've never seen a real *yakuza*?"

"Hawaiian golf courses are crawling with them year round, but your kind is a first."

Now it was my turn to snicker as I sat back down.

When Tyson went out, Owada took a scan of my driver's license and saved it to his computer. He returned the license but put my mobile in a drawer. "You'll get it back once we're done downloading your call record," he said. "*And* you cough up the photo."

"Photo? What photo is it you're looking for?"

His only response was to position a dining room chair by the front door and have me sit there, ready to go at a moment's notice.

"Must be a real hush-hush mission for them to send you two all the way from Hawaii," I said.

Owada squared his shoulders and tightened his lips in a regulation military stonewall.

"You're so used to your cushy Fleet Command desk jobs, no wonder you slip up."

"Slip up? Like how?" he finally said.

"You're shadowing Ackerman, right? He swings back through Japan, but you get sidetracked and can't even tail me without alerting half the cops in the city. And what's worse, you don't know Japan, you even think I'm *yakuza*."

After a while I asked politely if I could use the john, so he herded me to a door, which led to a hallway with a bathroom at the far end. It was spacious by Japanese standards, with a double-sink vanity to the right and bathtub to the left, ending in a toilet under a frosted glass vent.

The door opened inwards. Owada leaned back against it and stayed there watching.

"Shut the door, will you?" I asked. "I won't take long."

He thought it over, then nodded. "Fair enough. You're not in custody. But don't try to escape. A broken window in an officer's quarters won't help us get promoted." He removed a credit card from his wallet and slid it between the latch bolt and the strike plate in the lock. "Even if you tried, you'd never make it off base. You read me?"

I chose a simple time-honored trick. Luckily for me there was a big new bar of soap by the bath. I grabbed it and closed the shower curtain, then climbed up onto the vanity and knelt behind where the door would swing open. From there I hurled the soap at the window and broke the glass. Hearing the noise, Owada kicked open the door, but waited before reaching in to pull back the curtain. This gave me a second to slam the door on his arm, then yank him forward while I jumped down.

His first punch landed somewhere on my face. I groaned and tried to get up, but he kicked me. I managed to right myself, before his fist caught me on the cheekbone. Sparks flew behind my eye. I shook away the pain only to find him charging at me. Somehow I moved aside just in time for his head butt to ram into the counter. His bulk jerked as he fell flat on his back, grabbed his face in both hands, and curled up unable to move.

Dizzily, I stepped over him and went back to the living room. I was about to retrieve my phone from the drawer when I noticed a corkboard on the far wall pinned with dozens of photos and memos. One image stood out among the rest: a portrait of a US Navy officer in his dress whites. A career military man, to judge from his wrinkles and white hair, along with rows of ribbons and stars on his epaulets.

Immediately to one side was a picture of the same officer seated behind a large desk in an ordinary-looking office. Next to him was Ackerman, and sitting on a sofa close by was Yang. None of the three had his eyes on the camera. A covert photo?

I didn't have time to read any of the memos. I just peeled off the snapshot, shoved it in my pocket, and ran out the door.

27

I cut across the yard and down a driveway to the road before catching my breath, then started back the way we came, keeping the hill by the gate to my left. Larger buildings came into view along with more people, nearly half of them Japanese hires in hard hats. Signs saying REPAIR DOCKS seemed to diagnose the state of the old toolsheds and warehouses patched layer on layer with spackle.

A lead-gray frigate sat dead in the water opposite Shioiri. The shopping mall floated across the way, multicolored flags and flapping banners and concession booths lined up like sugar cubes along the seafront promenade. You could hear the distant bustle of crowds.

I turned my back to the harbor and kept to the road until I reached a fairly visible landmark building. I tried phoning Yamato, but he was on voicemail. Not once since I bought this damn mobile phone had he picked up for me. I left a call for help: "*Yahagi* to *Yamato*. Direct hit to the engine room. Mayday, mayday."

With no one else to call, I pressed Yori's number and out came a sugary voice. Was it a recording or really her? I couldn't tell at first.

"I'm on base. Got dragged in and now I can't get out—"

She cut me short. "Uh-oh, mustn't go chasing WAVES. They'll waste you."

"Hardly my intention, this is on-the-job trouble. Know any way out of here?"

"Just walk on out and don't forget to smile."

"Seriously. I barely made it away from a fight with a GI, who may have put in a call to the gate."

"Oh." She pondered my predicament. "Where is it you're at?"

"Like I said, I'm on base."

"Even yours truly knows *that*. I'm asking *where* on base."

"Right in front of me is a squat block of a building with a big antenna on the roof. There's a red *torii* gate sign at the entrance."

"Get walking! That's top secret—Seventh Fleet Communications Central."

I started walking. Sure enough, the building had a fresh coat of paint but not a window anywhere.

"A little ways ahead you'll see the main gate. Just trot on by and keep heading straight on Nimitz Boulevard. Pretty soon there's this little park where you can just about see the masts of the old battleship *Mikasa* and . . ."

"And then what?"

"Then you swim. It's real close there, calm water too."

"You must be kidding."

"Gee, so you don't go for swimming. How about dinner tonight, your treat?"

"Gotcha. My treat, wherever you like."

"Toward the back of that little park there's a food court. You sit on one of the benches out front, nothing suspicious about having a snack."

"I sit outside?"

"It's the best idea. There's twenty thousand people live on base, maybe five thousand Japanese. Staying where there's lots of other people and doing what they're doing, you won't stand out. Not unless you're wearing a sharkskin suit on a weekend," she said. "I'll be there as soon as I can."

Walking slowly under some shade trees, I came to a concrete bus shelter trimmed in red and blue. A base police patrol car drove by, BEWARE OF DOGS written on the side in Japanese. I kept walking for maybe a kilometer, arriving at the seaside park drenched in sweat.

The food court was a junk food convention center. They accepted yen, so I bought a tasteless burrito plus a root beer and took a seat on a cabana bench by the waterfront.

The setting sun cast long, building-block shadows, eventually splitting the park in two. By the time the Mustang Mach 1 pulled up, the sky to the east was a deep inky blue. Yori leaned out from the passenger side and called to me. In the driver's seat was her blond beau, Billy Stimwell. We shook hands and I climbed in.

"Isn't a car like this, you know, a bit conspicuous?" I asked.

"No problem," declared the cornhead.

"You'll see," Yori affirmed.

True to cliché, Yori smiled, Billy waved thanks, and the sentry at the checkpoint let the car through without a hitch. Seconds later we were on Japanese soil.

I reclaimed my car from the parking lot behind Central Station, drove back halfway around Shioiri Station, and was just nosing into a basement garage when my mobile rang. I stopped right at the foot of the ramp.

"It's me. Which sea you fightin' on?" asked Yamato. "And what's this *Yahagi*?"

"Light cruiser. Done in by the *USS Avenger* at Leyte Gulf."

"Half-cocked history's your problem. I'll have you know it sank off Satsuma headin' to Okinawa on a suicide mission with the great battleship *Yamato*."

I told him where I was meeting Yori and asked him to see me there. Then, leaving the car in the garage, I took Billy's photo from the glove compartment and walked to the appointed taco stand in Dobuita. There I ordered a Corona and sat waiting at a corner table on the pavement. Tied to a guardrail diagonally opposite was the same old dog. Not twitching a hair, it just lay there watching me drink my beer. We were almost on speaking terms when Yamato showed up.

"So, then," he said, taking his boater off and sitting down across from me, "where were we?" I spelled out the day's events to him, but ended up having to retrace the story all the way back to when I met

Billy, leaving out Aileen and Reiko Hiraoka. No particular reason, just the end of a tough day made me impatient.

"No wonder you got the wrong ship, you're too riled to think straight," said Yamato after hearing me out. "Those two were way out of line, could've just disappeared you."

"Damn right I'm riled. They hijack me, check my phone data ..." But something else bothered me just as much. "Tell me," I said, "during the Vietnam War, you think a young volunteer from Peru could have made fighter pilot?"

"Well, first of all, it takes time to train a fighter pilot. All sorts of tough screening an' qualifications, not something you do to get citizenship."

I belched, more burrito than beer. Why was I so pissed off? I didn't know what did or didn't make sense anymore. "You heard of a woman named Reiko Hiraoka, used to run a little *teppanyaki* place called Rei?"

"You mean that bomb shelter joint in Shioiri way back when? Sure I know the name. Hangout for your boys in blue. No foreigners drinkin' there."

I'd lost track of what I wanted to ask, so I changed the subject. "You think those guys were Naval Intelligence?"

Yamato gave me a wouldn't-be-surprised nod.

"It doesn't add up, though. There's NI here in Japan, right nearby in Yokohama. Why call in those newbies from Hawaii?" I wondered out loud.

"You said it. Ain't normal for them not to trust their own local branch."

"Yang must have some special connection with the American Forces here. He gets leaked a lot of information."

"Like what, for instance? Anyway, he must've lost interest in you soon as they found that cargo in Taiwan."

"Yeah, I probably served him as a link to Billy, but then he got the proof he needed."

A waiter brought a menu and, to my surprise, Yamato ordered a Perrier. I looked him in the face, but couldn't read the expression beneath his wrinkles.

"How 'bout this? NI catches Billy by the tail, so he gets no choice but to jump in bed with 'em and promise to deliver the goods. Then Yang gets wary at the last minute, changes the plan, and has Billy disappear, goods 'n' all."

"But that doesn't jibe with them finding the cargo. Also I can't see Billy crashing the plane just to pretend to be dead and get away."

"Okay, say this Yang fella finds out Billy betrayed him, so he blows the plane up?"

"Then why would he go to the trouble of threatening me? And down a pricey minijet just to seal one guy's lips?"

"Score you one point," he teased with a bob of his head. "But what if it's just ornery detective thinkin' that everything's got to have a reason beginning to end?"

"True. It could have been an accident. Billy tried to make a run for it, but the crash put an end to that, plain and simple. Still, why make for Taiwan? If he was trying to escape, wouldn't he have headed across the Pacific?"

Yamato crossed his arms and moved his mouth as though chewing. The dog yawned. The Perrier arrived but was left untouched.

I pulled out the corkboard snapshot, peeled off a yellow Post-it, and placed it in front of him. "You know this officer?"

"Know him? That's the Lord High Fleet Activities Commander hisself. Joseph Glidden, same name as the guy what invented barbed wire," he said, looking up with a smartass grin.

"It was tacked up front and center in their secret NI playroom."

"Yeah, well if this piece of work's involved, anythin' goes. Hear tell he makes the guards shine his shoes. A real badass, even steals this poor ol' seadog's business."

"So what does a Fleet Activities Commander do? Keep the fleet active?"

"Nosir, beached sea lion's more like it. Most GIs in Japan never see combat, they work on the bases. Haulin' supplies, providin' fuel and food. So this big wheel, in a company he'd be like the Executive Director for General Affairs."

Unconsciously, I found I'd been folding up the Post-it. On straightening it out I saw the handwritten words "Sneak Beak."

"What d'you suppose that means?" I asked.

"Got me. Isn't 'beak' like the sharp mouth-thingy on an eagle or a hawk?"

"Glidden's nickname, maybe?"

"Well, the eagle's your all-round American symbol. Pentagon slaps it on most everythin'. Not just the Navy seal, but all their armed forces' crests. That's all I know."

"There's something else. Here's what they were after." I took out the photo Billy left at my place.

Yamato raised his voice in surprise. "Yang an' Glidden together with . . . ?"

"The other guy's Ackerman. Mister 504."

Deep furrows appeared between his eyes. He was leaning forward to say something, when suddenly an excited voice was calling our names. Lights were coming on up and down Dobuita as if to welcome Yori and Billy Stimwell.

Before Yamato said, "Lend that to me overnight, will you?" the photo was already safely tucked away in an envelope on my lap. I nodded.

On weekends Dobuita bustled with out-of-town teens and old folks. They didn't drink, they just walked around buying dumb souvenirs, then headed home like good little tourists. Now every eye was trained on Yori in her hip-hugging leather micro-mini, with the American cornhead in tow. Before she got to our table, I took out my wallet and paid the snooping fee plus one dollar. "I'd hoped for a shoeshine."

"We're closed weekends, like any self-respectin' merchant."

"Fair enough. Count it as an advance."

Yamato picked up the bills and tapped them on his forehead. "Sure thing, till the next one. I'll see what I can dig up 'bout your Tyson and Glidden."

Yori wriggled past us over to the old dog and crouched down to pat its head. Her "Good boy, Musashi" produced a feeble wag of the tail.

"Yori, stop it with your made-up names!" yelled the proprietor from inside. "The old fleabag's senile anyway."

Yamato seemed to take this personally. I shook Billy's hand and asked where they felt like eating, but Yori just tilted her head. "Here's fine. Whatever, we're here already," she said, spreading open the menu.

"C'mon, don't you want to go someplace fancy? You worried about the depth of my pockets?"

"Uh-uh. I told you not to ask two questions at once," she giggled. "I want to have the taco rice here. Billy too. We've been talking about it since we got up."

Beef chilli over rice, cheap eats by any standard. "That's what you get when the dollar slides to a hundred-eight yen," said Yamato.

Billy just smiled and nodded politely, unable to follow the Japanese.

"Shall we have drinks too?"

"You go right ahead, but I'm driving, so not for me."

Cornhead Billy and Yori settled on vodka lemonades with nachos for nibbles.

Yamato suddenly slapped himself on the forehead and said, "I swear my mind's goin'. Damn near forgot." He pulled out a postcard-size pad device, powered up the screen, and gave me a this-PDA-does-apps-even-takes-hi-res-pictures spiel, only to give up squinting at it and put on a pair of folding glasses. "About your Vietnamese guy in the freezer. I did a little snoopin' and it seems this Chen or Tran, he rented an apartment. Address is Shioiri, but it's way up in the hills by Uragamichi."

"Could you find it?"

"Went all the way there for nothin'." He pressed a key, then turned the PDA in my direction. The screen showed an empty plot of land hemmed in on three sides by houses, two of which were shrouded under construction sheeting. "They said it burned to the ground. Lots of steps, no way a fire truck could get up there. Landlord had the place leveled last month."

"Nothing suspicious? Arson?"

"According to the firemen, someone was smokin' in bed. Fire started in Tran's room. They said a woman was livin' there, thirtyish Vietnamese lady."

"And the police are onto it?" I asked.

"Nosir. That's the thing, the fire was in July, but the incident with the stiff was reckoned to be in June, right?"

I breathed out hard. The corner dog and Yori both looked at me.

"So you tell me, how come the landlord swears Tran, who's supposed to have died in June, was still livin' there till the day of the fire, eh?"

"I give up, Musashi," I muttered at the dog. "Looks like I won't be driving tonight."

Yori smiled cheerfully and ordered a bottle of tequila.

The dog slowly stood up with tail on high.

28

Yamato set me up at a hotel on the edge of Dobuita, a swank nine-story place right by the steps up to Suwa Shrine. Nice clean room with bath ensuite, breakfast included, which he bargained down to half price. In the morning, last night's photograph and a free coupon for the garage where I'd parked awaited me at the front desk.

I caught the tail end of breakfast service and scarfed up the last of the buffet all by myself, then returned to my room and had some coffee. Once my stomach had settled I called Yang. The goods had been found, which meant he should be happily back in business. I was curious to know what his mood might be. Maybe I could get a lead on where Ackerman sourced his information.

Yang didn't pick up. His number just rang and rang with no indication voicemail might connect. I tried four or five times over thirty minutes but it was always the same.

By the time I got my car out of the garage and started back toward Yokohama my watch read almost noon. Through the first tunnel, signs directed me to where elevated railway trestles straddled between the hills. I abandoned the car and followed Yamato's hand-drawn map up a steep track barely wide enough for one person, passing houses clinging to their sloping plots until finally I got to where the sea appeared beyond the roof lines. The water was a deep cold October blue, the only indication of winter's approach.

Uragamichi was part of an old Edo-period ridgetop road that once ran all the way down the coast. The housing tracts up here were a nightmare for City Hall to supply with water or drains or fire trucks. You had to climb such a long, narrow flight of steps to reach the former site of the apartment it was a wonder only one building burned down.

The landlord, who lived next door, told me as much. He said it took a team of firemen over thirty minutes just to pull the hose up this far. The police only came to dig through the ashes for the cause of the fire. Up here the guy was Chin, not Chen or Tran.

"He had a British passport, so I figured him for a reliable sort." Apparently he'd had a woman living with him since spring, someone he'd introduced as his wife.

"And they both were here till the day of the fire?" I asked.

"Well, I saw him come home the morning of the twentieth."

"July 20?" I asked again. The date snagged in my gut.

"Came back around 9 a.m. Night shift, maybe? Can't say about the wife, no recollection of her, but I guess she was around," he said.

With no composite portrait to go by, this was about as far as a Police Archives name card would get me. Short of any sure way to identify Tran, inquiring whether it was the same person the whole time merely got me a puzzled nod. The only plausible explanation was that this Chin, the British passport holder who rented here, was not the Tran Binh Long I knew about.

"It was accidental, right?" the landlord now asked me. "Smoking in bed's what I heard from the firemen."

"It started in his room apparently."

He nodded. "He seemed nice enough, her a bit on the gloomy side."

"What did they do?"

"This and that. Wife worked as a maid, spoke passable Japanese. Husband washed dishes, that sort of thing. But he had a car, so I guess they made okay money."

"Is the car still around?"

"Sure, down in the lot below. I know the property owner and it's got him in a pickle. Takes all kinds of paperwork to dispose of another person's car. Costs money too."

I said my thanks and plodded downhill to the first intersection at the bottom, where a short jog toward the elevated trestles brought me to an empty pocket of unpartitioned land surrounded by houses. There were three parked cars, one of which stopped me cold. In the far left-hand corner was a vehicle painted all over in sandy brown camouflage, with a red R emblem on the nose of the hood—the WagonR that the aloha shirtmaker couple said they'd seen Reiko Hiraoka get into with a scruffy character. That had been on July 19, the same day she withdrew five hundred thousand yen from her bank book. And the very next day the apartment burned down, the occupants gone without a trace.

I circled the car. The tires were already starting to go flat, the windows were grimy. The inside was a mess of shopping bags and empty boxes. Predictably the doors wouldn't open.

I reached Nagai in short order. Not a semi in sight on the coast route, only a procession of cars hauling surfboards.

Remembering it was Sunday, I supposed Gagarin's owner's eatery would be closed. I'd need a reason to show up on her day off, I couldn't just say I was looking for a neighbor who'd gone missing. So I stopped by a liquor store and bought a small bottle of Urakasumi saké, then parked behind the condominium and walked toward Ukita Izakaya Cuisine. The shop curtain wasn't out, but the entrance to her house was right next door. I shouted hello through the sliding door but there was no answer. Walking around the hedge gave me a glimpse of the backyard, a parched flower bed, fishing nets and laundry drying on bare ground. Sitting on the plank veranda smoking a cigarette was a white-haired old man with incredibly broad shoulders.

I greeted him over the hedge. "Good afternoon. Mr. Ukita?"

He cleared his throat and nodded, but that was all. He didn't even look in my direction. His sunburnt face was furrowed with stubborn wrinkles.

"My name is Futamura. Is your daughter in?"

He gave me a quick glance, shook his head, then faced away again.

"I've been asked to look after Mrs. Hiraoka's empty apartment."

"How the hell's that my concern?"

"Mind if I come in? I brought along a little something by way of an introduction." I held out the saké for him to see.

That got a rise out of him. He eased down onto a stepping stone and into a pair of sandals, shuffled across the yard to open the picket gate, and showed me to a seat on the veranda. Then, over a can of beer, he abruptly launched into a tirade against windsurfers—they'd ruined the sea, turned the town into a madhouse. I managed to slip in a casual inquiry about the yellow truck, but he hadn't seen it.

It wasn't the windsurfers themselves he couldn't stomach so much as the fishermen who let out places to keep their boards. Even his own daughter tried to get in on the act, using the yard to earn a little "pocket money"—like dousing a flame with oil, she was! In her mid-thirties and still unmarried. Frittering away her life.

On and on he went. I did my best to commiserate, but it was a good half hour before I could bring up the day Reiko Hiraoka bought a lot of sashimi.

"Why'd you wanna know that?" the old man asked back. "The daughter's a musician. Her management handled everything, the bill was on the company tab."

I didn't probe further. Obviously he thought the sashimi was for a party to welcome back Aileen. He went to the restaurant kitchen to fetch a notebook, donned a pair of reading glasses, and flipped through the pages. "June 17," he announced.

It was well past two when I reached the condo. The reception window of the superintendent's office was curtained, with a NO SERVICE TODAY sign posted alongside.

While waiting for the elevator I heard a woman laughing somewhere, followed by a loud thud. In the passage to the pool patio I noticed a door marked 101. So there was a ground floor apartment here.

Up on the third floor, I searched through Reiko Hiraoka's cookie tin. In among the utility bills and assorted papers were three snapshots, probably from the time she went to Kamakura with her two friends. I picked out one that showed her alone. Stepping back into the corridor, I wondered what to do. Making inquiries among the neighbors would only spread word of her disappearance—as if that would make any difference at this point. No way would she want to live in 301 after all this.

I rang the doorbell of the next apartment. Three times and no answer. The neighbor on the other side was out as well. In the end not a single door opened on that floor. It might as well have been an abandoned building the corridor was so dead.

Down again by the elevator to the ground floor, I heard a loud noise, then a scream. I ran into the lobby without waiting for the doors to fully open. Standing there was a naked woman. Japanese, though no spring chicken. Her eyes were red and her cheeks streaked with tears, even though she was smiling. Her flesh sagged, but at least I didn't see any needle marks on her blue-veined thighs. If not for the handcuffs dangling from one wrist I could almost have pretended not to notice. Behind her stood a black guy in a tank top and cotton pants. He was barefoot and his pants were unzipped.

"What's going on here?" I asked.

"What's it look like? She's drunk," he drawled in bad Japanese.

I raised my voice. "So what's with the handcuffs?"

"Like you can't tell! We was just having some fun."

Right then the door to 101 opened. "What you doing! Get back in here!" called a voice in Japanese English. A woman's face peered out, then hurriedly withdrew. I couldn't help seeing who it was.

"Okay then, I'll ask her," I told the guy.

"Whoah, just a second there," the GI tried to stall me.

I made straight for the door and forced it open. Old man

Ukita's daughter stood on the threshold, trying to button her blouse. "Wait—" she gasped.

A muffled cry came from somewhere inside. I marched in without taking off my shoes, straight to another doorway at the end of the hall that let out some weedy-smelling smoke. This apartment was much bigger than 301 but only minimally furnished. Two folding cots and a sofa piled with cast-off clothes huddled at the epicenter of an explosion of bottles and glasses, junk food, strange silicone gadgets, rubber toys and colored ropes. Splayed on a dining table was a woman wearing only a red bra hiked up to her throat. Mid-thirties maybe, older anyway than her crew-cut white partner. Buck naked with tattoos on both arms, lifting her legs at each thrust of his hips, he turned as soon as he noticed me and grinned.

I did a quick once-over of the place to look for a surveillance camera, then grabbed Ms. Ukita and pulled her out of the apartment. She followed me to the poolside patio, arms crossed defiantly.

"You get money for this?" I asked.

"What's it to you?"

"Funny how your type always says money's no object, yet you get into money trouble anyway."

"You don't even know me," she sneered, barely containing her agitation. "Anyway you're lying. You didn't come to check on Mrs. Hiraoka's place. You're one of them."

"What's this now?"

"You're from the loan sharks. You people took stuff from her apartment."

I spoke even louder. "I said, what's this all about?"

She glared back at me. "Go ask the super, he'll tell you. Mrs. Hiraoka took off because of all the debts she ran up."

"The superintendent told you that?"

"Fuck you. You people don't frighten me. We're not doing anything wrong."

194

"Maybe not the sex, but dope is against the law. So is breaking and entering."

"It's all cleared with the super. That's just a showroom."

"Which belongs to the real estate company. A crime all the same."

She clammed up and pressed her arms tight against her chest.

"Listen, I'm not a loan shark. I'm here because Mrs. Hiraoka's daughter asked me to investigate a robbery. Or didn't the superintendent tell you?"

"I saw them make off with a Gucci handbag, saw it with my own eyes."

"Who's *them*?"

"Well, only one guy actually. Smart dresser, Japanese, I didn't get a close look. We were having a little get-together here, so I didn't want to be seen. But not the yellow truck guy. He's been coming around since July."

"Since when in July?"

"The fourth Saturday." She was absolutely certain. Her little "get-togethers" happened twice a month, the first Sunday and third Saturday. July 1 had been a Saturday, so that meant the fourth Saturday was July 22.

"You host these dos of yours regularly? How do you get your customers?"

"It's not like that. We're all internet friends."

"And your GI buddies, how do you recruit *them*?"

She hesitated, then started making excuses. "They get, you know, gratuities. Some older people still know how to show their appreciation."

I made to leave. "And your old man's not one of them. I just talked to him."

She covered her mouth with a hand, her cheeks puffed full of air.

My feet moved out of sheer anger. Anger toward whom or what I had no idea. I stormed out the front entrance and headed for my car at the rear of the condominium. Through the tall juniper hedge, however, I glimpsed the flatbed of a truck. I caught my breath and walked around the hedge for a better look.

Just as I thought, it was the same yellow pickup, parked where I'd seen it before. The rear license plate was hidden by the tailgate. I'd have to go all the way to the other side or crouch down underneath to read it. Against my better judgment I circled around the front. That was a big mistake.

Edging past the driver's cabin, I couldn't help seeing the large speakers inside. The floor on the passenger side was chock-full of audio equipment and the seat held an encyclopedia-size console connected to a compact video unit with its red RECORD light blinking. I tried the door. It was unlocked. On closer inspection, there was a lens cap on the camcorder but the tape inside was moving. I flipped open the LCD panel, but just as the screen lit up I sensed movement behind me.

"What the fuck you doing in my truck!" boomed a voice right at my neck. A weight bore down on the back of my head faster than I could swing around. I ducked, trying to deflect it with my left arm. It almost worked until something caught my elbow—a spiked something.

No pain or tingling, my whole left side just turned to stone. My arm hung limp, my hand was hundreds of meters away from my shoulder. Again the spike attacked my left shoulder and I crumpled over, knees meeting the ground with a thump.

I lay there on the pavement immobilized. All I could see was a pair of ankles in worn-down Nike sneakers. I wanted to raise my head but couldn't budge. A foot was aimed at my gut, only to freeze in midair with a groan from above. There was a bandage on the heel encrusted with dried blood. The guy took a short rest on the driver's seat, just long enough to shift to the other foot and tread hard on my chest. I choked out a cough, my mouth lolling open but my lips unable to move.

"You better choose who you mess with, dumbfuck!" Then he

straddled me, grabbed hold somewhere, and dragged me backwards out of the way. I casually noted the backs of my hands being scraped raw along the pavement. The door slammed, the engine started, and the pickup moved off. For one fleeting second I saw the license plate, but all I could remember was *Yokohama* plus four digits. I tried to follow it visually, but my eyeballs wouldn't move.

I could blink and my heart was beating. I hadn't even lost consciousness. Only my voluntary muscles were immobilized, so I knew the spike wasn't a stun gun. I hadn't heard any electric discharge or felt a burning sensation. Maybe he used a Myotron? They weren't readily available in Japan, but bulletins had circulated about a spate of nasty incidents on US bases in Okinawa. Myotrons fire high-frequency pulses that temporarily sever conscious muscle functions, all without harming bones or joints. I seemed to recall reading that the effects lasted anywhere from fifteen to forty-five minutes, yet soon enough I could move my hands.

After a little while I could move my feet too. I curled up tight and reached out wide, contracting and flexing repeatedly until finally I managed to sit upright, though the small of my back remained seriously out of commission. Dragging my numb butt, I was just able to crawl to my car like an old dog whose hips have given out. By the time I pulled myself into the driver's seat my whole body was soaked in sweat, which was some comfort. At least I knew where my skin was.

Sensation returned to my back before long, but I had no will to do anything. I just sat there exhausted for a good thirty minutes. Finally I got up the strength to get out of the car and stretch. I hurt where I'd been booted. My hands and knees were in bad shape. My mouth was all gummy and my throat dry.

I set off in the direction of the Ukita Izakaya. There was bound to be a vending machine on the frontage road. Sure enough, I found one and bought a bottle of mineral water. In two gulps it was gone.

That's when I heard a woman's voice from behind the eatery.

"What's wrong with you, Dad! Drinking at this hour! And without eating!"

The old man's reply was good and loud, though I couldn't make out a word of it.

29

It was going on dusk by the time I reached the Washington Hotel in Yokohama. I pulled over to the curb and called Ackerman, only to get an unexpected recording: "This number has been canceled at the customer's request."

I went in to ask for him at the front desk, but the clerk didn't even look at his reservations monitor before replying, "He checked out last night."

"That's odd," I wondered out loud. "He said he'd be staying in Japan for the time being."

"So we understood as well, but apparently something came up."

Was there any message from a Mr. Yang, I inquired. The clerk searched behind the counter, but no, there was nothing.

Heading back to the car, I drove past the lot and my apartment to my regular spot by Parklane Terrace and sat for a moment to work up the nerve to walk up the front steps. Just beyond the plate glass door was an intercom with a security keyhole and a number pad. I pressed 504 good and hard—once, twice—but there was no answer.

The graying concierge in a dark blue uniform poked his head out of the office. I knew those bulging eyes, that slouching posture. It was the same guard who'd been making the rounds the night Billy came for the suitcases.

"Remember me?" I asked preemptively.

"'Course I do," he said. "You're Detective Futamura from First Division Investigations. You probably don't remember me, though. Deputy Sasada? We were on the same task force way back. You know, the bar hostess serial killings in Kawasaki?"

Apparently he thought I was still a detective and seemed bothered that his handling of the situation might be to blame for the whole mess . . . so he told me at length.

I interrupted him to say I'd come to check out Jason Co., Ltd. in 504 and his eyes showed immediate interest. He retrieved a master key and strode into the elevator ahead of me. "Now this is what I call investigating. We could teach today's young slickers a thing or two, eh? They dropped the case before they even got to which apartment the sneak was visiting."

"Is it okay to go poking around now?"

"504? Why not? We can go in, no problem. A moving truck came this morning. It seemed funny to me, so sudden and all . . . Tell me, how'd you finger him?"

"Someone posted clues on a bulletin board in the train station."

He grinned a mouthful of yellow teeth.

"Was Ackerman present when the movers came?" I asked.

"No, there was an American, said he was his representative. Left his card, I'll show you later." Sasada was proud to say he'd taken down the license number of the truck too.

The hallway on the fifth floor was straight out of an old hotel, not a window anywhere. Maybe because it was Sunday, you could hear the tired buzz of fluorescent lights in the stillness. "Lease runs till the end of the month. Actually it's breach of contract, him moving out with no prior notice like this," he mentioned as he opened the door to 504.

The wall fixtures were all in place, but they'd stripped the shelves bare. The carpet was rutted from heavy office equipment—a photocopier or maybe a telex terminal—and a telephone cord snaked across the floor. A big oak desk had been relegated to a corner to make way for a conference table, but where were the chairs?

Sasada opened another door to show me the bedroom, a modest space without built-ins, now crammed with metal shelving. Ackerman probably used it as a storeroom. A square crater gaped in one wall.

"What the hell?" Sasada gasped at the hole. "This is criminal."

The bathroom door had been removed and the molding all around it drilled for bolts at regular intervals. Judging from a conspicuously unfaded section of wall and the trail of grime where a rail had been removed from the flooring, he must have rigged up some sort of movable panel to block access.

The hidden bathroom was spacious but unremarkable. That is, if you overlooked the unhinged door propped up in the bathtub and a commercial, refrigerator-size safe crushing the terracotta tiles. Otherwise it was quite tidy. The disconnected plumbing was tight and dry, not a speck of dust remained inside the safe.

We returned to the bedroom, where a few sealed cardboard boxes and crates as well as a plastic air freight case were left behind. All bore labels handwritten in English—MINERAL SAMPLES, SOIL SAMPLES— and all were empty. Atop one box was a large dusty envelope printed with what I immediately recognized as the Arrow Planning Associates logo and contacts underneath for Yasuichi Orimasa, Executive Director.

I brought the envelope back to the desk in the main office room, where I now noticed a wall map of Vietnam flagged with red pins right below Ho Chi Minh City. Next to it was a framed picture of a freighter with *Mineola* painted across its peppermint green hull. Probably in the hundred-meter 5,000-ton class, nothing special about it, certainly nothing that merited framing. The office was rather less shipshape than the bathroom; odd bundles of papers had been shoved under the desk along with some expensively printed pamphlets titled *Overview of the Val-Nam Development Scheme.* Inside the front cover was a simplified diagram of southern Vietnam marked with stars on the Mekong Delta corresponding to pins on the wall map. I stuffed a pamphlet in the envelope.

"Seen enough? Can't leave my post too much longer," said Sasada, already by the door. Though once we were in the elevator, he thought to ask, "Didn't Investigations mark Ackerman?"

"No. All they had in their heads was drawing curtains on the case. Well, given how the suspect escaped via a US base, I guess they didn't have much choice."

The name card given to Sasada turned out to be one of Ackerman's own, annotated on the back with "I hereby assign complete authority to the bearer." The movers were from the Kanagawa branch of a mid-size transport company.

I showed Sasada the photo from Tyson's corkboard, but he shook his head, no, he'd never seen any of them. Great memory: he couldn't even tell that one of the men in the picture was Ackerman.

Just in case, I also showed him the snapshot of Reiko Hiraoka. "I get so tired lately," he whined without even looking at it. "Sorry, my mind isn't what it used to be." Then, out of nowhere he asked, "What happened to the car?"

"What car? I'm not following."

"Us cops in the old days," he rambled on wearily, "we used to put ourselves on the line. Our own money too. I know I used to spend quite a bit on cases, figuring it'd get sorted out in retirement pay. Guess that's why so many of us got into debt. Now I can hardly afford cigarettes."

I just looked at him. I knew where this was leading.

He went on about his financial straits, then recalled, "That night, about two hours before I saw you, there was a strange-looking car. Already said so in the deposition."

"A red sedan?"

"No, some boxy thing. Parked out back, pretty much right where you did, but then it drives off when I come around to check. Thirty minutes later, I go take another look and it's parked a little ways up the street, some scrawny fella driving—foreigner by the look of him."

"Brown camouflage paint job?"

"Yeah, that's right, like guerrilla fatigues . . . The second time I spot him, the driver looks like he's crying there in the car." Sasada sounded a bit mawkish too.

I'd had just about enough of sappy ex-cops and crying foreigners. Luckily a foreign woman came through the autolock into the lobby just then, which was my cue to get out of there before he turned to mush.

I returned my car to the lot and walked toward the lights of Isezakicho. One block from the shopping arcade there's an eatery that dates from when these backstreets were lousy with streetwalkers cruising for GIs on R&R. A good enough place for a pork cutlet sandwich and beer while examining the contents of the envelope from Ackerman's office.

The main item, a plastic-bound folio of plain paper printouts, was a film treatment for something called "Hellboys." The manga cover sheet showed a GI and the tattooed back of a *yakuza* clutching a dagger, overprinted with the title in a lurid typeface. A brief synopsis laid out an adventure storyline set during the last gasp of the Vietnam War: a Japanese mobster goes underground in Saigon and infiltrates South Vietnamese military operations to abscond with their secret hoard of cash. Adapted from an original "based on a true story" novel by Orimasa, the production was credited to Tsunetoshi Inamoto, with the publishers of *Zoom* listed in the production group. An attached cost-benefit analysis admitted the potential box office plus income from distribution and secondary rights far outweighed any actual merits as cinema. Surprisingly frank for a come-on.

The other item, the *Overview of the Val-Nam Development Scheme* pamphlet I'd lifted, was a promotional glossy describing major suburban land reclamation and construction works underway near Ho Chi Minh. A landfill area in the marshy delta to the southeast of the city roughly equivalent to the twenty-three wards of central Tokyo was to be "reborn" as a Special Economic Zone combining bonded entrepot facilities with residential tracts fanning out around an "academic hub" and affiliated "research center," all touted as a "perfect location" for foreign investment, factories, and other productivity logistics. Some of the housing was already completed and people were said to be moving in, while the research center boasted the backing of top-name firms from France, Germany, Japan, and Korea. The entire operation was apparently a joint venture between Ho Chi Minh City and a Taiwan Cheng Long Investment Group, with an unexplained Nanyang Perpetual Holdings, Ltd. trailing afterwards like goldfish shit.

The scale of the scheme was so enormous, if there hadn't been a satellite flyover of the sprawling site and various on-the-ground photos of Stage 1 Development Works, I'd have taken it for an elaborate investment scam. Or no, in this age of computer imaging you couldn't even trust pictures like these. More suspicious, however, was how closely the two pamphlets resembled each other. There really wasn't all that much separating the gist of the film project from the development scheme: both promised big returns if successful and beggared belief big-time. The only hard and fast difference was the number of zeros in the amounts of investment involved.

Leaving the restaurant, I went looking for Orimasa's "true story" in a bookstore. It didn't take long to find, though the title had been tweaked for the film. *Hellboy in Paradise* was out in third-printing paperback from Inamoto's publishing house.

I bought a bag of ice at a convenience store on the way home, then settled in for a night of reading and drinking. The plot centered on a young Orimasa lookalike who gets expelled from his *yakuza* family for some breach of their code of honor and goes on the lam to Hong Kong, where he meets up with a triad maverick named Kang. Together they slip under the radar into endgame Vietnam. Not looking for money, at least not at first, they're after amphetamines from two labs operating in Saigon with the tacit consent of the military. Somehow they make off with ten million dollars' street-value of speed, then buy a minesweeper—captain and all—from the ARVN fleet to smuggle the goods.

Here the author pauses to explain that troops on the front line have always had their dope, often routinely provided to keep the boys in fighting spirit. At the height of the Vietnam War, GIs flown to Japan for R&R would bring in huge quantities of drugs, which they dumped on the market much to the chagrin of the undercut Osaka syndicates.

So now, back to the plot, someone fires an anti-tank rocket into the Saigon hotel where Orimasa is staying. He barely escapes with his life only to find himself on the US military's wanted list, though of course the ones who put the poke on our hero are Allied insiders. These "Khaki Mafia" types had been planning to steal the speed themselves, backed by a chain of command going all the way up to the top brass.

From here on the story turns into a four-way battle royal between thieves. ARVN goons smelling money set their sights on Orimasa, among them undercover Viet Cong agents receiving orders from the Liberation Army, which is steadily closing in on the city. Our hero and his Hong Kong sidekick get put through their paces, narrowly evading deathtraps time and again, and eventually learn their adversaries' real target isn't the speed but a seventy-million-dollar nest egg of "emergency funds" the South Vietnamese generals have stashed away against the inevitable fall of Saigon.

Better dosh than dope, the two of them start consolidating connections and weapons. Their first recruit is one Ernesto Fujikawa, a young Japanese-Brazilian who enlisted in the hope of gaining US citizenship—more than a little reminiscent of Billy. A loser who loves his drink, portrayed sympathetically as a fall guy you just can't hate, he's a Navy flunky working at Military Customs. That odd detail put an interesting spin on things.

Just before the climax, this Senhor Fujikawa shows his stuff. In order to rescue our hero from certain death he leaves his girl waiting on a rainy street corner, where she gets caught in Liberation Army crossfire. On hearing of her death, he tells the Orimasa character to stand him two tall shots of 50 percent proof. "The first glass is to thank me for saving you, the second is for me to forget her."

At last the day comes for their team of five comrades to infiltrate ARVN headquarters and crack the secret safe. Unfortunately the seventy million dollars proves to be gold bullion, not paper currency, much too heavy to haul in the helicopter they have on standby. Working feverishly until almost daybreak, they load up as much bullion as they can, but in the end the take is only five million in gold. As a parting gesture, they bombard the remaining pallets of ingots with napalm stolen from a US Air Force base. The explosion vaporizes the precious metal, sprinkling a golden shower over the rice paddies. Gazing down from the helicopter, our hero reflects, "Someday, someone's going to build houses here. They'll sink wells, dig irrigation ditches, plow the fields . . . and hit a vein of gold."

I shut the book and poured myself another drink. The closing ceremony for the Olympics had already begun on TV I turned it off and flipped through the pages again. The Hong Kong sidekick was probably modeled on Yang, but his age and general description didn't fit. Orimasa had made him into a movie montage, a strong sinewy Shaolin master, hard-nosed but loyal to the end. Nor was Fujikawa's commanding officer anything at all like Ackerman. Both were just paper-thin cutouts.

Okay, so Orimasa was no genius at character studies. The most believable people in the cast were those copied as-is from real-life models. Which I supposed meant Orimasa had his reasons for not cutting closer to the bone with Yang and Ackerman. But something else about the story struck me as flimflam. Artistic license or not, gold bullion doesn't just vaporize. The stockpile and the firebombing had to be window dressing for very different actual facts.

I scraped around in my desk drawer for Inamoto's card. There was no one at his editorial office on a Sunday and his mobile was on voicemail. I left a message saying there were things I wanted to ask about Orimasa's book.

Not thirty minutes later the phone rang, but it wasn't Inamoto.

"Hey, hanging in there?" My reporter friend Tomoda sounded a little drunk. "I dug up a few details."

"You're telling me the Taiwanese authorities found something at the crash site."

"Really? News to me," he blurted back in surprise. "Where'd you scoop that?"

"Secret sources. Taiwan probably hasn't made it public yet."

"Well, don't hold your breath."

"Right, so what's the NHK evening report?"

"It's that freezer business, remember? That warehouse where your Vietnamese guy got permafrosted."

"Now just a . . ." My voice gave out. Not once had Tomoda and I ever discussed Tran freezing to death.

He forged ahead, unperturbed. "The warehouse, it's been demolished and the lot sold to a Yokohama realtor, Golden Harbor Enterprises. Big Taiwanese operation under someone named Zou. Heard of him? And that dive in Yokosuka—you know, Kaput? Well, it's managed by the same company. Kind of odd, don't you think? A real estate mogul with fifteen-story corporate offices looking after a dump like that?"

"What's it got to do with the cold storage place?" I asked impatiently.

"C'mon, it's your Kaput connection, Billy to Mr. Freezer." He slurred his words, then coughed. "Still haven't tracked down the details, but for sure this Zou's in bed with Yang. Not only that, Billy's Palm Brothers House is also his property—hey, you listening?"

"Go on, I'm still here."

"Moreover, like I was saying, this Zou character had his eye on that warehouse from the word go. Three years ago half the site was sold to Golden Harbor. The warehouse company leased the land to stay in business. Now the remaining land and building get sold off, or repossessed is more like it." He chuckled, obviously pleased with himself. "Just maybe your frozen Vietnamese friend got in the way."

"What made you go snooping this story? Only a handful of the team at Headquarters even know of any link between Tran and Billy. I proposed it, but Investigations didn't take it up."

"Does it bother you?" Tomoda laughed. "It's not like I tricked you or anything."

"No, but you've kept quiet about your real objective. So what *are* you after? Billy's case isn't your kind of project."

"Didn't I tell you? I've been chasing down funds behind the prime ministerial election. Yang's got a hand in a major development project in Vietnam and some of that money wound up in the Liberal Democratic Party's coffers. Got word of it via informants in China, which conversely makes it all the more plausible."

"You mean the Val-Nam Scheme?"

"There you go. Bingo. So you knew about it? That there's a gold mine for journalists. Remember way back, those huge kickbacks to the LDP from postwar reparations paid to Indonesia? It's as big as that."

"Are you saying there was political pressure on the Department to have the cases dropped?"

"Can't tell if it goes that far. Your Prefectural Police have a grand tradition of sucking up to the US military. Word is the Chief of Investigations was rubbing his hands the minute he heard they'd found the body from the crash. Meant they could call it a wrap."

"You been drinking?" I asked.

"That I have. Drinking to keep sane. They assigned me to a special feature on child abuse. Believe me, Yang's a far more decent criminal than these parents who do things to kids." He trailed off into a sigh of pained resignation.

I clicked CALL END, then looked up the number for Palm Brothers House. There didn't seem to be anyone on Sunday night duty, only a recorded woman's voice repeating that weekend concierge service ended at 3 p.m. While trying to save the number to my mobile, I noticed a MISSED CALL/MESSAGE icon on the screen.

Aileen had called three times the day before. Twice she hung up without saying a thing. The third time it was, "I'm in Tokyo for work. I'll stay overnight here, then I'm down in Kansai most of next week." Her voice was irregular, breathy. "No, that's not what I wanted to say. It's just that I'm so phobic about people leaving without saying goodbye—sorry, I know I'm acting strange. Forget it . . . What's with this, why won't it erase?" Through muffled sounds of flustered fingers came a push-button double beep.

I listened to her voice one more time, then erased the recording for her sake. While I was at it, I took out all the name cards I'd accumulated, together with my address book, and entered the lot on my mobile phone. Then, once I was done, I reconsidered, wondering what would happen if the phone fell into the wrong hands. It made me nervous, so in the end I deleted half the numbers and changed the remaining entries to code names only I would recognize. Before I knew it, I'd been screwing around with the gizmo for close to two hours. Disgusted with myself, I buried it under a cushion.

30

I put on my official "we" voice when I called the moving company on Monday morning. "Prefectural Police here. There's a few questions we'd like to ask." Specifically, where had they moved the evidence from Parklane Terrace 504? "We believe your client was a Jason Co., Ltd. or a Mr. Chris Ackerman. Or would you rather we serve you a warrant?" Sometimes this alone works. This was one of those times.

The female staffer answered without hesitation. "The waybill says it was offloaded here in Yokohama. Joyo Storage, No. 4 Chiwakacho, Kanagawa Ward."

"A rental storeroom?"

"Yes, that's right. One of those container places, I guess. I'm not too clear about it myself."

I jotted down the address in my agenda and dialed 104 for directory assistance, but there was no listing for any Joyo Storage in Kanagawa Ward. Either the management was under another name or the corporate offices were somewhere else. And a rental storeroom was bound to be a dead end. I shut my agenda and gave it a think.

Next I rang up Yang and got through surprisingly quickly, to the man himself no less.

"Did you call me yesterday?" he asked first. "So sorry, I was tied up. It's about that little pact we made, isn't it? By rights, I ought to have called you. My apologies."

"They found the cargo, didn't they?"

"My, don't we have keen ears."

"Was everything there?"

"Most of it got burned, but that's neither here nor there. As I said previously, it's enough that I know the cargo was loaded on the plane. It's a matter of face."

"I didn't know there were so many high mountains in Taiwan."

"Yushan? You Japanese don't know your own history! You colonialists called it Niitakayama, 'New High Peak,' higher than Mount Fuji. It was even your Imperial Navy's signal code to launch the attack on Pearl Harbor. Nowadays there are military installations around the mountain, which is why it took so long to get confirmation."

"So Billy's off the hook and I'm no longer of service to you."

He chortled at this. "Don't taunt an old man," he said, about to hang up.

"Ackerman told me what was in that cargo," I cut in. "You said you had no connection with Park Lane Terrace, but his office is there on the fifth floor. You ought to know, he's your business partner in the development scheme on the outskirts of Ho Chi Minh."

"And an acquaintance of Billy's, too?" he responded calmly. "I can't count the number of corporations in that joint venture, and more sales agents than stars in the sky. Even I don't have a full grasp of the whole scheme. No doubt there are a few wild cards in the deck, Billy among them."

"I assume you're familiar with *Hellboy in Paradise*, the novel by Yasuichi Orimasa? Aren't you the model for the Hong Kong triad member?"

"I have no idea what you're talking about."

"It's a *yakuza* and GI crime story set at the end of the Vietnam War, and one of the characters is a dead ringer for you. And it's being made into a movie. Tsunetoshi Inamoto of *Zoom* magazine is in charge of the filming. If you want to claim defamation of character, he's the man to talk to," I rattled off. "One last thing. Could you possibly introduce me to Mr. Zou of Golden Harbor Enterprises? I want to lease a commercial property in Yokosuka he manages. I'm thinking of quitting the police to run a hamburger place. Actually, I heard you were the owner of that company."

"Please, I'm a busy man. Is this more poppycock your Inamoto fed you?"

Speaking of food, before Yang could hang up on me, I proposed we meet in Chinatown over some dim sum. Of course he wouldn't dream of it. I tried to picture him eating a pork bun, but he probably only ate Chinese at some high-class hotel on days when the American Club was sold out of steak and fries.

Lunchtime came, so naturally I headed for Chinatown. Once again I parked my car in the courtyard at Kagacho Police Station and called up to Notomi in Forensics. Once again he came down, to say sorry, he'd already ordered a lunchbox. "It's been delivered and is sitting up there." Then, as if in apology, he handed over the bullet in a ziplock bag together with a word processor printout. "I've written it all down but anyway, it's from an 8 mm Nambu handgun, military issue from around 1925. Almost unmistakable."

"8 mm? Must be pretty rare."

"Nowadays, yes. But at the time, 8 mm automatics were the weapons of choice. They had different ideas about military ordnance. Only America used 11.9 mm models or what they call .45s. They were fighting Indians coming at them with tomahawks and needed something bigger to wham them in one shot."

"Does the bullet itself date from back then?"

"Yes, also in the report. After the war, some gun enthusiasts had a few made by special order in America, but the manufacture differed slightly. It's amazing, that California website. Not even their police have so much data." He rolled his eyes in admiration. "Oh yes and, sorry to say, this baby did not hit a human body. You see that white stuff? That's mildew, enough to corrode the jacket. Even if it had hit someone, it would never have gone through."

"What makes you think that?"

"The gunpowder had deteriorated. Would have significantly reduced the initial velocity and impact." Quite possibly, he speculated, it might have jammed the gun. He lowered his eyes. "Mind if I hold on to it as a keepsake? It's a rarity."

"Okay, but on the off chance this later becomes a case, it's your headache."

"No problem. I'll just brilliantly discover it in its original location."

I handed the bullet back, then went for chicken rice at a Cantonese place I know. No matter how impossible the lunch hour crowds, you can always get a seat there. Everything else they serve is terrible.

After lunch, I decided to drop by Palm Brothers House, but the concierge I'd met that night wasn't around. Instead, a fifty-something man in a dark suit informed me there were separate day, night and weekend shifts. He had weekday daytime duty, though he did remember Billy. "He'd come in dead drunk and sleep in the lobby, who can forget that?"

"But I thought you said you're on the day shift."

"I am, but he'd still be sleeping there at noon. Funny thing, though, not a soul complained. Except for one of our more prudish customers."

I handed him my card and said I was investigating Billy.

"So you're police, then?"

"Yeah I'm police, but this isn't an official investigation. Billy was a friend of mine."

"Fair enough, but what's the story? If a murder suspect dies, doesn't that more or less close the case?"

"Well, since dead men tell no tales, how about you tell me instead. This property belongs to Golden Harbor Enterprises, doesn't it?"

He believed so, though he himself had been sent there by a hire operation and had no contact with the actual owners. What he did know was that Billy's deposit money had been forfeited and the lease terminated as of the end of August. All the personal possessions he left behind, about two trunks' worth, mostly clothes, had been transferred to the company warehouse. Which was not uncommon among short-term foreign residents. "The thing is, he lived here quite some time, maybe four years all told."

"And only two trunks of stuff?"

"Yes. He'd come and go, wasn't here half the time. The longest absences, he'd show up after close to two months away. He must have been flying around somewhere. I think he had a home in San Francisco."

Billy had moved in with a big trunk, a classy Louis Vuitton ocean liner number—probably the same one the dead woman had been found in. Then, as if he'd just remembered something, he withdrew behind the front desk. "Would you know a Paulita Maxwell?"

"From where?" I asked.

"From Nago, down in Okinawa," he said, pushing a slip of paper across the counter.

I quickly copied down the details before he could change his mind. "Did she call?"

"No, she showed up in person, during my shift. Last Friday it must have been. Said she'd tried phoning him dozens of times."

"Pity. Wish I could have met her. I'll give her a call."

The concierge leaned over the counter and lowered his voice. "Right after she left, two men barged in and demanded to know what the woman wanted."

"Not cops, I take it."

"Hardly. They didn't show any credentials, let alone badges. It was just *Tell us*."

"Japanese?"

"Well, sure. They said they were from a credit agency running a background check at the request of a relative. I told them she was just asking directions and sent them on their way."

I walked back to Kagacho to get my car. The rookie I recognized by now spotted me coming from far off, but looked away when I greeted him. Sitting in the car, I phoned Paulita Maxwell, introducing myself as a friend of Billy's and saying they'd given me her number at his apartment.

"I'm so glad you called," she answered in a deep, husky voice that reminded me of the golden age of cinema. "Do you know where he is?"

"Didn't the receptionist tell you?"

"All he said was they'd terminated his lease, so I should go to the authorities if I wanted to find him. His English was so bad I could hardly understand him, but I wasn't desperate enough to go to the police. Is it bad news?"

"The man probably meant they could fill you in on the details. Are you back in Okinawa by now?"

"No, I'm just on my way, at Yokohama Station waiting for a bus to Haneda Airport, but I can take another flight if you want to meet up."

I told her to wait outside Yokohama City Air Terminal on the east side of the station, and stepped on the gas. Even from a distance she was easy to spot: wavy blonde hair, low-rise jeans, and short white blouse, standing by the taxi rank with a red roller bag. I pulled over to the drop-off curb and honked.

"Mr. Futamura?" she said, hopping in on the passenger side. "Call me Paulie. I didn't think it got this cold here, I'm fr-eezing."

"I'll drive you to Haneda, we can talk on the way," I offered, U-turning sharply through a department store loading zone toward the on-ramp right under the expressway. We barely had time for introductions before we reached the toll booth. She was from San Francisco, an art school graduate. She'd met Billy while part-timing in an office at San José Airport. I didn't ask, but she couldn't have been more than thirty.

"Well, enough about me." She spoke with quiet resignation. "Tell me the bad news."

"Billy's jet crashed in Taiwan, two months ago now."

"Jesus—"

"Hardly made the papers. Small plane, one fatality, plus the

Taiwanese have a history of sitting on information. And Japan being Japan, there's the police and there's politicians, neither of whom want the story made public."

"He's the fatality, isn't he?"

"I can't be sure, but everyone says so. Lately I don't know what to believe."

"I'll go there. Where in Taiwan?"

"Were you married?"

"Us?" She shook her head and smiled, but her eyes brimmed with tears.

I turned my attention to the road ahead. Brushing past the factories of Kawasaki, the Yokohama–Haneda route traced a graceful arc toward the Tama River. "If you're not family, it won't do any good going there. Chances are the police have turned him over to some national security corps by now."

"Wouldn't they at least show me his grave?"

I canned further comment. If she'd already made up her mind, there was nothing more for me to add. "Since when were you and Billy . . . ?"

"Two years . . . but we weren't living together. I'd always dreamed of moving to Hawaii, so I could paint. Working at the airport, I got this crazy idea that if I had a pilot for a boyfriend, maybe he'd fly me there." She grinned through her tears. "But Billy, he'd never let me set foot in that jet. He wasn't allowed to, being a hired hand and all."

I reached over to open the glove compartment where I kept a box of tissues.

She blew her nose and continued. "He invited me to Okinawa the winter before last. I'd planned to stay till summer, but ended up liking the place and rented a beach house up at the north end of the island. Billy would show up from time to time, maybe three weeks at a stretch, but it's not like we lived there as a couple. He just wasn't the type."

"What type was he then?"

"Him and me, we drank. A lot. Sometimes until morning. The League of Insomniacs he called us, we pulled so many all-nighters. I told him it seemed like we only existed for each other when we met. Which seemed to surprise him, like, did I actually exist when we were apart?" She mussed her hair and gave a raspy laugh.

"In whose name did you rent the house?"

"Mine, but Billy chipped in for his lodging. Ten thousand yen a night, meals included. Him staying half the month paid the rent and covered all our groceries. Everything's cheap up north in Okinawa."

"Sounds like him."

"Oh? It was my idea."

"So let me guess, he bought the liquor."

She bent forward and nodded like a sniffing cat. "Well of course."

"Any friends in Okinawa?"

"Him? Occasionally he'd bring friends by, maybe four or five in all. Base types, but only one still in active service."

"Anyone named Ackerman?"

"I don't think so. This guy was Latino, an airman."

"He had friends in the Air Force too?" I don't know why that struck me as odd.

"Yeah, not that I'd go out of my way to see them, so I never took down their numbers. I really don't like military types, and the Americans you run into over here turn me off."

"That's mighty un-American of you." Now it was my turn to laugh.

"Funny, Billy said the same thing."

I got off at the Haneda ramp and followed the surface road around the runway fence.

"This whole thing has me spooked. First he doesn't answer the phone, then they close up his Yokohama apartment . . ."

"What've you been doing since visiting the apartment?"

"I remembered Billy once introduced me to some friends who live up here."

"Named Yang and Orimasa maybe?"

217

"No, Vietnamese. They were my last hope, the only ones who might know how to get in touch with him, but the phone number didn't seem to work. I'd pretty much given up."

"These Vietnamese, were they named Tran?"

"No, but *she* was," Paulie corrected. "Tran Kinh Hoa."

Before I knew it, I'd stopped on the side of the airport access road and cars were swerving past us honking.

"What's the matter? What's so important?"

"The husband, he wasn't Tran Binh Long?"

"No, he was introduced as Lê something-or-other. Lê Ngữ Thanh, was it?"

"Vietnamese married couples have different last names?"

"At least according to Billy they do," she said, giving me a puzzled look.

I asked her for Tran Kinh Hoa's number and jotted it down, then parked in the short-term lot and saw her into the Departures lobby. We still had a little time to spare. When she stood on tiptoe at the check-in counter, red T-back panties showed over the top of her jeans. I averted my eyes.

As did a man at the far end of the airline counters. I don't know why, but something about him didn't seem right. A light raincoat out of season, an earphone cord trailing out of one ear. Airport security maybe, but no necktie. When we moved toward a café stand, he motioned with his chin and another man got up from a bench by the lobby clock and slowly walked in our direction. I hurried us to the furthest queue and ordered some coffee.

"This Vietnamese couple, where did you meet them?" I resumed.

"In Okinawa. He worked at the Naha docks. Cleaning warehouses, moving freight, odd jobs. She sold who-knows-what brand-name goods in the free trade zone."

"Is that something American military-related?"

"No, I don't think so. It's right on the waterfront by the airport, a tax-free compound with workshops, food courts and stuff. I'm pretty sure it's got some special status under Japanese law, and not just for buying and selling. Say you bring in a half-built computer from Taiwan to finish assembling there. Presto! Your Taiwanese laptop becomes Made in Japan, without import duties. There's probably all sorts of other angles to the place, but I'm no expert. Okinawa has no industry, but it was supposed to be an easy fix."

"Okay, then what? Did Billy herd them up here?"

"No, nothing like that." She shook her shiny blonde hair under the café lights. "There was the Okinawa Summit last summer, remember? On account of which, security was real tight from early spring. Police came knocking, wanting to know who lived where, making a clean sweep of illegal overstays, so it's like they were chased out."

"And they wound up in Yokosuka?"

"They did? I wouldn't know, they left without a word. I only found out when I tried calling her mobile and the message said they'd moved up here. Her English isn't great, so it was hard to understand over the phone. And he doesn't speak any English at all."

"The wife, did she get headaches?" I asked, firing at random.

Paulie went wide-eyed and nodded. "You know her? Sometimes she'd have to go lie down. She never told me why, probably didn't want to worry me, but I'm sure it was trauma or something to do with the war. Poor thing."

"How about Aileen Hsu, do you know her?"

"No, afraid not. Is she a friend of Billy's?" Naturally the name Reiko Hiraoka wouldn't register either.

It was almost departure time, so we headed for the hand-carry scan. The second man hadn't touched his coffee. The raincoat appeared out of nowhere and slipped into the queue ahead of her. Just before the metal detector, she turned and waved—*Thanks!*

I started toward the escalator, then quickly looked back mid-step. I watched the second man, now at the tail end of the check-in queue, head through toward the boarding area, then lost him in a blur of movement.

31

The restaurant across the way had hung out a BLOWFISH NOW IN SEA-SON sign. Reason enough to go there that evening. I had just downed my first glass of *shochu* when my phone rang. The grumpy proprietor glared at me, so I stepped out under the eaves and pressed TALK.

"Inamoto here," came a nasal voice. "Thanks for calling. I'd been meaning to get in touch."

"I was trying to get in touch with Orimasa," I said.

"Ah yes, difficult man to get hold of. He's been in Hong Kong for some magazine job until today. More like he went there to gamble," he chortled.

"I read *Hellboy in Paradise*. Have you started filming yet?"

"No, and that's the stinker. It seems our author has turned prima donna on us."

"He doesn't like the script?"

"If only. How shall I put it? He now says he wants us to film a different novel of his. And this is after we've already committed to budget for the present one."

"Did Yang's company invest too?"

"Who? Which company?"

"Nanyang Holdings. Yang Yun-shi."

Inamoto practically squealed in disbelief. "You must be joking. He'd never risk ten yen on a film, though we did approach him."

"Then how about Jason Co., Ltd.? I found a copy of the film treatment at their office."

"Promo packs are like name cards, you toss them wherever you smell money." No, regrettably Inamoto had never heard of Ackerman's firm, which prompted him to go off on a tangent about losing a pile of money on some other project.

Okay, I cut in, so what was it he'd wanted to talk to me about?

"Ah yes, sorry. About Mr. Bonney. What's become of him? I was told he'd suddenly returned to America. Was there a problem? You must know something. What is it with him anyway—claiming to fly a private jet—is he wealthy? Or his family?"

"Could be. Hawaiian royalty or something?"

"Really?" he cried incredulously. "You mustn't tease me like that! Though I was wondering, mightn't Mr. Bonney have had something to do with this sudden whim of Orimasa's? It's just a hunch, but perhaps he took offense at the book?"

"So the Japanese-Brazilian character *is* modeled on Billy, then."

"They both deny it, but it's got to be him, absolutely. Our author only writes from personal experience, on account of which he's had his share of run-ins with people he uses for models. He says he makes them colorful, but to them it's libel." Inamoto trailed off, as if chewing his words to mush.

"Mr. Inamoto, would you know someone named Tran?"

"Ah-ha," he perked up. "Ever the policeman, leaving no stone unturned." This didn't sound as unconcerned as he may have hoped. An uneasy silence hovered between us. When he next spoke, his voice had lost its edge. "Just how much do you know about Tran, Mr. Futamura?"

"This is the Vietnamese living up in the hills in Yokosuka?"

"Oh. I dare say you're more informed than I am!" He started to laugh, then stopped himself mid-breath. "Actually, when was it? I'd been wanting to have a look at the Dobuita area, so I asked Mr. Bonney to show me around. Thinking back on it, I believe I may have said something rather unfortunate to Tran."

"What was she doing in Dobuita?"

"She? This Tran was a man. He ran a little hole-in-the-wall called Kaput. You know, the one who died in that freezer accident."

"You mean Tran Binh Long?" I asked in surprise.

"Yes, that's right. Mr. Bonney got drunk and fell asleep in the bar. I wasn't too sober myself. Well, I started talking with this Vietnamese fellow and we got along famously, though I suppose that's not so uncommon when you're drinking. But you know, this Tran was quite the intellectual, and a former Viet Cong guerrilla to boot! When he learned I was an editor with *Zoom*, he asked all sorts of things. And I, being the person I am, probably got carried away and said something remiss about Mr. Bonney. Then later, out of nowhere, our author Orimasa gets cold feet. The story's based on actual events and everyone in it is a criminal of sorts, so I'm afraid my little faux pas may not have gone down well."

"What was this 'something' you said about Billy?"

"If only I could remember. I haven't a clue, no idea whatsoever."

"Does Tran figure as a character in the novel?"

"I wonder . . . not that our author would let on. He didn't exactly take kindly to my having met Tran." Again Inamoto stifled his chatter only to come back impulsively, "What about meeting up, say tomorrow? I'll be in Yokohama."

We settled on ten o'clock at Minato Mirai. He had a lunch appointment nearby.

When I stepped back inside to finish my meal, the gruff old proprietor thought I was a new customer and gave me a proper welcome.

For some reason I remembered Père Guignard mentioning that Tran's sister, a Madame Lê, lived with her husband in the vicinity. But by then Investigations had bought the accident story, so any chance of searching out the couple was pretty well nixed.

Come to think of it, what had Precinct done with Tran's corpse? Had they even tried to contact the couple? Not likely. Even the priest didn't know their whereabouts, they showed up so rarely for Sunday Mass. Nor would Investigations have bothered to ask the Frenchman to relay a message to the next of kin.

Père Guignard had called the sister Madame Lê, but maybe that was just an assumption on his part, not realizing that Vietnamese couples keep their own surnames. Assuming either the husband or wife or maybe even both were illegal immigrants and Tran Binh Long rented a house in his name for his sister, the Tran who met the realtor and the Tran the landlord saw every day could easily have been two different persons. Not much chance anyone ever compared notes. Which would make the couple Mr. and Mrs. Tran—and Mr. Lê simply vanishes from the picture.

While talking myself through the possibilities, my glass of *shochu* on the rocks also vanished. In the end, I ordered another and made sure I drank it before settling my bill.

32

Even so, I was back in my apartment by eight o'clock. No live TV game on a Monday, but that didn't stop me from stretching out on the sofa with a stiff drink. I'd dozed off staring at the blank screen and when I jumped to get the phone it wasn't even ten.

"I'm on the coast route now." Aileen's voice trembled slightly.

"Weren't you down in Kansai?"

"My fault. But you should've called to know I wasn't."

I couldn't think how to respond. I got up from the sofa and looked out the window, waiting in silence. The paper lanterns of the restaurant across the way were still lit.

"Today's my transit day. But I can still make it in time if I catch the bullet train tomorrow morning," she said. "I'm in a taxi on my way to Yokosuka. Just crossing the bridge—I can see your neighborhood."

"If you're on the bridge, you can make a detour."

"Well, naturally," she laughed in a lonely way.

Before I could arrange where to meet, she said she'd call when she got to where she'd dropped me off the first night, then hung up. It took me a second to figure out what she meant. I quickly tossed down the last of my drink, threw open every window, and leapt into a frenzy of cleaning. I gathered up all my crap—old papers and magazines, stray shoes by the door, dirty dishes from the sink— and ferried the lot to the bedroom. I barely had time to do a quick vacuum of the floor, then practically bungee-jumped into the shower. My hair was still wet when Aileen called. I toweled dry while closing half the windows, tossed the damp terrycloth into the bedroom, grabbed a clean shirt, and after rolling down the divider blind to cordon off the kitchen, ran out the front door.

Aileen waved from far off the moment I hit the pavement. The mercury vapor lamps in the park put a glow on her cream-colored jacket and short skirt. I grabbed her Boston bag and asked if she'd had dinner as we passed the blowfish restaurant, hoping I could interest her, but no, she never ate much at night unless she'd had a marathon concert.

"There's a nice bar nearby," I suggested.

She reached out a smooth hand and pulled me to a stop. "I don't want to go anywhere there's lots of people."

"Well, my place is in no shape to invite you up."

"Did you forget? You're talking to an orphan raised in a bomb shelter."

"I don't have any champagne."

"Oh, but I do. Bought it for a nightcap."

Yes, her bag did seem a little heavy. I hoisted it onto my shoulder and started toward my apartment when I noticed, with a sigh, that she was still holding my hand.

Among the things in her bag was a bottle of Louis Roederer Brut, unchilled, of course. I showed her to the sofa and ducked through the lowered blind to the kitchen.

"Why were you heading to Yokosuka?"

"To collect something I forgot."

We'd both combed her mother's condo from top to bottom, but I didn't ask what the something was.

"I don't have the right glasses," I added, excavating leftover ice from the freezer.

"Hey, may I?" She'd slipped into the kitchen and held out a shopping bag containing a tomato, a lemon, a piece of cheese, and bread. "For breakfast," she said calmly, placing the cutting board on the counter. "Knives?"

"All useless."

"You don't cook, do you?"

"Don't need more hobbies." I dug a folding camp knife out of a drawer and handed it over, then returned to the living room with a half-bowl of ice for the champagne. While waiting, I decided I might as well roll up the blind, just as she brought out a plate of toasted black bread with melted chèvre. It smelled like a haymow after a sudden shower.

I took the armchair and offered her the sofa, but she claimed a cushion on the floor instead and jostled the champagne bottle. "Not cold yet," she complained.

"Sorry, no ice bucket either. Never thought I'd be throwing a house party here. Not much of a host, am I?"

"No, *I'm* sorry, barging in like this," she said. "I just didn't want to go out anywhere." She placed a hand on my knee to rest her chin. I felt like a teddy bear. With my knee held captive, I stretched back to the low cabinet behind me to grab a bottle of Bacardi and filled two glasses.

Aileen went ahead and popped the champagne, then topped my drink with a foamy splash and squeeze of lemon. I was about to scold her for wasting good bubbly until she took a sip and gave it a thumbs-up. "Yum, tastes like unsweetened ice cream."

The concoction wasn't half bad. It went well with the cheese on toast too. We each drank two rounds while the rest of the champagne chilled.

"Impromptu is always best," she said with a snicker. "How about you? Gone back to drinking your friend's special cocktail?"

I shook my head. "No. He was a murder suspect, and he made me help him escape from the scene of the crime."

"Wow. And that's why he hasn't returned?"

"Making me help him wasn't so bad. At the time I could have asked him to his face, was he involved? Or even earlier—but I didn't. Not that I avoided it. We'd be drinking and he just kept coming out with all these unbelievable stories."

As I set down my empty glass, Aileen pressed my hand. "Ouch. How'd you do this?"

"Scraped it on the street."

She drew the sore hand up to her cheek, then casually snuggled into the crook of my arm. "I really didn't forget anything at the condo," she confessed. "I just couldn't think of anywhere else to go, not until I looked this way from the bridge."

"I didn't think so. I turned the place upside down."

She didn't seem to hear me, she was looking through me somewhere. "Since Mom disappeared, it's like I don't know who I am anymore. And it scares me. I wasn't really worried about her—I'm a bad daughter."

"You've had other things to worry about."

Her big eyes glistened, ready to spill.

"I could help you find out about your background if you want. Your Signor Duecento, I bet he knows who you are." That many roses would make a nice big wreath for a pachinko parlor opening. "Do you remember flying in a plane?"

"Coming to Japan? No, only a ship." She was still holding my hand, tight enough to almost pull me up with her when she moved.

"I'd like to take a shower. Please."

I held her back and spoke gently but firmly. "You can't stay here. The bed's a tiny hand-me-down from when they were renovating the holding cells at the station." I probably should have booked her a hotel room, but she'd just checked out of a hotel.

Aileen gave me a long look and slowly lowered herself onto the cushion, breathing uneasily, somewhere between a whistle and a laugh. She raised her empty glass for some champagne, and after a sip to see if it was chilled, sat straight up to drink the rest. Then, pretending to be sober, she announced, "Well, better be going. Got an early morning ahead of me. Could you call me a taxi?"

"You can stay in Yokohama."

"Please."

"I'll drive you."

"No you won't, you've been drinking."

"Not as much as you that night." Nor as much as me on another night.

She didn't answer, she just stared in silence. I called a taxi. And when the cab arrived out front, I carried her bag downstairs for her.

"So bye," she said with a wave. "It was fun, for a one-time thing, even if it won't happen again." She spoke right at me, but it wasn't me she was telling this to.

I watched the taxi turn the corner and returned to my apartment, went straight to the bedroom, and tidied up. Which left the living room and kitchen and entryway still cluttered. It occurred to me that if I really wanted to be doing this, I could have done it while she was still there, looking on.

The ice in the bowl had all melted and there wasn't any more in the fridge. I drank a warm glass of rum and did the dishes. She'd left the tomato on the cutting board. I picked it up, but stopped short of tossing it in the trash. It tasted like mud.

33

The sky weighed low and heavy from morning on. Yet the city was bathed in a hidden glow, the fat underbelly of clouds shining like bluefish.

I skipped out of work early and drove to the much-hyped new urban hub out behind Sakuragicho. It's theoretically a five-minute walk away, but the moving sidewalks and skybridges and underground passages linking all the new high-rises always flummox me whenever I try to go there on foot. Much easier to set my sights on one particular multiplex structure and park in the garage, then take the central elevator to the second floor as Inamoto had instructed. Out on a cedar-decked esplanade around a sunken courtyard, I spotted the awning of the appointed café and a vacant table.

Below in the courtyard, young people lazed about, enjoying a waterfall spilling down a concrete cliff and the view along a canal to the giant ferris wheel and roller coaster across the harbor inlet. A leisurely scene accented here and there with splashes of color, and music playing somewhere.

A waitress came with a teapot and lengthy instructions, before flipping over a miniature hourglass. I couldn't be bothered. I took off the tea cozy and poured a cup.

A little over ten minutes later, my phone rang and an out-of-breath Inamoto apologized, saying he was still at Yokohama Station. "I'm getting in a taxi right now. Something came up just as I was leaving. A phone call from guess who. Remember yesterday, we were talking about Tran's brother-in-law? Well, by a strange coincidence—"

The line cut off, but I didn't try to call back. Nor did he. Yokohama Station was less than ten minutes away by car. Soon enough a taxi came into sight from the harbor end of the road beside the canal and pulled over to the opposite curb. Inamoto got out and hurriedly paid the fare, then went behind the cab to cross to the other side. When he reached the middle he paused to check the oncoming traffic. As the taxi moved off, a white station wagon waiting right behind it released its brakes and made straight for him.

There was a dull thud. I ran to the railing to see Inamoto lying in the middle of the road holding his leg, trying to get up, white in the face. Two men climbed out of the back of the station wagon. One in a blue jersey who didn't look Japanese, the other in a mechanic's jumpsuit with a gauze surgical mask hiding his features. They yanked Inamoto up and dragged him into the car.

I dashed down the courtyard steps and dodged an obstacle course of garden statuary and fountainside seating to reach the roadside just as the Subaru Legacy station wagon pulled away. Cars had stopped in alarm, drivers stood by gawking.

"They just took him. Some kinda nasty business," was a delivery man's obvious comment.

"Wasn't anything we could do, was there?" a young pedestrian summed up for one and all.

"Anybody get the license number?" I asked.

"I did!" shouted another bystander, but she'd only seen four digits. I told her to call the police and ran. Way up ahead on the canal road the white Subaru had stopped at a red light. I ran flat out through a barrage of honking horns. Just twenty meters more . . .

The light changed. The Subaru turned right onto the main avenue and my lungs gave out. I slouched over to the sidewalk to catch my breath, when I noticed a middle-aged Chinese man with gold-rim glasses on the far street corner squinting in the direction the vehicle had gone.

A patch of sunlight through the clouds lit up Wang Lun's face as he jaywalked, unaware of my presence, to a shiny blue-black Mercedes parked across the street. He got in on the passenger side, the turn signal blinked, and the car sped off.

I gave up on trying to follow him—never a taxi when you need one—and returned to the scene. There wasn't a soul around now, either on the street or the sidewalk. No police either. Had anyone even called? This was no hit-and-run accident; they'd abducted Inamoto with premeditated intent and the life-or-death clock was ticking. I had to go get my phone.

Back at the café everything was just as I'd left it. The waitress came to refill the teapot, then replaced the tea cozy and lectured me on the proper way to partake of one's second infusion.

Cutting her short, I called First Division Investigations. The Chief was out but I got hold of a squad leader, a serious type several years my junior named Yoshinaga, and told him I'd witnessed an automobile assault and the injured party being forcibly removed. Judging from the circumstances, the odds were they hadn't taken the victim to a hospital. The car in question was an old model Subaru Legacy, white, only four digits of the license number known. I duly reported Inamoto's name and occupation, saying I'd had an appointment with him at the time. I said nothing about Wang Lun or Yang.

Next I called Yang's mobile, but to my surprise the number had been discontinued. So I pulled out my agenda and found the number for Nanyang Holdings.

A Japanese woman, not a particularly young voice, answered, "Please hold." Then after a moment or two, "I'm sorry, the Chairman is presently unavailable."

"Very well, then, can you please give him a message. It's urgent. If the Chairman can't be reached, then Mr. Wang—I saw him just now at the Minato Mirai waterfront."

"What is it you wish to tell him?"

"A mutual acquaintance was just hit by a car and Wang was there on the scene." I spelled out Inamoto's name and the make of the car for good measure. "His injuries probably won't be fatal, but the police have been alerted. Just tell him that, it's urgent," I insisted. "It might affect Mr. Yang's business affairs."

As I hung up, I felt a cold sweat moving down my spine. For the last few days, pretty much as Tomoda said, I'd been beating around a bush. Only I'd picked the wrong bush. Or no, I got the right bush, but the snake in it had bitten a harmless tourist.

I drank the tea. I was upset to learn the café didn't serve alcohol, so I slapped down the exact change and left. Then, waiting for the elevator down to the garage, I had a sudden idea and rang up Orimasa. His answer message came on, though the day before his phone hadn't been powered up.

Inamoto had said he had a lunch appointment nearby and Orimasa was back from Hong Kong. Putting two and two together, I blundered my way through a shopping mall passage to a different bank of elevators and up to the seventy-first floor. Arriving at Orimasa's sports club, I was told he'd reserved a conference room from eleven-thirty.

"Afraid I'm a little early," I said looking at my watch. It was barely eleven.

The desk manager offered to show me into the room, but I said I'd wait in the lobby, and I settled on a corner sofa where I had a discreet view of the entrance. Even before lunchtime, a remarkable number of dark suits shuffled to and fro between in-house meetings. The rest were of that charmed species who don't work afternoons.

Not ten minutes later, the reception telephone rang and the desk manager looked furtively my way. A short hush-hush later, he asked me over to take a call from Orimasa.

"Oh, it's you," intoned the voice of a late-night rerun villain. "Been up to all sorts of fun, have we?"

"Just stirred things up a bit."

"Well, thanks to you, I can write one thing off."

"So is your editor going to be okay?"

"Why can't you sit still and shut up for once? I got a call from Inamoto. He said he was still in the car. He wasn't that hurt, but they were waving a blade between his legs."

I put on a businesslike tone. "And what are their contractual terms?"

"Get real, Futamura. A man's life is in danger. No, make that three lives, counting you and me. Push your luck and you're asking for a hitman visit. Hong Zhi-long's been quiet lately, but you never know, for a while there he'd do a job for the hole in a five-yen coin. A population of a hundred-fifty million does tend to lower the price per head."

"Better a guy who takes money for it than a creep who does it for fun."

"You know, you boys in the police need lessons in risk management. Listen, I'm going to disappear for a bit. So don't try to find me, and leave Inamoto be as well."

"I can't promise. But just let me ask you something. One time, didn't you say Billy saved a lot of lives?"

It was the first time I'd heard him lose his cool. "Drop it. You've run out of time. But after all you've done to try to clear Billy's name, if he's still on your mind, do us all a favor and do nothing. Have yourself a few drinks like him and forget about it. You know your Hamlet? 'The rest is silence.'"

"Those were last words . . ." I hung up no wiser, except for one thing: if Billy always downed a few drinks to forget, then the Ernesto Fujikawa character had to be him.

"Scotch, sir?" The desk manager was suddenly at my elbow. "It's on Mr. Orimasa." A waiter appeared from the back carrying a tray. I hesitated for all of three seconds, then followed him to a room where floor-to-ceiling bookshelves lined every wall, the perfect padded cell to drink and think about Billy Lou Bonney. Not about all the lies and missing pieces of the puzzle he'd left behind, but about the times we drank together.

Try as I might, I couldn't muster enough lenience to find him innocent. Even supposing he did kill that woman, what did it matter now? Very little of his spiel was fact. He wasn't a fighter pilot in the Vietnam War, he couldn't even fly a plane at the time. He wasn't American by birth, he was half Peruvian, one of thousands of enlistees scrambling to get citizenship. But so what? None of it made any difference now.

For all his faults and crazy nonsense, I'd enjoyed his company. If not for him I'd never have had cocktails at midday while on duty and so close to Headquarters at that. I didn't want him to see me drinking coffee in a bar, as if that were some kind of betrayal. Nothing strange about befriending a drunk, any more than befriending a liar—even if the liar turned out to be a murderer. I guess there were better policemen around.

34

The two trolls had gone to their old canteen for lunch. No way they'd be back before three. Nine times out of ten they'd head straight home afterwards.

I rang up a nearby lunch delivery place, but they didn't do single orders until two o'clock. So I was brewing some tea to clear my thoughts about Tran's brother-in-law when the mobile I'd found in Reiko Hiraoka's car started ringing.

"Hey, is that you, Futamura? Where the hell d'you get this phone?" asked Sato in lieu of a greeting. "Must've pinched it from that dive where your Vietnamese guy worked."

"And hello to you, too. Why'd you ask?"

"I'm calling there."

I took a deep breath, but couldn't think of a comeback. Sato kept going regardless.

"You asked me to check four numbers. The Yokosuka landline number, it's for that bar. What gives?"

"You tell me."

"Two were mobiles, right? One was contracted in Okinawa, shut down on account of unpaid phone bills. Don't ask how I found out. Sneaky is as sneaky does."

It was the incoming call number that Reiko Hiraoka received three times in two days. Something clanged in my head.

"Just a sec." I set down the phone and grabbed my agenda. The number was identical with the one Paulita Maxwell had given me for Tran's sister. Sato asked what was up, but I kept it to myself.

"The other mobile number was contracted to a company in

Yokohama. Real estate and transport. Unsubscribed as of June. Ever hear of a Golden Harbor Enterprises?"

I had indeed, no surprise there. "But what about the other land-line?"

"Hold on, there's something about this I don't understand. The phone you got is probably a quick-cash resale. The number's on ice for now."

"On ice?"

"Not currently being used, but the dealer—some scalper who trades in phone contracts—he's keeping it in reserve because it's a saleable number. Go down to the bottom and it'll show you."

Down to the bottom? "Whatever you say." I figured out what the ex-snoop meant.

"So now call up the menu and tell me the number on that phone," he said.

I did as told and punched a few buttons. Right away a number appeared on-screen.

"Hey . . . that *isn't* Reiko's phone," he said loudly.

No, I thought to myself, but how would he know? "I didn't know you had her mobile number. You must've been pretty friendly."

Quelling an outburst, he admitted, "All us old folks got to have mobile phones nowadays. Any idea who this one belongs to?"

Flipping through my agenda again I happened to see a row of four digits: all I'd been able to make out of the license plate on the yellow pickup truck. "Think you could run a vehicle registration search for me?"

"Come on. Get serious, will you!"

"Compared to phones, cars ought to be a breeze." I read off the number, explaining how I'd seen the truck apparently staking out the condo.

"But a civilian accessing Records Office files, that's actually illegal."

"Actually nothing, it's completely illegal. Just like cops all over Japan do 24/7."

He hung up without another word.

Somebody had called the Kaput number on the day I met Billy there at the bar. A somebody who, the very same day, called the Yokohama real estate company that owned Billy's apartment house and the cold storage warehouse and managed the Kaput property—a company whose ties with Yang ran deep.

Somebody had also called Tran's sister, who called back two days later. It wasn't hard to picture Billy as that somebody. The second time I met him, he said he'd lost his phone and asked if he'd dropped it in my car. Which meant he thought he lost it the first time, the night of June 17. So what was his phone doing in Reiko Hiraoka's car?

The answer had to be in plain sight, but I just couldn't get it. Like a carrot dangled before a donkey's eyes, goading me on.

I ran out the front door, forgetting to write a message on the blackboard. Stopping by a hardware store, I bought some 2 mm-diameter wire and a metal file, then headed south on the Yokohama–Yokosuka route. As the sun broke through the clouds, the glare off the road surface made all the cars look like they were standing still.

From the bypass exit, I hung a U near Shioiri and doubled back on Route 16 through a tunnel and up into the hills. The raised Keikyu trestles came into sight. An old woman waited at a bus stop, bowed under the weight of the huge basket on her back.

After parking, I fetched a pair of pliers out of the trunk and straightened a length of wire, filed it to a point, and bent the tip. It hid easily inside my jacket while I walked around checking the houses that backed onto the parking lot, making sure no windows were close enough to see.

The camouflaged WagonR was still there. I sidled over to the driver's door and took out my gizmo. Time was they used to sell readymade lock-picks at filling stations, though nowadays of course people protect any car worth stealing with electronic locks or anti-theft devices. I jimmied my wire down between the glass and the window frame right behind the keyhole and jiggled it. Almost immediately the hook caught enough to claw up the safety bolt. The lock clicked and the door opened.

The interior smelled like shit. A filthy jersey and a dank blanket lay balled up in the passenger seat, the back seat was buried in old clothes and defunct appliances, many of them charred black. Half-eaten leftovers were everywhere, along with scattered food wrappers and drink containers, even a worn-out toothbrush—like household effects salvaged from a fire. Someone had obviously camped out here a few nights.

At the foot of the passenger seat was something strange: a 1.5 liter plastic bottle filled with dirt. I unscrewed the cap to smell and shook out a bit in my hand, but it was just soil mixed with wood shavings and sand.

There was no car permit in the glove compartment, only a magazine and an old newspaper. I recognized the magazine, the *Zoom* issue I'd seen at Reiko Hiraoka's condo, earmarked to the page with Aileen's photo. The paper was a *Herald Tribune*, folded to the culture section, which featured a review of Aileen's latest European tour.

When I unfolded the paper, a leaflet slipped out. A single-fold affair with Bible quotes and hymn lyrics printed in three languages—Japanese, English, and something else, something alphabetical with accent marks all over. On the reverse side were the proceedings for a funeral service, under a fancy heading in Japanese:

Farewell gathering for
Chen Bin-long
July 3, 10 a.m.
Midorigaoka Family of God Chapel
Père Guignard

35

Every last house up the steep slope had been done over in faux-brick or plastic tiles. Only Père Guignard's chapel still had wood siding, reinforced here and there with rusty tin patches. A washload of men's underwear and socks was hung out to dry under the eaves, dripping audibly by the door.

"My washing machine is broken," said the French priest by way of excuse.

Telling him I'd come to see Monsieur Lê didn't change his expression. Not a wrinkle disturbed his forehead, he just stared unconcerned. "He's no longer here. He has gone."

The hall just inside the door, cobbled together from an old tatami-matted room and a Western-style parlor, had rows of folding chairs on vinyl flooring. He pulled over a chair for me. The door to the office where we'd talked before was shut.

"I'm not here today on official business." I brought out the funeral leaflet. "I found this in Lê's car."

"Those three Kachin boys are still here in Japan for now, but I could not persuade your authorities to imprison them. I will appeal to the *communauté internationale.*"

"I didn't know Japanese prisons rated so high."

"It is not a joke," he told me, brushing the leaflet aside.

"Did Tran's sister and her husband attend the funeral?" I asked.

"*Oui, mais certainement.*"

"But you said they weren't both here in Japan as a couple."

"That was what I heard at the time," said the priest, noticing the *Herald Tribune* on my lap. "Was *that* also in Monsieur Lê's car? He took it from here. The *Asahi Shimbun* sometimes delivers for free. They think all foreigners are *Américains*," he said scornfully, then pointed to the article on Aileen and added, "I was surprised about this woman."

"What about her?"

"The photo of her as a girl, Monsieur Tran said he knew her at that age. And now she's a famous violinist. Two weeks before the accident, his brother-in-law brought it to show."

"The magazine, too?"

The priest nodded.

"Why would Lê have had them? Did they seem proud to know her? Or was there some profit in it for them?"

"*Alors, qui sait?* I do not pretend to know."

On an impulse, I rose quickly and opened the office door. A brown-skinned foreign youth sitting on the sofa looked around startled and nearly spilled his box lunch.

"Mr. Lê? Lê Ngữ Thanh?"

"*Non, non*, Adelon is Filipino, a volunteer who helps me clean up here," came Guignard's voice.

Admittedly, he didn't really look Vietnamese, and he was way too young to be Tran's sister's husband. I apologized and shut the door.

"You are free to look in all the other rooms," the priest offered.

"Tell me, why did you cover for them?"

"Monsieur Lê was illegal, an underground émigré, not like his wife. At risk of being deported, *le pauvre*."

"But you said he wasn't in Japan, and you didn't know where she lived. Isn't lying against your religious teaching?"

"According to your *gouvernement*, I am a pretend priest holding a non-authorized assembly." He smiled and stroked his nicotine-stained beard. "I did not go to a *séminaire*. Until I was forty, I was an academic, and not very devout. You know of the student protests of May 1968, which shut down the Sorbonne? I protested with them against the bombing of North Vietnam by the *Américains*. I found the path of God soon after that."

"Why become a priest? Why so suddenly?"

He turned to look at me. "We were trying to solve the world's problems all at once—but only God can do that. In the end I was not up to the task, better to leave it to God. All I could do was look for answers one by one. Forget grand *idéologies*, just untangle knots. That is the way of our church." He shook his head, smiling sadly. "You said this is not business. Why then do you look for Monsieur Lê?"

"I'm not sure myself. There was a guy named Billy, he's suspected in a murder case, and I drove him to an airfield. In other words, I helped a suspect escape."

"So he was your friend." The priest was a practiced listener.

I nodded. "I knew he was up to something shady, but that didn't matter to me at the time. Whether he committed murder or not, I didn't care. And I'm a policeman."

"I also am willing to lie if it helps." His knowing smile prompted a quiet laugh from me.

"Billy promised to return, but he didn't. The plane he was flying crashed, but the reports aren't clear if he died. Maybe I just can't accept that."

"Who is he suspected of killing?"

"An unidentified woman I believe to be Tran Kinh Hoa, Lê's wife."

"*Ah, je comprends . . .*" The priest pressed his big knuckles to his brow, then wrung his face in his hands.

The office door opened and the Filipino volunteer entered carrying a vacuum cleaner nozzle, then bowed and left.

"When was the last time you saw Tran's sister? Do you remember?"

"Not the exact day. For a week after Tran's funeral at the beginning of July she came in every day to pray."

"So you didn't see her from the middle of the month. Did Lê say anything about her?"

Père Guignard looked straight at me, drew his lips tight, and shook his head.

"Did something happen, something that affected him?"

"Nothing I can tell you. I have given my word to God. Even if you bring a court order, I will not talk."

"Okay, how about I ask this? Tran and the couple were desperate for money, right?"

"That I can answer. Madame Lê had to have surgery. She was playing in the bushes when she was a little girl. An *Américain* mistook her for a guerrilla and threw a grenade. A fragment pierced her head, so she always had headaches. Terrible headaches. But if an unskilled doctor tried to remove it, she could go blind. So Tran came to Japan and saved up to bring her here with her husband. The travel was cheap, but the operation would cost much, much more. *Des millions.* He was devoted to his sister."

"And that's how he came to work for Yang."

"I do not know any Yang. He got jobs from a merchant in Yokohama named Zou."

"Did he have any other shops besides the hamburger place?"

The priest thought for a moment. "Not a shop, shipping. Zou bought a cargo ship that Tran was to helm. They transport cargo, then they sell the ship."

"Contraband?"

"Maybe nothing so special. They could sell the ship for scrap in Vietnam."

"How did Tran come by such a big job?"

"He was a merchant marine captain, *vraiment certifié.*" The priest sighed and patted the pockets of his loose black smock.

"Here, have one of mine," I said, offering him a cigarette.

"*Merci.* I am trying to quit," he admitted.

"So where is Lê now?"

"*Il a foutu le camp.* One day last week his things were gone."

"You know his apartment burned down."

"*Oui,* he was very upset. He was drunk and smoking and the sheets caught on fire. *Normalement* he did not drink."

"Why was he drinking, then? The fire was on July 20. Did something happen on the night of the nineteenth that drove him to drink?"

"Excuse me, I cannot answer that."

"Which is an answer in itself. Any clue where he might have gone?"

"He talked about making quick money, maybe *en Amérique.* He has cousins there."

"Did he have a mobile phone?"

The priest frowned, took a deep drag on his cigarette, and exhaled before walking into his office and returning with a piece of paper, a torn half of a handbill scribbled with a phone number. "Call this number with your caller ID on, then ring off. Never call *anonyme.*"

"Why all the fuss? Was someone after him?"

"*Aucune idée.* Like I said, I only lend an ear. Come one come all, no questions asked. *Voilà notre chapelle.*" The priest sat up straight in his chair, facing me directly. "And if you find Monsieur Lê, what do you propose he should do?"

The question caught me off guard. I looked up at the ceiling, where a poster of a curiously Asiatic Jesus with arms widespread looked down.

"Wish I knew," I sighed. "Maybe once I pack this whole thing in I'll have an answer."

The priest rose and smiled at me serenely. "Same here, *j'espère,* same here."

36

I raced downhill toward Shioiri Station and parked the car up against the stone wall of an elementary school where they'd posted a sign in English:

OFF-LIMITS TO US MILITARY PERSONNEL
BY ORDER OF FLEET COMMAND

I got out my agenda and called Lê Ngữ Thanh. As soon as I clicked off after the fourth ring, my phone rang back.

I hurriedly picked up. "Mr. Lê?"

"You late. You real late." I could feel the desperation behind his accusing tone. "Where the money? The money! No can wait no more."

I slipped into the role. "Do we have to bring it to you? Traffic's terrible."

He held back for a tense blank moment. If he got wise to the deception, that'd be it.

"What you talking? You promise, big money cash! Belong to family, you owe us!" The frantic burst of angry words left him no time to doubt who I was. "Come quick here! Kaput! Kaput! I waiting."

I'm on my way, I told him, and clicked off.

Clouds swept in over the bay and the sun withdrew behind a seawall of high-rises. I drove via a shortcut, but traffic still slowed to a crawl. Two bright-red plastic traffic cones were positioned at the head of the alleyway. I pulled to a stop a little further along.

Grabbing a flashlight just to be safe, I walked up the cul-de-sac and checked either side of the premises. Kaput was hemmed in on three flanks, no other access but the front door. I reached out and forced my hand to turn the knob. It was unlocked.

The dim interior was mottled with dust. A sour smell stung my nose, yet the air wasn't particularly stuffy. Had someone just left?

"Mr. Lê?" I called into the gloom. There was no answer.

I called out a second time, then closed the door behind me and switched on my flashlight. The corner booth was heaped with empty instant-noodle cups, store-bought lunch packs, and soft-drink bottles. A kettle sat on a tabletop cooker. I went further in. Something rotten squished under my shoe.

There was no one in the place, only a lingering human presence. Nowhere anyone could hide except the john or behind the counter. Sweeping the flashlight around toward the back, the beam came to rest on a nearby table where a dark stain glinted. I touched it, easily breaking through a soft crust to the sticky layer underneath. My moistened finger came up red. A third of the tabletop was covered in blood.

The place had been under police scrutiny all through June and there'd been no report of any blood, so this had to have happened since the beginning of July. Blood had also dripped onto the floor and trailed off in a confusion of smeared footprints, some directed toward the door.

I crouched down with my flashlight to take a better look. No detective, not even on *yakuza* duty, gets into constant fights or whacked from behind every day. By the time I noticed someone else in the place, I'd bent too low to turn around. The flashlight left my hand and the narrow beam rolled away.

Next thing I knew I was sitting in a booth rubbing my face with both hands. Only then did I realize I'd been knocked unconscious. How did I get up, claim my flashlight and seat myself here? Luckily I hadn't blacked out for too long, maybe thirty minutes by my watch.

If I sat still I didn't hurt, but when I moved, my knees were gone and a sharp pain ripped up my spine. Thrusting my hands left and right for support, I staggered over toward the counter. My assailant had to have been waiting there.

I smelled trouble ahead. A small man with prominent Indochinese cheekbones lay face up behind the counter. His face was red as a tomato, though I could see no bleeding. Most likely Lê Ngữ Thanh had died in a headlock. Strangulation leaves bruises, but there were no marks on his scrawny throat. Generally that means lifting the victim from behind in a choke hold, so the killer must have been big and strong.

Lê's fingernails were gritty, his T-shirt a diary of stains, his trouser legs streaked with dirt. He hadn't changed clothes for days. After living in the Uragamichi apartment with Tran Kinh Hoa until the fire, he had camped out in the camouflaged car, then moved to Guignard's church, only to breathe his last here in hiding. Lê wasn't just on the run, he'd had a definite purpose. He needed money to pay for an expensive operation on his wife, though in the end everything they had scraped together he needed for himself.

Stepping over the body to check the kitchen area, my flashlight picked out the old American ice-maker, now a reservoir of dirty water. I remembered that first night here when the Fifties-era machine had suddenly groaned and Billy scooped up those round ice cubes. Every little detail pointed to the same scenario—one I just didn't want to believe.

A heap of rotten vegetables had dried on the cutting board by the sink, as if some emergency had interrupted the cook mid-prep. I opened the cabinet under the sink and located the knife rack, but found only a serrated bread cutter and a small fruit peeler, nothing for chopping. I groped around by flashlight, but there was no knife on the blood-smeared table or amidst all the rubbish and overturned chairs on the floor.

Experience told me to accept the most likely story: Tran's sister was murdered here, packed in a fake Louis Vuitton trunk filled with round ice cubes, and hauled by Range Rover to Parklane Terrace—all on July 19. The driver was my friend. Did he kill her too?

But I wasn't quite through, not yet. I went to check the john, but when I opened the door the scummy brown toilet bowl gave off such a foul stink I had to bury my nose in my sleeve. No one in his right mind would hide in here. Flushing didn't release much water. I waited for the tank to refill and flushed again. For some reason water wasn't coming in.

I lifted the porcelain lid of the tank. There was something wedged inside at the bottom. I reached down and dredged up a duct-taped bundle. Twice the size of a brick, wrapped three layers thick in plastic, the watertight parcel contained fifteen bundles of hundred-dollar bills in a paper bag, for a grand total of a hundred-fifty thousand dollars.

I thought it over and decided to put the money back where it was. I drained the tank using a coin to turn off the water valve and erased any clumsy traces of my search on the way out. I even wiped the doorknob with a handkerchief.

The rank air of the trash-filled alley was positively refreshing by comparison. Already twilight, the corner bakery lit up the pavement where the traffic cones had been moved for a milk truck. The aproned baker who came out to see off the driver now turned to greet me. There was no avoiding him. Still sweating, I dusted my clothes and straightened my tie before asking, "See anyone hanging around hereabouts?"

"You mean those two guys a little while ago? Yeah, saw 'em go in."

"What'd they look like?"

"Well, I was watching through the shop window . . . but, uh, one of 'em was real big."

"And the other, on the small side?"

"Hmm, I s'pose. Might've been wearing a suit, well dressed any-way." The baker picked up a cone, then looked at me quizzically.

"Y'know, maybe he was American. They had Y-permit plates."

"So you saw the car?"

He nodded. "Couldn't not have. They parked right in front of the shop, so I told them to hike, and they moved on beyond where you're parked. I swear, those foreign plates think the whole country's their private parking space."

"It wasn't a Camry, was it?"

"No, a four-wheel drive job. White, as I recall." He was losing interest and began rearranging the cones to stake out his streetfront.

"When the police arrive, be sure to tell them what you told me."

"What's with that? Aren't you police?"

I bought a drink from a vending machine and returned to my car, took a swig, and picked up my phone. Like it or not, I had to abide by regulations for reporting homicides. I braced myself and called Yokosuka Investigations. Desk Sergeant Takabayashi picked up. We weren't exactly friends, but no strangers either.

"Violent death at a bar called Kaput in Honcho, sighted five minutes ago. All indications it's murder."

He didn't miss a beat. "Isn't that where the Vietnamese deep-freeze worked?" I was put on hold to a muzak rendition of "Happy Feet" until his voice returned. "Okay, we'll send over a team in four to five. So, was this work-related or what?"

"No. I was just driving by and saw two people come running out. Got curious, so I went to check. The door was open, and the victim was inside."

"Must've given you quite a start. Anyhow, thanks for the information." And that was that. Concise as ever, he hung up without any further remark.

Twenty minutes later, a call came from Section Chief Komine. By then the CSI boys had arrived and sealed off the mouth of the alleyway with blue plastic tarps and laid down a tangle of lighting cables. When I asked Komine how he got my mobile number, he just snorted that anyone who keeps his caller ID on is hardly incommunicado.

248

"Your Takabayashi's right on the ball," I told him.

"Unlike some of us. More to the point, what the hell are you up to?"

"Can you please not yell for fifteen seconds?"

"I'll give you five."

I repeated what I told Takabayashi, leaving out the part about getting whacked from behind and passing out.

"Know why I'm not yelling louder?" he said. "Because I had to get off a train to call and, just your luck, the station's full of people."

"Why don't you just stay there?"

"Like hell I will. It's wise guys like you make public servants think they can slack off."

"Can't argue with the facts. Thanks to you I've got nothing but slack time."

That shut him up. I asked if they'd identified the corpse found in Billy's car, but he didn't reply. Not one breath until he said, "Now listen up. I'm putting Takabayashi on your tail, so beat a path home once you're done there. We'll talk tomorrow, and I'll ask the questions. Meanwhile, don't get in the way, this is Precinct business. You're no longer a detective, remember?"

"Understood."

"One other thing. Don't mislead the initial investigation with any of your lies."

"Lies? Since when was I ever lying?"

An outside voice interrupted Komine's lecture. Through a gap in the tarp I saw the irate baker waving his cones at a cop. "How's I s'posed to do business with your big fat squad car blocking my shop? I'm not telling you a thing!"

I hung around until they took away the body. None of these snoops seemed in any hurry to discover the stash in the toilet tank. Fine. I suggested there must have been yet another homicide: the blood was too old and there was too much of it.

"How long was this place under wraps for the warehouse case?" I asked.

"Till July 2," announced one detective off in a corner.

"But the blood, it's been here at least since August," noted a young forensic. Not only that, someone else was staying here and had compromised the crime scene. They used the sink, there were fairly recent food scraps and signs of a cleanup. And yet the toilet was filthy, which was strange—and a hairbreadth short of a hundred-fifty grand discovery.

"Hey, what's that?" The forensic was looking at the seat of my pants. "Did you fall or sit down? There's something on your trousers." Without waiting for an answer, he took out a spatula and a plastic bag from his toolcase and proceeded to scrape off a sample.

"Now how'd that get on me?"

"Still sticky. Seems fairly fresh. Maybe from the stiff, or else the perp."

Luckily the stash came to light just then and everyone forgot about me. Everyone except one older detective who eyed me like a barman seeing a drunk to the door.

I drove nice and slow for thirty minutes in the outside lane to Yokohama. By the time I got home, took off my jacket, ran a hot bath and switched on the TV, it was well past ten o'clock. I felt lean and hungry. Come to think of it, I hadn't eaten a thing since morning. While waiting for the tub to fill, I poured myself a scotch on the rocks and watched the sports news. The Hawks were on the way to winning the league pennant.

Five glasses later, close to midnight, Tomoda called. "Inside word from Taiwan confirms they found the goods." He sounded hyper, but I couldn't tell if he was drunk or not. "Burnt greenbacks mostly, some stocks and bonds too. They're running carbon analyses now, but off-the-record a senior official estimates at least a million in cash."

"Probably'll never go public."

"Nope, everyone's under gag orders. Think about it, even with

Beijing right next door, they've never allowed us to open a local NHK bureau."

"Fair enough, no burden on taxpayers," I said. "But thanks to you, seems I beat a big snake out of the bush." I told him about Orimasa's editor getting hit by a car and hauled away. "Yang's behind it, saw one of his boys there at the scene. Inamoto's still captive."

"Serious stuff," he exclaimed. "You really mainlined those Val-Nam cronies."

"You understand why I'm telling you all this?"

"You want me to raise a stink on TV to put pressure on Yang and the police, right? So the goons don't waste this editor guy. Can't promise you, there's lots of news lately."

Before he could hang up, I asked him to get me corporate details on Golden Harbor Enterprises. Tomoda sounded reluctant but agreed. If a quick skim of the net was good enough, he'd send over whatever sludge came up right away.

As soon as he clicked off, I fixed myself another scotch and sprawled out on the sofa. The booze swirled into my system and switched on a nice warm glow.

Yang knew I was investigating a case that involved him. He probably knew I was still on the police payroll. He knew all this and yet he'd tried to threaten me. What the hell did he hope to gain by taking such risks? Not money, or so he said, but face. And yet only money and stock certificates had turned up.

Yang was rattled. Why else would someone of his caliber even bother with me, or tell me his mobile number? What could possibly disturb a big fish who played cool about a million bucks charred to a crisp? I hadn't a clue. Even if I had a million and a private jet to burn, I still wouldn't have a clue.

37

Kanagawa Prefectural Library smelled like black suits returning from a funeral. The half-lit hall was hardly empty, but the readers' presence was studiously muted. I took a seat on a hard bench and looked around. A miniature waterwheel whirred in my brain, payback for drinking on an empty stomach.

Someone coughed. I turned and smelled cigarette smoke. Not that anyone had lit up, it was just the years of tar creased into my own clothes.

"Sorry. Got tied up in a phone call just as I was leaving," whispered Section Chief Komine when he arrived, "then I got lost. Who'd've guessed this place was here?"

"Well, you said somewhere out of the way."

"You come here often? For research or what?"

"Not research, I used to drop in to read the sports pages."

A librarian came to raise the blinds on the window opposite, throwing a dart of sunlight at my feet.

"Your friend, the hit-and-run victim, turned up," Komine said.

"Unharmed?"

"Unharmed and unruffled. He called in late at night to say he was back home. His wife had put in a report."

"Verified in person?" I had to ask. Inamoto's mobile hadn't responded this morning, while his editorial office reported he'd been taken ill and would be away until further notice.

"Someone from the Precinct went by to check up on things, and out he comes, cool as a melon, to apologize for bothering us."

"Think they put the squeeze on him?"

"I wouldn't know. He's saying the car just grazed him and he lost his balance. So they took him to Emergency and paid the bill, end of story. Says he didn't get their names, believe it or don't. Legs hurt bad enough to need crutches, so him not getting names doesn't wash. Whatever, no way he's going to bring charges. Who *is* this guy?"

"An editor who was close to Billy. And also involved with Tran."

"Oh great, him again."

"Him and everyone else, they're all connected."

"Who, to which case?"

"It's all one big case."

He stretched out, kicking his feet into the sunlight with his hands folded behind his head, while I spelled out yesterday's events. The camouflaged WagonR, the phone call to Lê Ngữ Thanh, everything. Only when I'd finished did he open his mouth.

"Enough, I've heard you out, and I'll pass it all on to the squad slated to cover Yokosuka."

"Tran's sister and her husband came up from Okinawa this spring and stayed in an apartment in Yokosuka rented in her brother's name. They also had dealings with Billy, and Inamoto apparently had some kind of handle on that."

"Some kind of what on what? Sounds kind of half-assed for a detective."

"You forget, I'm no longer a detective. But you people, you haven't even identified the dead woman found in Billy's car."

"You mean his murder victim—"

"Murder victim?" I nearly shouted. "He's not accused of murder, only of disposing of the body." Stares were leveled at me from across the reading room.

"Fair enough, you're entitled to that view," said Komine, trying to cool things down.

"The autopsy found a metal fragment lodged in the head of the corpse. Tran Kinh Hoa had grenade shrapnel in her head and came to Japan to get it removed, but needed money for the operation."

"So the whole family shipped in and buckled down and worked their butts off, till they ran up against sharks who killed the lot of them, brother, sister, and husband in turn. Is that what you're saying?"

"The weapon used on the woman—the sister—was a kitchen knife, right?"

Komine looked spooked. That detail was presumably still classified. "Yeah, uh, probably professional grade. Stabbed all the way through the liver, leaving twelve hundred mils of blood in the abdominal cavity."

"An upward thrust from below, apparently. In a standing position, that would mean whoever knifed her had to be pretty small. Billy's slighter taller than me."

"Don't jump to conclusions. The perp could've done it from a crouch."

"There's a knife missing at Kaput—or didn't you know?"

He didn't say a word. He merely dug his hands in his pockets and stared at his feet.

"When I called Lê, he mistook me for someone else and told me to rush 'the money' over to him. But the money was already hidden in the shop."

"Payoff for what?"

I felt a twinge deep inside. I was about to mention the magazine and newspaper I found in the camouflaged refuge on wheels, the ones with Aileen's childhood picture, but I went on the offensive instead. "Are your hands out of commission?"

Komine stared, puzzled and indignant.

"I'm asking why you're not taking any notes?"

"You've got some nerve talking to a superior like that."

"So now you're angry? That makes two of us."

Komine stood up, which still didn't make him very tall. The lowered blinds in the hall shaded him in stripes. "Okay, pal, have it your way," said the slatted figure after a long breath. "Yokosuka has staked claim to the inquiry, but if need be we'll reinvestigate the woman in the trunk and your frozen fall guy as related cases. We'll even question Inamoto. *If need be.* But what is or isn't needed is not for you to decide. Meanwhile you do nothing more. Got it, Futamura?" He looked plain stupid as he lectured me.

"This has to be the Public Security Bureau's doing!" My outburst made him glance about nervously. "They had Billy marked, they had us on their radar from the beginning."

Komine zipped his lips tight, stole past the bookshelves toward the door, and strode out into the sun. "Not PSB," he corrected, "an Organized Crime Control squad. Crossed the river onto our turf."

"An OCC squad? From Tokyo?"

Komine smirked and shook his head. "According to the Chief, this is something cooked up by the PSB as an anti-terrorist whatnot. They're not based at Metro HQ, no declared home base at all. Rumor is it's part of a general post-Cold War reshuffle of police agencies. Whoever they are, they've taken center stage."

I remembered those two creeps at Haneda Airport. The raincoat by the check-in counter and the sideman who shadowed us to the café stand. Their nondescript clothes, their circumspect behavior. Sure bet one of them tailed the girl all the way to Okinawa. Only one act could straddle nationwide links like that: some kind of special outfit.

Komine turned to face me. "That's how it is. Their investigation's been in progress from way back, and all we know is we're not party to it."

"Except the body in Kaput is a new tie-in."

"That's precisely why I'm telling you to stay out of it." He started down the library steps. A black Cedric stirred on the square below and swung around closer. "What *is* it you're after?" he asked. "If you wanted to investigate, why didn't you stick it out? If you'd just listened to me and laid low in the boonies for a year—"

"It'd be the same difference, wherever. Lately it occurs to me, I only get involved in cases that somehow interest me."

"Is that any kind of motto for a cop?"

"I draw a cop's salary, but I never really apprenticed in law and order."

His short frame looked tense and he stared at me. His receding hairline glinted with pomade. The car was ready and waiting, the driver standing by the open door. He let out a big nasal breath, then turned and climbed in.

My interim workplace was only a stone's throw away. The two trolls were off at Prefectural HQ as usual, which meant I could smoke in peace and peruse the contents of the envelope Tomoda sent over by bike courier: a printout of the Golden Harbor Enterprises online company profile and a photocopy from an old newspaper.

The article detailed how the company had bulldozed over local resident opposition to launch a large-scale construction project at the edge of Chinatown. After the Eighties economic bubble burst, they'd snapped up defaulted properties in the area, earning the disfavor of small restaurant owners nearby. But considering how big shots like Yang no longer dined anywhere in the vicinity, this can't have been a big issue.

Moving on to the company profile, Tomoda had crossed off various entries, probably indicating things discontinued or on hold. One of these caught my eye: "Warehousing operations: Joyo Storage, No. 4 Chiwakacho, Kanagawa Ward."

I pulled out my agenda to double-check. The name and address matched the place where Ackerman's effects had been stored. I rang up the telephone listing and got a "No longer in service" announcement.

Predictable, but worth another try. I was about to key in REDIAL when my throat knotted up. I flipped through my agenda to find the four call-record numbers from the mobile in Reiko Hiraoka's car. Laying the page side by side with the company profile, I ran my finger back and forth just to be sure. The Joyo Storage number and the Yokohama number that had yielded no data were the very same.

38

It was already dusk by the time I found myself at Higashi Kanagawa Station. Not wanting anyone tracking my car, I'd returned it to the lot, then taken the train from Kannai. I didn't know what to expect, but thought I'd better leave my options open.

The rear of the station had changed completely. The loading area where stevedores and freightyard hands hustled for day jobs had been upgraded, and decorative roadside plantings left no pavement for food carts. The little red lantern bars were all gone, as was that striptease joint the sports tabloids used to tout. There were several signs for buses toward Chiwakacho, but only one read Mizuho Pier.

"Don't even think about it. Nothing heading that way this time of day," warned a heavyset lady at a nearby newsstand.

"Any buses coming *from* there?" I asked.

"Maybe one or two. Lots running in the morning, though."

I examined the route chart. The fourth stop was Block 4 Chiwakacho, beyond which was Mizuho Pier, a US military installation. "The bus goes all the way inside the fence?"

"You bet, it's for Japanese who work on base. A city bus you have to show a pass to board, can you imagine?"

I bought a pack of gum from her.

"Mister, you got manners," she said with a belly laugh.

I started on foot toward the pier, cutting across the Dai-Ichi Keihin waterfront route, under the Yokohama–Haneda Expressway, and over a canal where pleasure craft bobbed hull-to-hull with old hire launches. The road ran between a gigantic water treatment plant and a golf driving range to yet another canal and a forlorn rail crossing that looked like a low-budget movie set. I didn't meet another soul out walking. The center line vanished and the tarmac buckled, a dump truck sat abandoned among weeds on the shoulder. Up ahead, over an iron bridge, was the American pier.

Just before the arched iron span an orange stopline and military roadblocks halted traffic, but there was no guard post. Two cocktail bars slumped at the water's edge, ready to topple in. Only one had its sign lit. A gaudy purple microbus was parked outside.

I stood there chewing my gum, trying to get my bearings from a photocopied map. Running alongside the road behind a wire barrier were narrow-gauge tracks as if from some long-lost amusement park ride. The address had to be across the tracks, but all I could see was a salt depot. I walked back to the second canal, where a road forked off between a recycling yard and a home delivery sorting center, then crossed a spur line and curved across a wide ditch to a large landfill tract. Flanking the far bank, a long stretch of low saw-roofed industrial sheds reached a compact crane out over a barge.

Another orange stopline slowed my steps. I had to squint to decipher the tiny sign:

RESTRICTED ZONE

PERSONS UNCONCERNED WITH US ARMED FORCES

AND JOYO WAREHOUSE CORP.

KEEP OUT

It read like a bad translation from GI jargon. Even stranger, it put Yang Yun-shi's ghost company under the same roof as the US Forces in Japan.

According to the map, the entire block was held in common by the Americans and Joyo with no walls or fences between them. The low stretch-shed was apparently some kind of US military equipment depot, while the featureless three-story structure behind it belonged to Joyo Warehouse. The rest of the zone was dotted with minor prefabs.

I ventured across the line and casually strolled toward the structure stenciled in large letters JOYO WAREHOUSE – GOLDEN HARBOR TOTAL LIFE PLANNING. They must have regraded their corporate identity. Despite some noise and glints of activity up ahead, there was no sign of an MP, nor any Japanese security guard. The hard hats I passed paid no attention to me. Some "restricted zone." Japanese police might cuff me for trespassing, but no extraterritorial authority was going to shoot me on sight with an M-16.

A path led between the prefabs, past a jumble of bicycles and motorscooters, to an open area by some warehouse loading docks. The shutters were all closed—well, one was half-raised, but I still couldn't see in. Forklifts buzzed like flies around three trucks parked broadside. The workers loading the trucks wore full-face respirators, others had on white gauze dust masks. I don't know why that bothered me, but I kept my distance.

Just then, a gunmetal-gray minivan arrived from somewhere and several men jumped out. Hurrying up a steel staircase—an important delivery, perhaps?—they went inside a room whose two small windows had lowered shades, probably an office. I walked on. The path ended at the water, looking across to Mizuho Pier. During the Vietnam War years, the place would have been solid with tanks and armored cars waiting to be loaded onto freighters. Today the berths were idle save for one rusty, peppermint-green civilian ship. Even from here I could make out the name *Mineola* across the bow, the sluggish flapping of the Stars and Stripes on the stern.

I hiked back the way I'd come and caught a cab. At Yokohama Station, no rent-a-car place had two-ton trucks, so I opted for an ordinary white commercial van.

I still had time. I drove to my apartment, changed into overalls, a windbreaker, and rubber-soled walking shoes, stuffed a folding multi-tool and penlight in my pockets, and backtracked to Chi-wakacho. On the way, I stopped by a discount drugstore and picked up a box lunch of *siumai* dumplings at a station kiosk. Back to the bus street and off onto the side road, I pulled over into the brush near several other vehicles just past the spur line crossing. There I spread a sports tabloid wide open on the steering wheel and ate my dumplings, deliberately keeping the reading light on until I'd finished, then stretched out across the seats and waited.

By eight o'clock incoming traffic had died off. Around nine, the warning bell on the train crossing started ringing. A steam whistle shrilled through a sudden glare, wheels screeched and weeds whipped about as a big diesel engine rumbled past pulling boxcar after box-car, so close I thought they might hit the van. When the last one cleared the crossing, I got out and chased the red taillights up the tracks to a railhead quay. Night blacked out everything beyond the iron bridge, but as soon as the train groaned to a stop a signal flashed on the far bank and a white-helmeted soldier appeared.

I quietly made my way back to the van. Not long afterwards, a microbus full of workers whizzed by, followed by a truck and a blue Toyota Crown. Then, just past eleven, after close to an hour of no traffic, along came a Chevrolet van with square headlights. I'd seen it somewhere, there couldn't be more than one clunker like that in Yokohama.

A minute later, I started my engine and swung onto the road. No need to hurry, I gave them plenty of lead time. Across the first canal, just before the expressway, the Chevy blinked left and turned in at the golf range. The clubhouse lights were still on and the blue Toyota was there in the lot.

Slowing past the clubhouse, I saw a short man get out of the Chevy. His face floated up in the streetlight. It was Wang Lun, fol-lowed by the guy who tried to kick me out of Wang's van. Probably the thug Orimasa had called "Hole in Five"—Hong Zhi-long. They both entered the clubhouse restaurant.

I did a U and pulled over onto the shoulder halfway to the iron bridge, where bright lights now flooded out of one of the bars and people were milling about, as if someone were shooting a movie. Then, pocketing a few bills but leaving my wallet and mobile in the glove compartment, I set off on foot. Beyond the spur line crossing and orange stopline, I crept all the way around the perimeter fence to Joyo Warehouse, approaching this time from the seaward side. Waves lapped at the embankment below, wind carried the distant sounds of expressway traffic. Night breathing a low moan.

The building from this angle showed its age. Brickwork was visible through flaking concrete, iron staples reinforced earthquake cracks, only the office up top seemed a recent addition. I saw no lights, no surveillance camera anywhere. The loading dock shutters were down, but the service entrance on the side looked promising. I pulled on a pair of drugstore-bought latex gloves and pointed my penlight at the lock, a simple pin-tumbler job. I had just the thing. I unfolded my handy multi-tool, addressed a slender prong to the keyhole and, hearing it engage, pressed down slightly. The door opened just like that—a little trick I learned way back from a burglary expert at the Precinct.

The very first step inside immersed me in a harsh acid smell like the industrial cleansers they use to scrub down public toilets. I covered my nose and mouth with the dust mask I'd bought. A sweep of the penlight revealed I was in a long tunnel of plastic sheeting tacked to a frame a handspan bigger than the door, a wrinkled tube sagging across a dark void. I felt like a tapeworm exploring a large intestine.

All I could see through the plastic was a dim interior piled high with unknown goods. The tunnel extended to an opening at the far wall that funneled into a gap barely wide enough for one person that led behind a chipboard partition under a row of bare lightbulbs. The narrow passage dead-ended at a door that hummed like an air conditioner. Next to it on the exposed brick wall was a control panel with operating instructions printed on the cover and a switch marked EMERGENCY FORCED AIR VENTILATOR, with a handwritten warning: *Do not run for more than 30 minutes continuously.*

Obviously they'd rigged up the plastic tunnel to access the control panel without breathing the warehouse air. I remembered the fork-lift operators' respirators.

I returned to the tunnel. The only way into the main warehouse seemed to be via the loading docks, though the locks would surely be stubborn and the big shutters heavy. But hey, what did I care? I was already trespassing on a US military facility and had broken into a building for no good reason. Now was no time to start worrying about damaging property. I unfolded the multi-tool knife blade and cut through the plastic.

Immediately my eyes began to hurt, sparklers burned inside my nose. My dust mask was almost useless. The choking sensation wasn't just from the acrid odor, the interior was sweltering. I stepped through the plastic and shone my penlight at a wall of lidded acrylic pails reaching halfway to the seven-meter ceiling. The place was too steamy to see the contents clearly, nor could I break one open without upsetting the stack.

A more immediate problem was the smell. It was getting harder to breathe, my lungs ached. Eventually I found a pail that wasn't quite so misted up, but I still couldn't tell what was inside. Syringes and pumps? Drug paraphernalia? Emergency life-saving supplies? There were transfusion tubes and empty drip-packs, gauze and bandages stained with blood and secretions, who-knew-what-else medical refuse. Crammed down in the bottom was a shit-smeared adult diaper.

Another partially visible container was full of disposable vials with different colored caps. Lab test discards? All had tags with cryptic abbreviations: O1/2LT, E7/SFC . . . I could only guess that "2LT" stood for Second Lieutenant and "SFC" for Sergeant First Class. One tag read GS15 SAKAMOTO. The military organized everyone and everything by rank, General Schedule Japanese employees included. Even the drip-packs bore names, ranks and Navy Bureau of Medicine BUMED stamps.

There were easily ten truckloads of acrylic pails here, all presumably containing medical waste. I took out my agenda and started walking around the stack recording the tags and labels, when further back I noticed other shelves with uniform packages. Fewer than the pails, they looked like oversize dice, just under a meter on each side, wrapped in dark plasticized paper. I jabbed my knife blade into one and dug out what appeared to be ordinary soil, if maybe a little denser than normal. Was something else mixed in? It smelled funny, like a sewer leak laced with burnt chemicals or solder. Crumbled between my fingers, it gave off a slight warmth as if fermenting.

What was this stuff? I peeled off one glove and shoved a sample fingerful down inside, tying it at the wrist. Then, stepping back, I did a quick penlight survey of all the shelf units. A plaque fixed to an upright support on the closest one read FAC3099—probably a Fleet Activities Command code. There were fourteen rows of five-shelf units in all, nine marked FAC3117 holding twice as many packages as the others combined, though they didn't feel as warm. Maybe they were just old. I jabbed one and wiggled the blade about—this one seemed harder—and a trickle of concrete bits mixed with soil spilled onto the floor. Compared to the FAC3099 soil, this was a more vivid red.

Having gone this far, I made the hole bigger. Inside was something like a tin can lid along with wire and metal parts. They were wedged in tight, as if everything had fused together under intense pressure. I collected enough to fill the thumb of my glove and tied it off before jotting down the shelf code number in my agenda.

There was no law against the US military hiring a private contractor to handle its medical waste. Not as long as the company was properly licensed and didn't just dump the stuff in a vacant lot or into the sea. For a fact, Japanese home delivery trucks had been hauling their weapons and explosives for years. They merely had to display CAUTION: DANGER stickers and it was all perfectly legal. The US–Japan Status of Forces Agreement didn't require filing any special notification. Trucks traveled between on-base arsenals at Yokota, Atsugi, Yokohama and Yokosuka once a week on average and, for what it's worth, the Prefectural Police kept an eye on their movements. Just to make sure no local precinct clowns did anything stupid.

I wouldn't have put it past the US military to do the same with their hospital trash. The contractor wouldn't even have needed a permit. All they had to do was load the stuff and go dump it somewhere. Complain all you like, that was the law of the land.

Once when I was a student, I saw an MP fire a .45 at a civilian car on a city street. A cop came out from the nearby police box but didn't say a word. I still have no idea if it was legal or not. What I do know is that no one took issue . . .

Just then, I felt my pupils dilate. There was no change in the smell, but suddenly I got a sharp burning pain in my eyes as if some new odorless irritant had seeped in. The ventilator fan came through louder, rattling the partition wall. So I headed back through the plastic tunnel, heart pounding, until I got outside and could feel fresh air in my lungs. The whole building seemed to be vibrating behind me.

Up above, the office door opened and footsteps came clanging down the steel staircase. I flattened myself against the wall, just out of sight from the stairs. I heard spoken Chinese, something that sounded like "Naha FOB". Another voice laughed and repeated it back in a heavy accent. I crept behind some backhoe digging equipment, not a moment before two of them headed my way. I heard the click of the service door, then a squawk of alarm when they realized that someone had tampered with the lock.

I took a peek. A crew-cut kid stood at the door cautiously scanning the surroundings. He seemed to be empty-handed. A voice called from inside, having no doubt discovered the rip in the plastic tunnel. The voice barked a command. The crew-cut disappeared around the corner of the warehouse and footsteps raced up the stairs.

Resisting an urge to run, I moved off from the backhoe and followed the wall around to the far side of the building. If I could just make it past the loading docks over to the prefabs, out of sight of the office, the rest of the way back would be easy. I checked to see no one was about and bolted across the open ground. But one breath shy of cover everything went white in a blast of arc light.

Zŭzhĭ tā! Zhuāzhù tā la! Bùyào ràng tā pǎoqù! Angry shouts sprayed around me. I knew what they were saying even if I didn't understand a word. All I could do was keep going, but I wasn't even as far as the orange stopline when headlights came at me from up ahead. The blue Toyota braked, rear wheels kicking up dust as it skidded sideways across my path. The car door opened and some-one big got out of the driver's seat. I threw a ray of penlight at the figure and fled to the spur line tracks, jumping from tie to wooden tie. My own panting drowned out the shouts behind me.

The tracks slipped into the shadows behind the salt depot and eventually emerged beside the road where I'd parked, but I couldn't get to the van. My path funneled between a wire barrier and a chain link fence toward a railway trestle parallel to the iron bridge. The cocktail bars glowed half a world away, islands of comfort in the darkness. Not that they would even notice if I called for help. Once the tracks mounted the trestle, there was nothing between the ties, only the sea below. One false move and I'd be in the drink. I'd been too harried and out of breath to notice whether I'd lost my pursuers, but now that I slowed down I still heard their angry voices.

I maneuvered onto the narrow steel-mesh maintenance catwalk and was halfway across when an MP squad car idling on the far side drove onto the tracks, blocking the way forward. "Stop where you are!" commanded an American over a loudspeaker.

"Where do you think you're going? Get down off there!" came a scolding voice from a Japanese police car over on the roadway bridge.

"I need help!" I shouted. "They're trying to kill me!"

"Halt! This is a US military installation!" boomed the Americans. Two MPs stood there, one gripping a bullhorn, the other with a hand on his holster. Their helmets shone blue in the revolving light.

"Help!" I pleaded even louder. "Can't you hear them?"

"This is your last warning. Come no closer or we'll shoot."

"I'm a policeman. I'm unarmed."

"Yeah right, what would a Jap policeman be doing trespassing on our train tracks in the middle of the night?" He put down his bullhorn and brandished a nightstick. His partner drew his pistol and started walking toward me.

The Chinese were closing in fast, but the gap separating me from the roadway bridge was too far, too dark and deep. Could I shimmy up the diagonal truss high above the tracks? For the first time I felt really afraid.

I hurled myself into the void. Air rushed up my legs. Would I hit one of the pilings? My eyes must have closed, then suddenly I was in the water, even before I felt the spray or heard the splash. My windbreaker ballooned up. I pressed my sides to release the trapped bubbles and was buoyed up to the surface. A bridge piling came into view. I kicked off my shoes and swam for the concrete outcropping.

The MPs' bluster echoed down to me. This bridge was US military property, come peacefully and they'd turn me over to the Japanese authorities. The MPs only shut up when the Chinese shouted, "We from Golden Harbor. He break into our warehouse!"

My best bet was to swim from piling to piling toward the lights on shore, hiding between the moored launches and rowboats. The water wasn't so cold by now.

Music drifted across the harbor, a J-pop ballad with diluted English lyrics. The closer of the two bars straddled the seawall, couples mingling on a low terrace decked out with parasols and old dock tires. The next thing I knew people were pointing at me. One man, "the producer," he said, pulled me out of the water and told a waiter to fetch me a towel.

A woman in a party dress laughed, covering her mouth with both hands. "This has got to be a promotional stunt, right? What's the gimmick?"

"No gimmick's the new gimmick," quipped her male companion.

I stripped off my waterlogged windbreaker and dried my face and hair, but was still soaked through. I apologized for interrupting the film shoot, but my host explained it was a wedding, not a movie. "These 'found locations' are big money nowadays."

I climbed the ship-ladder stairs to a round of applause from the terrace. A few guests lingered at the mood-lit bar while others were starting to head home. I found the waiter who'd brought me the towel, handed him some soggy cash and keys, and asked him to bring the van around. It was only a few hundred meters away, but better to play it safe. Those Golden Harbor goons might still be scouting the bridge and I was barefoot.

Nothing simpler—the waiter delivered the van promptly to the entrance of the bar. "Please be real careful," he said. "The Americans aren't spending lately, and if us Japanese have too much of a good time, their MPs lean on us and cramp our business. And like, this is supposed to be Japan?" He thrust his chin at the orange stopline, not three steps from the front door where the Yokohama patrol car now blocked both lanes and an officer was busily arranging traffic cones.

In the van I spread the sports tabloid under my damp butt and got going. Passing the side road, I didn't see anyone on the lookout or any of their cars waiting. The Chevy van had also vanished from the golf clubhouse. As I crossed the last canal, I met another patrol car turning in from the Dai-Ichi Keihin with its light flashing.

I was angry at everything and nothing. As my body warmed up, my wet clothes began to smell of ditch water and spilled oil.

39

Driving south on the harbor side of Yokohama Station, my mobile phone rang in the glove compartment. I pulled over. It was Tomoda.

"Got time to talk?" he asked. Did he know what time it was? 1:09 in the morning to be precise. "I have something for you," he insisted. I told him I wasn't going anywhere without hosing down first.

"Make it a quick one. See you in, say, fifteen? Keep us company, I'm on an all-nighter too." I didn't know what he thought I was up to, but he wouldn't be dissuaded.

I left the van in front of the apartment, shed my wet things, and had just turned on the shower when Tomoda rang the doorbell. "Whoah, you look terrible. Like a wrung-out King Lear in a Ninagawa production."

"I wish. At least that would've paid."

A soak in a nice hot bath would do me more good than a shower, decided Tomoda. He'd kept his taxi waiting, so without further discussion we drove straight to a multiplex commercial center in the new waterfront redevelopment where there was an "Ultra Bathhouse" on the top floor. A great big leisure center with lots of different hot tubs, even a dry sauna and a mist sauna, though the fancy reception counter at the entrance made it look more like a karaoke club. Tomoda pushed me out of the way and paid for two.

The thermal waters really hit the spot, piped up from an underground spring, or so they said. The cypress-wood outdoor tub on the rooftop was a pleasant place to watch the night sky dawning over the Bay Bridge and try to sort out what I'd just been through. Those goons would have killed me. Why else had they chased me so far?

US military installation or not, they'd have taken me out and no one would have been the wiser.

Finally relieved of the shivers, I stretched out on a massage recliner in the lounge. Half the chairs were occupied by towel-wrapped zombies plugged into headphones, either listening to music or glued to LCD movie screens.

Tomoda treated me to a beer and started in. "Believe it or not, I've been tracking this Val-Nam thing a good four or five years now. I did a news special when they completed phase one of the project, but stuff happened, so NHK dropped the investigative reporting and treated the piece as financial fodder. Vietnam's international ascent, incentives for concerted Taiwanese investment, that sort of whitewash."

"But you had a different angle, I take it?"

"Hell yes, I cover real news. Nothing's out in the open, but plenty going on behind the scenes—bribery, election fund irregularities, foreign exchange fraud, banking scams, you name it. If any of those backstories broke, senior politicians' heads would roll."

He grabbed the controller from his sidetable and lowered his backrest to full recline. "It all began with a little whisper from an opposition legislator acquaintance. One of our reporters inherited his father's constituency and became a parliamentary deputy. So I go meet him and—you remember a Yoshimura of Tonichi Planning? Former professor, taught civil engineering at Tokyo University, got real friendly with certain construction firms—*that* Yoshimura. Well, Yoshimura was telling our boy things, and it turns out the whole development project is shallow landfill, no solid ground at all."

Tomoda took a swig of beer and sized up my reaction. "The scoop was too hot right then, he said. When things cooled down a little—once phase two was underway—he promised to reveal more. Meanwhile, they're filling in marshland, for which they need Japanese drainage technology."

Here Tomoda paused and got up to get us more beer at the self-service bar by the entrance.

Someone seemed to be staring. The man in the next chair was looking our way. Thirtyish, balding, long face, unshaved shadow of a goatee. As our eyes met, he nodded hello and turned away. He was wearing headphones, but one earpiece was half off.

Tomoda returned with two beers. I took one and set it on my sidetable.

"So tell me about the Taiwan Cheng Long Investment Group," I said a tad louder than necessary, then stole a glance at the goatee. The man appeared to have dozed off.

"They're a dummy corporation, a front for the ruling Kuomintang Party, invented as a joint venture with Ho Chi Minh City government." Tomoda spoke pretty loudly himself, but the goatee showed no sign of rousing—which somehow bothered me even more.

"The Val-Nam project is in the river delta southeast of Ho Chi Minh, a swamp that can't even be farmed. Misguided is not the word, the idea of building a whole new city on a marsh is insane. A 500-hectare industrial zone plus 3,000 hectares of commercial and residential, then another 2,500 hectares come phase two, for a grand total of 6,000 hectares? The Taiwanese pitched the thing to Ho Chi Minh, and they offered the land, no money changing hands. A good part of the layout is earmarked for the City, port facilities will be entirely theirs."

"But isn't Ho Chi Minh inland?"

"That whole delta's been diced up with channels connecting the Mekong to the South China Sea since forever. Any channel that can handle five-ton freighters should make a dandy container port with a little dredging. The City not only gets a logistic hub for shipping, they square away their housing shortage, too. And if foreign manufacturers locate there, their tax income soars. They aim to be a Southeast Asian Shanghai."

"And what does the Taiwan side get out of all this?"

"Cheng Long develops land obtained at zero cost and sells it for two thousand dollars a square meter." He hooted like an owl.

"What's so funny?" I asked.

"Oh nothing, it's all just so ironic. Maybe you've heard of the Viet Cong Liberated Areas, where the VC dug in ahead of the siege of Saigon? One of their strongholds was right there. Had the Americans scared so shitless they carried out dozens of clean-sweep operations. Huge body count, and still the VC held on. The Americans finally napalmed the place flat, a full-scale scorched earth campaign, but they never could capture it. Dig a bit and you'll strike blood. The 'Val' in Val-Nam could stand for 'Valiant.'"

"I thought Val-Nam was some kind of realtor jargon."

Tomoda shook his head, without looking up. "Well, it is and it isn't. The story goes that one of the American generals had read his Shakespeare, though obviously not too closely. He thought he was being clever by ordering his men to 'burn 'em woods' after the famous scene where Birnam Wood moves against Macbeth."

"Yeah, the climax of the play," I said, not wanting to be thought ignorant.

"And the wood defeats him, just like the VC behind every banyan tree defeated the Americans. Somehow the Vietnamese liked the sound of Birnam, which they heard as Vàng Nam—'Golden South'— only now it's been given a 'value' marketing spin."

"It's a stretch, but okay. What I don't get is why the VC vets who fought on the front line don't object. To them the place must be a sanctuary, no?"

"Well, you know what they say: no good deed goes unpunished. The most lauded ideologies eat their own." He yawned philosophically into his beer. "Most of those VC heroes were purged after the war. The rest lead very quiet lives now. Nah, the pageants of history aren't worth a rat's fart against the coin of the realm. Big money's flooding into Val-Nam from mainland China. Nanyang Holdings is just a pipeline."

I took another look at the goatee. He was awake but making a show of unconcern.

"Ho Chi Minh's chronically short of electricity"—Tomoda was starting to trip over his words—"so they also went in with the PRC to build a power plant especially for Val-Nam. An oddball joint venture with no money involved, only used hardware. Gave them a generator stripped from a plant in Fuzhou built with Japanese ODA funding, a black market hand-me-down—and Nanyang Holdings brokered the deal."

"Sounds kind of messy . . . Incidentally, do sand imports figure in the picture?"

"Sand? What's this now?"

"Something Yang mentioned, that lately there's a demand in Japan for Vietnamese white sand. Said he's importing the stuff to make artificial beach resorts."

"Could be. When Asia's economies scraped bottom, it was anything goes. They were selling off whatever, hand-to-mouth. Sand's probably one of the cleaner things."

The goatee had rolled over asleep and his headphones had slipped all the way off his scalp. I sat up and looked around. Everyone else had dozed off, too.

"These last few years, though, China's given a real boost to business," Tomoda continued. "America lifted sanctions, the embargo's been dropped. Major multinationals have homed in on Ho Chi Minh and factory incentives are all on track. They're building condos and high-rises, they've even got container port facilities. It's boom, boom time. And as of the first of this year, after much delay, Val-Nam started in on phase two."

"Construction's underway?"

"Yessir, right in the thick of it. Phase two is completely Yang's baby. The recent election in Taiwan that unseated the president has their judiciary examining everything with a magnifying glass. Got the Kuomintang so antsy they withdrew any direct party links to

Val-Nam. Enter Yang's company. His investment percentage suddenly jumps tenfold. In name only, of course; the politicos still pull the strings."

The goatee glanced this way, then rolled back as soon as I looked up.

"Just a metaphor, mind you, but there's all kinds of gems in that swamp," said Tomoda. "Whole veins of hidden stories. Foreign exchange fraud and bribery are just the beginning. Take overseas Chinese in America, they're shitting themselves trying to invest in Vietnam without the local powers-that-be finding out. But even if they stuff trunks full of cash, they still have to figure out how to physically move the stuff."

"So you think that's what Billy was hauling by private jet?"

"No proof, but that'd be one way to do it. Up until five years ago, Yang's biggest business was covert banking. Had quite a reputation, moving money from right to left with no ledgers or traceable records. Only now his clients aren't just overseas Chinese. He's got rackets going with US military boys and mainland Chinese corporations, too."

"In this digital money day and age? Why would anyone lug around trunks of cash?"

"Because they're Chinese, dummy!" he sputtered through a frown of beer foam. "For them that's the bottom line, what they can trust." All this was going on, and he couldn't make news of it. Very likely the Tran case and Billy's disappearance were just minor episodes in the whole screwball affair. "There, that's what I got. So how about it?"

"How about what?"

"The Yokosuka case. Someone I know finds a body at a bar in Dobuita? That story." He sat up and grinned.

"Didn't think you'd treat me to a bathhouse for nothing," I said.

"And don't forget the beer."

"Okay, the dead man was Tran Binh Long's brother-in-law. Two men driving a foreign Y-license car were spotted leaving the scene."

"Spotted by who?"

"I leave that to your imagination. Everything's in the police report. After Tran's death, his sister and her husband were goners, but Investigations didn't do a damn thing."

Just then it hit me like a winning red token at a lucky draw. What was it those Chinese goons at Joyo Warehouse said?

"Just a sec." I excused myself to go get my phone from the locker. The signal was clear in the dressing room. I took a seat by the mirrors and called Paulie in Okinawa. Mornings were no good, she'd told me, but I should feel free to ring however late. Was it morning now or night?

I got through right away, though I could hardly make out what she was saying. The background noise sounded like a festival dance on a rush-hour subway platform.

"Sorry to call you at this hour. Futamura here. Remember me?" I shouted.

Paulie shouted back for me to hold on, then paused while the noise blared away. "Okay, I just stepped outside. I'm at a club," she said once things quieted down.

"Disco?"

"No, island music. Please tell me you've got good news."

"No news, good or bad," I said. Which was true.

"Same here. Though I do have something to tell you. Last year, Billy, he bought a grave here in Okinawa, way up north on the island. I only remembered after I got back."

"A grave for who?"

"Dunno, himself I guess. Grave mounds down here look like spread vulvas, birth canals connecting this world to the next. The Okinawans say we return to the holes where we were born. Once the body's gone to bones, they seal it in the grave with all the other relatives and have a party."

"That was in the old days?"

"No, I believe he said they still do this in the countryside, even here on the big island. He really liked the idea. Well anyway, today I drove up north to sketch and went by to see it. And y'know what, there were flowers at the grave. Wilted, but they couldn't have been offered too long ago in this heat. What d'you think that means?"

"Anyone else know he bought a grave?"

"No idea. Don't know any of his friends, other than the ones I told you about."

I heard somebody else's voice. She covered the phone and answered whoever it was. Her ride was heading home, she told me. "Gotta run. Y'know, I think I will go to Taiwan after all. See if I can find a way to bring him back to his grave."

"But Billy's American. And you're not even related. And an Okinawan funeral's bound to be a hassle. You'd better call the Consulate, they can probably clue you in on details."

"Will do. Thanks for the tip."

"Oh, one last thing," I shouted before she could hang up. "Mrs. Tran's husband worked at the Naha docks, right?"

"Mr. Lê? Yeah, at a warehouse by the port."

"You remember the name of the company?"

"Joe? I think that's what he said, Joe Warehouse."

Someone passed behind me. In the mirror I saw the same bearded man greeting my reflection. He then ambled over to a seat two mirrors away and began to brush his teeth.

"Do you think it could have been Joyo Warehouse?" I lowered my voice to ask.

"Hmm, I guess. You can find out easy enough, it's a big place. Right by the Meiji Bridge." Suddenly the line cut out, then her voice swept back in a loud swell of music.

Unjun wannin iyaan wannin kampo nu kueé nukusaa . . .

"Hear that? 'You and me, we all shall die, but this place is forever . . .' It's poetry. I'll never know why Billy hated these folksongs."

I couldn't understand a word of Okinawan, but what did I really know of Billy either?

"Uh-oh, gotta go. My friend's—" She broke off, then came back out of nowhere. "Hey, so what about the warehouse? Who are you looking for?"

"Same as you, I bet." My answer silenced her for a moment.

"You think? Well, you tell me and we'll both know," she laughed.

On signing off, the phone clicked twice. How could you tell if someone was bugging a mobile? I'd always been in Violent Crime, I didn't know jack about wire tapping.

Across the dressing room a chair leg scraped. Rising to his feet, the goatee came to a halt right behind me. His right hand was out of the mirror frame, I couldn't tell what he was holding. He took a step forward and spoke through his nose. "Wha's your name?"

When he sidled another step closer, I tucked in my chin, powered up, and whammed him on the nose with the back of my head. Then, swinging around, I grabbed his bathrobe collar and wrestled him down on his side, pinning him under my knee.

"Who put you up to this?" Another blow forced open the hand I thought might've held a razor blade, but out tumbled a mauve card inscribed with a telephone number, email address, and heart doodle. I let go and the goatee sat up slowly, face in his hands.

Back in the locker room, I stowed my phone and retrieved the latex glove from my jacket pocket before returning to the lounge. Tomoda had his massage chair going strong while watching a movie without headphones. I plunked down the glove with its two fingers of dirt on his sidetable. "I want you to have some things tested."

He looked at me, then the glove in turn, and switched off his video screen.

"There's a Joyo Warehouse near the American pier," I said. "The company has ties with Golden Harbor. They've got tons of this stuff in there, probably from on base."

"I hope you're not going to tell me this is plutonium."

"Well, whatever it is can't be too healthy. They also had lots of medical waste."

Tomoda's eyes lit up. He raised his backrest and lowered his legs as I planted myself across from him.

"Down in Okinawa there's probably another warehouse under the same name and management on the Naha waterfront. Tran's brother-in-law most likely worked there until he came up here. That warehouse is probably in the same line of business."

"I'll check it out. Port of Naha, Joyo Warehouse, right?" He looked me in the face.

"Before Tran died, seems he said he'd be making good money soon. He'd lined up a job as captain of a freighter owned by Zou of Golden Harbor. The French priest said they planned to sell the ship in Vietnam. The freighter's berthed at Mizuho Pier right now."

"Sell the ship? Or sell the cargo? Which was it?"

"Both? Or maybe some other scheme? Tran wouldn't have told the priest if it was illegal."

"There's our breakthrough," Tomoda exclaimed, nodding to himself, "what they load and unload from the ship. Even if it's only garbage they haul away, what do they bring back? A freighter returning with an empty hold's not making money."

"How about Yang's white sand?"

"I suppose, though there must be tons of other things to bring in from Vietnam."

Just then, a sudden "Fuck you!" rang out across the lounge. The goatee glared at us from the locker room doorway, then stormed off.

"Who the hell was that?"

"A goat with a grudge?" The clock on the wall read well past four. I yawned as I stood up and heard myself say, "We'd better be going home too."

"Going home for what?"

"Breakfast. A one-pound steak, eggs, pint of milk, lettuce, *natto* beans and rice."

"How domestic. Me, I'm gonna get a little more sleep, gotta be at the studio by six."

"There's limits to liking your job."

"Not enough time to go home." He smiled weakly. "Always one thing after another."

The newspaper delivery guy was just coming out of the building when the taxi dropped me at my apartment. He seemed to know me. "Your mailbox's full of junk," he called out.

Several large envelopes were crammed inside. Mail-order catalogues I'd never requested and pamphlets from unknown charity groups. I excavated the lot and went upstairs, then bunged it all into the trash. No wait, there was one clean white envelope. I fished it out. Aileen Hiraoka's handwriting was like hieroglyphs, my name printed Western-style left to right looking like an overdesigned logo for some upscale restaurant.

It was a ticket to a concert at Minato Mirai here in Yokohama this coming Sunday, the last date of her Japan tour. That was nice of her. But with it came a strange feeling I was missing some angle, something in plain sight yet just out of reach. I turned the envelope upside down and gave it a shake, but it yielded no secret of any kind.

40

Sunlight slanted through the curtains to tickle the soles of my feet. My eyes wouldn't open, but the alarm drilling at my ears sent a hand roaming the nightstand in search of the clock. No lazing in the morning sun for me, I vaguely realized, then dozed off again.

When next I awoke it was past nine. I hauled myself out of bed and called the Archives. I let it ring maybe ten times before the answerphone kicked in, at which point I dispensed with any excuses for being late and just said I was taking the day off. No reason given. The sun spilling into the room would hardly count as an explanation.

After a sweaty lie-in till noon, I had two cups of coffee. Then the phone rang. "Hey, Futamura, why didn't you tell me sooner?" Sato started right in. "It was on my old Yokosuka beat, after all. Nobody thinks to keep me in the loop."

"Don't you read the papers?"

"The papers didn't mention Kaput by name. Who was the dead man? You found the guy? Why'd the Department clamp down on details? This is Komine in charge, right?"

"Cut me some slack, I'm barely awake," I said. "Before the inquisition, tell me if you figured out who the phone belonged to."

"Registered to a company. Same number as in your call record, contract under the name of Golden Harbor Enterprises."

"But the contract was canceled. Did you find out when?"

"Nothing escapes the old pro," he replied, clearly pleased with himself. "Mm, let's see . . . that was June 19."

It was past midnight June 17, Saturday gone Sunday, when I first ran into Billy. The next time we met, he asked if he'd left his phone in my car, so most likely he only noticed it was missing that Sunday afternoon. Naturally he'd ask the mobile company to stop service. But the contract holder Golden Harbor wouldn't be answering their office phones on a Sunday, so he must have waited till Monday to cancel and get a new phone.

The phone in Reiko Hiraoka's car had to be Billy's, it was obvious now. OK, but why was he still looking for it if he couldn't have continued using it? Was the number such a secret? Was he afraid someone might have stolen the thing?

"Hey, you still there? Can you hear me?" Sato demanded.

"There was another question mark, the Yokohama landline."

"Nailed that one too."

"Was it by any chance Joyo Warehouse in Chiwakacho?"

Molars grated on the other end of the line. "What the hell, were you *testing* me?"

"No, Joyo's a subsidiary of Golden Harbor. And there's something fishy about the warehouse."

"Well, their service was suspended as of June 19, too. The old 'removed at the customer's request' thing, shall we just skip it?"

I got up, phone in hand, and opened the window to let in some air. A few clouds idled about the harbor under a high blue sky. "You tried phoning all the numbers on the call record, right," I said. "Three of the four didn't get through, but the one that did was a mobile Tran's sister used. That would've been on June 19 or just before."

"Why would Reiko have called it? What's the connection to her?"

"No idea. But on June 17, she had guests over to her condo. Ordered sashimi from a nearby restaurant, bought liquor and meat too, so whoever they were they meant a lot to her."

"You suppose *they* could've forgotten the phone? And if so, why would she wait a whole month before calling in mid-July?"

"Hmm, didn't think that far. Maybe she was in no hurry for them to come get it. Or else she didn't know them too well—where they lived or worked."

"No, that doesn't make sense. Reiko wasn't one to invite strangers home for a party."

"There's a lot here that doesn't make sense. I'm just trying to piece together what little we do know."

Sato tapped a cigarette on the receiver. It was just like old times, talking over leads at Investigations. "Okay, I'm with you, keep going."

"Say something happens after a month that makes it necessary to contact whoever forgot the phone, but all the numbers in the call record are already out of service except one. The number for Tran Kinh Hoa, the frozen guy's sister. Either the sister or her husband tells Reiko to come to Kaput. There was a handwritten memo in Reiko's car, something about Kaput and Tran."

"Fine time to bring it up, Futamura!" he growled. "Why am I hearing this only now?"

"Sorry, I'm doing my best. Reiko Hiraoka was sighted in Yokosuka near her bank with the sister's husband. On July 19, when she withdrew five hundred thousand yen."

"The very same day? That's a recipe for extortion." His voice was shaky.

"The strange thing is," I went on, "a friend of mine lost his mobile right around that time—the suspect I drove to Yokota, you must've heard. We met late at night on June 17 at Kaput. The next time I saw him he asked if he'd left his phone in my car."

Sato said nothing, but I could tell he was on edge.

"The following month when I drove Billy to Yokota, he flew off in a minijet, abandoning a woman's corpse in his car. That was July 20."

Sato grunted with displeasure.

"The dead woman in the trunk of Billy's car was Tran's sister. The body I found at Kaput the day before yesterday was her husband, the man at the bank with Reiko."

Sato started to say something, but held back, swallowing a ragged breath.

"I'd rather not speculate any more than this, not over the phone anyway," I told him.

He suddenly perked up. "Ah yes, the license plate you asked about, the yellow pickup truck. I got it for you." He read off the address, an apartment in central Yokohama, above a seedy strip of former gambling houses. "Shogo Kudo by name, a young hood with the Shinseikai family. Just yesterday Yokohama South hauled him in."

"On what charge?"

"Animal abuse," he said dismissively. "Article 27, Welfare and Treatment of Animals. Apparently admitted to the charge."

Slipping on a jacket, I stepped out in the bright clear day. The sun was strong, but a breeze kept the air nice and cool. Perfect autumn weather. I returned the van to the rental office, then called the Detective Division at Yokohama South. Sergeant Kemi, a young Violent Crimes guy I'd worked with before at Headquarters, said he'd be manning the desk for another two hours.

I hopped on the subway. As soon as I walked in, Kemi looked up from some reports with his usual sour expression.

"Real open house you got here," I said. "Strolled in this far and no one asks a thing."

He peered around. His superior was nowhere in sight. Sitting up, his tired smile aged him years. "What's the story? We don't have any donations for your stacks."

"Don't need any books. I'm collecting doctored reports."

"Got plenty of those. Help yourself."

When I told him I wanted to see Kudo, his face skewed at a difficult angle. "No can do. He's Public Security's catch. What's more, they ran a search and turned up a handgun."

Off the top of my head I said, "What kind? Don't tell me it was a Nambu."

"Holy shit. Is that what you're after? The gun's got a history?"

I looked out the window so as not to lord over his surprise and thought quickly. "C'mon, let me see him. He might just own up to another offense. If so, he's all yours."

Kemi called over to Public Security, but the Chief was out. Lucky for me, he muttered, and took me downstairs.

The officer in charge was in her forties. No makeup, rimless glasses, hair done up in a bun. The school building framed in the window behind her made a perfect backdrop. Kemi introduced me with some formality as Detective Futamura *who was with* Investigations at Headquarters. I related how Gagarin got doused in the pool and suggested Kudo might have been keeping an eye on the woman owner's movements. Immediately the officer showed interest. Stalker crimes come under Public Security.

After some back-and-forth about possible motives, she led me to the interrogation room. I took a seat with my back to the door and waited. Presently they brought in Kudo, print shirt unbuttoned and untucked, loose jeans barely riding his underpants.

"You dislike dogs?" I asked.

"I hate 'em." He smirked, his eyes vacant. He might have been handsome if he didn't look so stupid. The holding tank had turned his bleached blond hair into a dusty mop. "Haven' I seen you someplace?" he wondered out loud.

"And what's with this dog you hit-and-ran?" I countered.

"The mutt wouldn' stop yappin'. Blame the stupid bitch that left it tied up in the parking lot while she's sayin' her prayers out loud. All mornin' long, twice the racket."

"And double the offense. You could be here for quite a while."

He looked up and cackled. "You gotta be kiddin', in this dump of a lockup?"

"Tell it to the family lawyer."

"Like I told you people how many times, I quit the family ages ago."

"More like they kicked you out," the woman officer put in. "No loss, says your boss."

Kudo didn't protest. If anything, he looked a little abashed and scratched his head.

"Last Thursday in Yokosuka," I said, picking up the slack, "you threw a dog into a pool, didn't you?"

His eyes flicked left and right, then looked down. "'Cause it bit me. You all got the wrong idea, I'm not some jerkoff that gets a kick outta hurtin' animals. I had my reasons."

"But the dog only bit you after you kicked it, right?"

He huddled down in his chair and the other two showed me out of the room.

"Can I have fifteen minutes alone with the suspect?" I asked them.

"Sorry, that's out of the question," said the officer in charge.

"No third degree, no tricks, I assure you. There's just something else I wanted to ask. I promise to tell you later," I pressed.

"About the pool incident?"

"No, about another case."

She looked at Kemi for a flicker of consensus, but he kept his head turned away. "Alright then, ten minutes only."

I returned to the room and was about to sit down when I noticed a dark patch on his scalp, a tattoo hidden under his blondish mop. It was the same punk who rifled the mailboxes at my apartment. That was two months ago, plenty of time for a hairstyle to go surfing or a nose to mend if it wasn't busted too bad.

"How about this?" I proposed. "Everything we say here stays here. I'm no dog lover myself, so you help me and I'll help you. Tell me what you were doing at that condo."

"What condo, where? I got no idea, honest."

I moved in behind him. "Next time, keep fucking track of who you hit with that stun gun of yours," I hissed in his ear. I had his neck in an armlock.

Once I got his full attention, I eased up and sat down across the desk from him. "Use that gadget on an officer, you're looking at five years," I lied. "But I'm investigating another case, and if you just answer my questions, I'll forget about it. You don't want my buddies to hear how you zapped me. So tell me, did you hide a spycam in condo 101?"

Kudo nodded tamely. "I was just hanging out, but there's a sexy milf got this, like, whole setup. Pulls in the GIs, pimps 'em to four or five women apiece. All day long, morning to night, humpty-hump."

"So you regularly go keep score?"

"Does me better'n any porn site on the net, that's for sure," he snickered. "Might even help you for evidence."

"No use to me," I told him. "But you stole a handgun from condo 301, am I right?"

"Didn' steal it, I, like, borrowed it," he quickly hedged.

"Who from? Mrs. Hiraoka?"

He went quiet. He seemed to be tapping at a calculator in his head.

"If you'll confirm it belonged to her, you're in the clear."

"That's a low blow. If the Brother Man finds out, he'll have 'em beat me to a pulp."

"When you looted her apartment, was that on orders from him?" I asked as calmly as possible.

Kudo looked up and pleaded, "Don't squeal on me, please, whatever. I'll take the rap for the gizmo, just leave him outta this."

"Your Brother Man's no stranger to us. He's been a loose cannon since when he was high up in the family."

"Then you know what he's like. He blows his stack, he goes all *yakuza* apeshit."

I threw out a blind ball. "I'll put in a good word with Orimasa for you."

Kudo stared at the edge of the desk, then slowly acknowledged this with half a nod.

"Any further information won't get to the detectives here. So talk. What were you poking around the mailboxes for?"

"There was an airmail deliv'ry I was s'posed to get from one of them, forget which. But then that cunt slugs me," he said, rubbing his nose.

"And what about condo 301?"

"I was told to keep watch on the place. Or more like, to help someone out. Granny in 301 got deep in some loanshark shit so, like, I gotta protect her."

"When did you hear about these loanshark debts?"

"July, middle of the month. Or maybe a little later, like, around the twenty-first. I get a call late at night. The Man's at the condo, says he has to step out awhile, could I spell him keepin' an eye on her?"

"So you actually met Reiko Hiraoka?"

"The old lady?" Of course, he said, but they didn't talk. He spent close to twelve hours at 301 until Orimasa returned the following noon. During which time the lady had gone to the toilet once or twice, which involved a passing nod but no conversation. Otherwise, she slept in the back room the whole night. Sometimes he heard her crying.

"And did you go keep watch there again after that?"

Kudo shook his head. "Play nursemaid, no way. Anyhow, she run off the next night."

"Did Orimasa chase her out? Where'd she go?"

"Like I'm s'posed to know? I split. Only later I get a call to clean out the place."

"But all her things are still there."

"All 'cept a handbag and a cardboard box. A big heavy mother. Had to use a wheelie to, like, wobble it out. Wasn't for my pickup, it'd still be there." The box, he said, was the size of a 37-inch TV Orimasa was waiting with everything already packed when he arrived. The two of them barely managed to load the truck and drive to Orimasa's place, where they stashed it in his storage unit. "More like a garage, big as my whole apartment."

"What was in the handbag?"

"Hell if I know. But like, get this, a grandma with a Gucci tote?"

I walked over to his side, put my hands on the desk, and stared right at him. "But you went back to the condo, didn't you? Did Orimasa tell you to?"

"I seen the rod when we wheeled the box out and I still had the spare key the Brother Man gave me, so—"

"So you went back for the gun. Where in the condo was it?"

"Under her pillow. Knocked it off the bed tryin' to move the box."

"Any bullets?"

"Three rounds in the clip. But, like, the action was jammed, messed up from a misfire. Way dangerous, specially for an old lady."

"That must also be when you found out about the goings-on in 101."

Kudo gave a sloppy grin. "Made such a racket, you'd gotta be whacked not to notice. Good as got me off."

Again I moved behind Kudo, this time tipping his chair back to glare down at him and say, "Let's keep quiet about 301, eh? You were just spying on the woman with the dog."

"Huh? What d'you mean?"

"The dog can't identify you, and with all the video you got, the woman's not going to bring charges. So you were just chasing a piece of ass . . . Unless, of course, you want to go up against Orimasa."

"Gotcha. I'll just say I, like, found the rod somewhere." The words caught in his throat as I righted the chair. "Hope they're gonna believe that."

"You stick to your story and I'll tell Orimasa you're doing fine."

I went out into the corridor where, as expected, the other two were standing right by the door. "I take it there were spycam video-tapes confiscated from his apartment?"

"What did the suspect say?" the woman officer asked back.

"The men in the video are GIs from Yokosuka. They also threw the dog in the pool."

"So if we can identify the stalking victim, we've got a case."

"More important is the gun. Would you mind showing me?" I turned on her abruptly. "Spycamming and animal abuse charges will get you nowhere. If you're going to take him down, the gun's the thing."

Without saying yes or no, she walked to Public Security and returned with a file opened to a page with photos of an old Japanese Army handgun, a Nambu 14 automatic. From the enlargements, it looked badly rusted. I examined a close-up of the pistol grip. Engraved on it was a dedication, which someone had duly transcribed on the page:

To Mr. Phan Ai Quak
from Capt. Kiyotaka Miyazaki,
Head, Hainan Production and Testing Center
Aug 17, 1945

Two days after the end of World War II. I committed the names and date to memory before the officer shut the file with a snap, then said my thanks and left.

"US military mixed up in this?" murmured Kemi as he followed along after me. "A gun turns up and all I can think is, what's Headquarters doing about it? Bet you Organized Crime Control's butting in again."

If that was the score, it didn't bode well, I agreed. And I wasn't just humoring him.

41

Outside the Precinct, I called Yamato but only got his voicemail. Leaving word I was on my way, I made for the station and was in Yokosuka in twenty-odd minutes.

As I crossed the pedestrian bridge out of Shioiri Station, the town shone here and there beneath a sky streaked with sunset. Lights were coming on in this window and the next. The parking lot at the seaside shopping mall was restless with housewives driving in and out. I picked my way through them, under a stairway, and there was Yamato, bent over, repairing shoes in his little hut of a shop.

"I switch off the phone while I work," he told me with a yellow-toothed smile, without looking up.

Could I buy him a coffee, I asked. The counter opened and out popped the impresario, dressed today in a pink jumper and white suede shoes. He lowered the shutter and off we went. Up the tall glass atrium escalator, past store after store, all the way to the opposite side of the megamall and out through a glass door onto a cedar-decked terrace built over the bay. We bought drinks at the self-service cabana, then claimed a pair of plastic chairs among a cluster of beach-parasoled tables.

Across the water by the far seawall a missile cruiser gleamed in the sunset. I remembered seeing this shopping center from over there only a few days before. The warship looked much closer from this side, more like a massive iceberg than an iron hulk.

Yamato eyed the surroundings and muttered, "Every last damn place near the sea they have to turn into Hawaii."

"And they've turned every seaside in Hawaii into mainland America with giant park-and-shop discount stores."

"Yeah? Never been there myself." He pulled out a cigarette and looked around for an ashtray, but seeing only families of non-smokers he tapped it back into his pocket.

"I'd like to meet Tyson," I said. "There's something I want to discuss without his sidekick present. I think he might take an interest if he knows I'm a cop."

Yamato curled his lips and scratched his head. "It's a secret op. Even their own team here don't know they're here on assignment. How's ol' Yamato gonna find them?"

"I didn't bring it up till now, but I didn't forget," I said. "That night I got knocked out on the Mabori coast road, didn't Tyson contact you? I think they have your number."

"Slow down, I ain't followin' you."

"How was it you could tell me out of nowhere that Ackerman's office was in Parklane Terrace? Now that I think of it, there's only one place you could've got that lead. Those two had Ackerman marked from way back."

Yamato drank his coffee in silence. His eyes were those of a sailing man, watching the day sink slowly toward the water. "There's all kinds of leads that don't go nowhere, probably more don'ts than do's. No matter what you ask for, Bro."

Something flashed in my head like the setting sun glinting off the sea.

"You must've had dealings with them," I said. "They scanned my driver's license, but afterwards they didn't lay any traps. Nothing. That's how I got out of the base so easily."

Yamato's face didn't move, he just kept staring quietly into his paper coffee cup. He barely had enough teeth to smile with anyway.

I changed my tack. "Yang's got close connections with the US Forces, right? And Tyson's been investigating those connections, illegal ones. Maybe something to do with the Khaki Mafia?" In

Orimasa's novel, they were depicted as a secret organization within the military who used MPs as their frontmen to hunt down the hero's comrades in arms Kang and Ernesto Fujiwara.

"Khaki Mafia? Wasn't just a few Army no-goods banded together," said Yamato, shaking his head at me. "During the Vietnam War, it was big-time. Pushin' dope to GIs, takin' cuts from showbiz types, showgirls, jazzmen, you name it. Squeezed everyone for margins, brokerin' all kind of deals. They used military mail pouches for smugglin' and fenced commissary goods on the black market. Back then, His Lordship Glidden was well placed as head of Saigon Customs. Kids nowadays wouldn' understand, but back in the day the PX was like their holy of holies, and the Khaki Mafia had the keys. Come the end of the war, rumor is they were even sellin' off helicopters."

I sipped my American drip coffee, a cup of colored hot water. "I heard similar stories from a friend of mine. So has Glidden simply scaled up in the same line of work?"

He ignored me and forged ahead. "More recent-like, in the Gulf War, when the Allies made off with so much stuff from Iraq? Ain't half of it been recovered, no trick one or two Joes can pull off. You need Joes to steal it, Joes to move it, Joes to cash it in. Organizin' teams like that's easier in the military. Wartime, peacetime, don't make no difference. Where armies go, money and materials go with 'em. Expenses get padded, goods get fenced. Put your winnings back in the game, pump up the stakes, you're in the gold."

"And now it's gone independent of the boys in khaki? Is that the Sneak Beak?"

"No comment." He croaked a laugh, his voice was giving out. "Durin' the Gulf War, water was a nice little niche. Water don't come cheap for a hundred thousand troops on desert maneuvers." At that his grin soured. "Lately, tho', they're outsourcin' this, that, and the other. Remember, time was the US Navy bakery used to smell so good? Now just look, they get their bread from Japanese companies.

292

Hell, there's even McDonald's on base. Next thing they'll be puttin' drive-ins on aircraft carriers and sendin' GIs to the front on passenger planes. Door-to-door munitions by home delivery. They farm out prison warden jobs and interrogatin' prisoners to private firms, pretty soon they won't even do the killin'. And just like gov'ment, all the cushy contracts go to military retirees."

I withheld comment and waited for the foregone conclusion.

"What I'm gettin' at is, this last decade your Khaki Mafia's grown from a mom-and-pop shop into a chain of department stores. By hookin' up with outside int'rests, they've built a system to rake in profits from any conflict. And *that*, Bro, is the way of the world. With venture business, ain't nobody knows where legal stops and crime begins."

"And Yang's in bed with them."

"Not just in bed, he practically runs the whorehouse. Wanna know who's his khaki connection?" Yamato leered at me, but I already knew what he was going to say.

"Who was Tyson tryin' to jimmy up as witness? Who'd he get in touch with when they wanted to trade amnesty for testimony? I know you know, Bro."

I pulled out a cigarette and lit up. My coffee was gone, the cup made a better ashtray.

"Word is, Acting Commander Joseph Glidden got called back suddenly to Hawaii. And Tyson's gone *aloha* too. Must've scored his goal."

"But Tyson was still in Yokosuka a couple of days ago," I protested. "I guess you heard about the dead body at Kaput. That was Tran's brother-in-law. A big guy and a short one were seen leaving the scene in a white four-by-four with Y-permit plates."

"You got it wrong, that weren't them. The Tyson twins flew out from Atsugi the very next day after they done you, Bro."

He tottered to his feet, walked over to the terrace railing, and began tossing out breadcrumbs from his pocket. All at once seagulls converged to fight over them.

"Know anything about a Hainan Production and Testing Center?" I asked to his back.

"Some kinda covert op, no? Back then, Japan's wartime *Kempeitai* run a spy school on Hainan Island for trainin' Southeast Asian militia. Trainees outta there joined their countries' independence movements after the war, some of 'em become local heroes and foundin' fathers." He turned around and the seagulls scattered in confusion. "About that Sneak Beak you mentioned, it's like a code word for the whole Khaki Mafia. Their lot got a different peckin' order than your official bald eagle. They divvy up the spoils right on the battlefield, hungrier and faster. Try to cut 'em out, they sprout back like bamboo."

"But profit's been the name of the game since the Roman wars."

He let out a sigh and gazed out to sea, but it wasn't the sea he was looking at. "America's changed. Just like with railways and public services, don't do no good to privatize war. Private enterprise puts profit first."

"Sounds like you miss the good ol' US military," I said, a little too loud even for me.

"More like I miss the last war. Or maybe the war before that, or wars way back when." He went quiet. So did I.

I broke the silence. "Sorry, shouldn't have said that."

"Don't mention it, Bro. Weren't me you was shoutin' at." He gave a let's-go flick of the head. I tagged along after him into the shopping mall. Yamato's back was bent, as if weighed down under a big duffel bag. Seen from behind, he looked like an elderly patient climbing hospital stairs. Then, without stopping or even looking around, he spoke up. "Bro, you asked if I ever had dealings with Tyson? That snapshot you loaned me, the one with Yang and the Lord High Fleet Activities Commander, well I showed it to 'em. That was your friend Billy's insurance. And now it's yours. But no, I didn't cut no deal, s'all in a day's work for ol' Yamato."

Just outside the atrium we stopped and looked across the

intersection up at the hotel tower with the heliport on top, the last place to catch the last of the sun. Down below was the chatter of neon lights.

"Sure, times was good in the Vietnam War, everyone on Dobuita says so. Not me tho', I never say that. Sure I made some money. But them soldiers' eyes was like dead fish. Nineteen-, twenty-year-old dead fish." Still without turning he said, "America's like a dog fightin' its own reflection in the mirror. Never realizin' till the mirror gets broke. Kinda the same as you now, eh Bro?"

"What's the same?"

"Like you're lookin' in a mirror."

"What is it you're trying to say?"

Too late, Yamato had already walked off, his retreating figure slipping into the crowd. We hadn't said goodbye, but I didn't follow him.

42

I walked up Dobuita toward Yori's club, not that I intended to go there. I was heading to the taco place for a drink, which took me right past it. A brace of high school girls occupied the corner table, the big old dog sprawled at their feet as relaxed as could be. Flower wreaths and barkers announced the opening of a new bar nearby, bright light from the big front window illuminating half the street.

An American NCO appeared with a blue-haired Japanese girl in tow and pressed his nose against the glass trying to decipher the katakana:

OOPUN EBURI NAITO UI NEBAA KUROOZU

In halting English the girl read it out for him—OPEN EVERY NIGHT WE NEVER CLOSE—eliciting a puzzled snort and a shrug from the soldier.

I stood there puzzled as well. Why was I here? I turned around and hurried back the way I came. I had to get home to my apartment while something was still on my mind.

Catching a special express at Shioiri, I changed to the subway at the fourth stop and was at my local station in no time. I ran the rest of the way, only to pause for a second in the entrance. Much to my surprise I suddenly remembered what I'd come back for: my mailbox, inscribed with the two characters *futa* and *mura*.

Billy said he'd once seen me park illegally beside Parklane Terrace, then later saw me enter this building, and found his way to my apartment thanks to my name on the mailbox. There was of course no alphabetic lettering anywhere. The lock hadn't latched properly since a few days ago and now I saw why: the bolt catch was bent out of shape.

The ground-floor resident had caught Kudo tampering with the mailboxes the morning after I met Orimasa. Then that evening Billy's letter arrived. It was Orimasa who alerted me to the tricky postmark date, saying his old friend just might still be alive, yet reasoning away all likelihood of it. Is that why he invited me to lunch? At the very least Orimasa knew the letter was coming and when.

Up in my apartment, I reread it for the first time in weeks.

I'm in San Francisco. Sorry I can't keep our appointment, but stuff came up. So I decided to write what you'd been wanting to know.

Billy suggested that Tran's death wasn't an accident but suicide. He'd made some serious business errors and Yang was leaning on him, so in the end he probably saw dying as the only way out. Billy also warned me not to get too close to Yang. As if I had something going with his employer when in fact I didn't even know Yang's name at the time. He sounded like he'd been beating himself up over something. What, he didn't say, only that it was his own fault. He didn't confess to killing Tran's sister, all he said was: *Use your half of that hundred bill and drink yourself some Papa Dobles at Brunhilda's on me.*

I rang up Takashi Kishimura at the wedding hall in Chinatown. I had to hold a while, he was still working, but he told me he'd call back in a few minutes. While waiting, I used my landline to track down the expert I needed, the manager of an internet café.

I told him I'd drop by the café later, then popped open a beer and had just about finished reading the evening paper when my mobile bleeped. Before Kishimura could say a word, I blurted out a question. "When Yuichi Hiraoka had his accident, what happened to the car driver? Would you know?"

"Hmm, I doubt I can remember. It was in the papers, though, I know I read about it. In those days it was pretty rare for Japanese to get in a traffic accident overseas."

I charged out of the apartment without changing clothes. I needed to grab a quick bite of supper before things got busy.

Things had changed in Kominato. The US Forces housing compound had reverted to Japan ages ago, though some of the old-time GI bars nearby held on long afterwards. When those finally gave up the ghost, they were replaced by regular counter bars and karaoke boxes. And recently an internet café had moved in above a convenience store.

My contact, the manager, was a kid with pierced ears and a tattoo around his thumb. He'd said he was busy, but I saw only one customer.

"Pentagon's no-go lately, they've initialized a proprietary hacker warning system," he said, dispensing a scrap of information an oldster like me might find interesting.

"I need some code numbers used in the US bases."

His eyes bugged out and a high-pitched voice told me, "*That* you can pull up anywhere." And to prove it, he promptly produced a whole directory. FAC3117, the most frequent code at Joyo Warehouse, was listed as the Shibasato Warehouse District.

Could he get me more details on this? He immediately logged onto an anti-base activist website and retrieved a contents page for *Pollution in the Shibasato Area*. It seems the Shibasato warehouses were located on a small outcrop in Yokosuka between Oppama and Nagaura, a square kilometer in size, shaped like a fist thrust into Tokyo Bay. A short hike over a hill, the Imperial Japanese Army had built an arsenal there, which was handed over after the war to the Occupation Forces, then to the US Navy until after Vietnam, when urban sprawl pushed residential tracts up against the headland and a citizens' protest movement had forced the Americans to stop storing explosives on the site.

Since then, however, "Worse than imminent explosions near our homes, a far more insidious threat has arisen." The website accused the US Navy of using it as a dump for hazardous waste. I skimmed through the polemic, then asked for a printout.

BUMED was even easier. An acronym for the US Navy Bureau of Medicine, it took all of half a second to find. Obviously my hunch about medical waste had been right.

"Is that all? Anything else?" We looked at each other almost disappointedly. Well, since he asked, I had him access a Japanese newpaper database, then old Mexican news items about traffic accidents.

The kid pouted. The website demanded a password, whereupon he keyed in a sequence of taps, and immediately the screen seemed to have logged onto a pay-per-view datastream for free, and I now entered my keywords MEXICO and TRAFFIC ACCIDENT. The search yielded a simple article stating only Yuichi Hiraoka's name and address, with nothing about the driver. The accident had occurred on the outskirts of Otatoclán.

The car tried to steer clear of an oncoming vehicle and veered off the steep mountain road. The victim, Yuichi Hiraoka, had little money and was hitchhiking.

The reporter then soapboxed against young people setting out on long journeys without plans or funds. The article was two decades old. By now the writer was probably on the editorial board, still railing against something from the comfort of his easy chair.

While I read, the kid reached out and with a "May I?" began to search something new. His fingers danced over the keyboard like he was playing Chopin, and presently an American news article came up. I was amazed, but the kid just curled his lip. "El Paso paper, for Hispanic readers. There's more, but this seems to be the only English page."

"How did you . . . ?" I stammered, but he didn't even look around when I thanked him.

This article was even less informative than the Japanese one, but at least it spared me the sermon. There was no mention of Yuichi Hiraoka's name, only the suggestion that since the crashed car had

California plates registered in Los Angeles, one or more of the persons involved must have been American.

I hit the date for further reports, but an ERROR message blinked up and the screen shut down. Feeling every cursor-stroke my age, I switched the monitor off.

Back at my apartment, I rang up Tomoda and got his voicemail. He wasn't at his office either. I gave up and wrote a few notes on the news article printouts, then went to the local convenience store and faxed them over to him.

Now I had time for a shower, followed by a thorough cleaning of my whiskey tumblers. I'd been meaning to get at the grime in the etched crystal for ages. A peg of scotch in a squeaky clean glass raised my spirits. The ice clinked clearer, the single malt aroused a noseful of peaty fragrance.

Still no call from Tomoda, for once I dozed off after one drink—but not for long.

"What the hell's this fax?" Tomoda wanted to know.

"Wondered if you could do a little more inquiring. Either via Spanish-language papers or the local police."

"You must think we have overseas bureaus everywhere."

"If anyone can do it, it's you," I said, and he took the bait with a leave-it-to-me laugh.

"About that photo, the one you gave me a while back, I figured out two of the guys. One of them's Tran, your frozen friend. Didn't you look at the picture of the corpse?"

"How can *you* be so sure?"

"I got hold of his passport photo. Much younger, but no mistake. He must've been in some real scrapes, he was thinner when he died than in his twenties."

"And the other guy?"

"Sitting in the rattan chair in the middle, this one totally by chance. One of our staff had seen his picture in a memoir of a purged

Viet Cong who escaped to Paris. So I went to the library and there he was, a guy missing one ear. The face is a match, no mistake."

"So he's Viet Cong?"

"No, the author's his younger brother, a big shot in the VC command by the name of Phan Bửu Kiếm. He eventually got the cold shoulder from the government up north and was exiled. The older brother, the one in the photo, a businessman in Saigon, seems to have been an influential wheeler-dealer in deep with the US Army and ARVN, then ten years after the Liberation he gets reinstated as a secret member of the VC."

"And do we know the older brother's name?"

"Phan Ái Quốc, fifty-one years old at the time."

After goodbyes over the phone, I just sat there staring at the empty glass in my hand. The name engraved on the pistol was Phan Ai Quak, but that margin of error was hardly surprising. I filled my polished glass with more scotch. It took another hour to get to bed.

43

A yacht from the marina cut its engine a short way out in the water and raised sail, close enough to hear the wind flap the canvas. The afternoon sun glistened off the waves.

I parked under the pines along the bayside drive, grabbed a polyethylene spray canister from the passenger seat, and locked up. Last night's whiskey still brooded in my gut. I hadn't downed even half a bottle, but this morning I was a wreck. Making the most of my two colleagues' absence, I'd taken a nap on the sofa in the corridor, had some soothing rice soup for lunch, then driven down here. Why should I still feel so strung out?

Reiko Hiraoka's condo was dead quiet. I had only one thing to do there. I headed down the ramp to the garage and lowered the red Nissan Sunny from its pallet, pulled out the driver's floor mat, then sprayed the muddy footprints with reagent: a mixture of potassium hydroxide and hydrogen peroxide with just a drop of luminol diluted in distilled water, prepared for me by Notomi in Forensics.

Before my eyes the footprints began to glow a lurid fluorescent green. It wasn't the mud and it wasn't tar from the road either. There were also faint traces of the stuff on the steering wheel. When I sprayed on the test liquid the same fluorescent color showed up in a chemical reaction to the presence of blood: a nauseating reminder of the sticky residue on the floor at Kaput—stepped in, squirmed through, smeared in all directions, a dance of grimy footprints. Curiously, these offhand associations are often a useful tip-off.

I returned the Nissan to its pallet and went up to the main entrance. While I was waiting for the elevator, the superintendent came bumbling down the stairs with a vacuum cleaner but turned away as soon as he saw me.

"A minute of your time?" I asked.

"Er, no, I'm busy. Lots to do."

"Sorry to bother you while you're doing the rounds, but . . ."

He gave me a sour look and hurried to unlock his office.

"Hey, just a second . . ."

Kicking off his sandals at the door, he scrambled toward his low table and started shuffling piles of envelopes, shoving them away into shopping bags and scattering a few onto the tatami mats in the process. I picked one up and, brushing away the super's hands, extracted a printed document from an unsealed flap.

"You can't just do that!" he protested.

The paper was a signatory campaign addressed to all occupants, claiming that condominium maintenance recently was in breach of service standards set forth in the resident agreement. The responsibility for this neglect rested entirely with the present superintendent. *Moreover, said employee has been seen to antagonize and otherwise provoke conflict with individual residents while trying to disclaim any wrongdoing on his part. Isn't it high time we demanded that the management replace this person?*

It was marked "A Common Interest Group" under the sender's name, "Mr. Shimazaki, a senior, Unit 204."

The super nosed in to snatch the letter out of my hands before I'd finished reading, so I pushed him down onto the tatami and grabbed it back.

"No rough stuff or I'll call the police."

"Go ahead, call them. Waylaying mail isn't theft, but it *is* against the Postal Code. I'll bet you filched all the management surveys too. That's jail, my friend."

His eyes dropped to his lap. "Please, it's this one old duffer, he hates me, he's turned everyone against me. It's all his doing."

"That's something else. Bad-mouthing the super isn't a crime."

"Yeah, but . . . a man's got to protect himself, hasn't he? Don't report me, please."

"Not even concerning Miss Ukita? How much does she pay you for the key to the vacant unit?" As he looked up, his sunburnt face was now pale, his eyes dull in their sockets. "A punk's been spy-camming the goings-on. He's now being held by the police."

"It's him, isn't it—the one with the yellow truck?" His voice was beginning to crack. "You don't really believe what he—"

Enough. Without letting him finish, I pulled him up by his work jacket and made him get the key to 101, then prodded him along the passage to open the door. A tawny light filtered through the curtains. The room had been cleaned, the cot stored away in the closet with all the bedding. The spacious living room now contained only a large settee-and-coffee-table combo and a dining table.

Hidden cameras aren't always easy to find, especially not CCD ones, though the lens will generally be visible. Admittedly, some newer equipment has tiny photo-receptor functions mounted right on the remote control, but I couldn't believe the punk would be so tech savvy. No, the camera was disguised in a big dictionary slipcase up on a decorative shelf. He'd punched a hole through the publisher's logo on the spine, but the lens glinted slightly and a power cable trailed down stupidly to a wall socket.

I handed the camera and transmitter to the super. Fidgeting, he said, "I didn't know nothing about this, I swear, I'm innocent. It's that woman and her girlfriends' parties . . ."

"Don't play dumb. How could you not see what dirt she was into? That and what happened in unit 301."

He clammed up, clutching the antenna-twigged device in both hands.

"A man from the daughter's office came at the beginning of August, no way you'd be unaware of developments at Mrs. Hiraoka's place before then." I sat down on the settee and just watched him refusing to look at me. "Or should I call the management?" I said, reaching for my phone.

"Please, if I get fired, I don't know what I'd do."

"You were supposed to keep tabs on people going in and out, weren't you?"

"No, I was asked to keep quiet," he said.

"By who?"

"The old lady's nephew. Said she was ill and had to go away two or three months for treatment. Didn't want visitors and all disturbing her, so I wasn't to let on."

I went with a hunch. "And you were paid off?"

"Wasn't much. Honest, I just wanted to help and—"

"Was that on July 17?"

"No, later than that. After July 20, I think."

"This nephew, what was his name?"

"Wasn't Hiraoka, as I heard."

"Address? Contact number?"

"Just a mobile number—but it doesn't connect, not lately." He scratched his head and smiled like an idiot. "When the man from the daughter's office came by I got in touch first thing. That's all I did, honest. Didn't want any trouble, least of all for myself."

"And what did he say?"

"To keep quiet. Said there were inheritance issues, I figured maybe loans or whatnot. Old folks are always getting suckered into scams and wind up with huge debts."

"You told him I'd been here, didn't you?" I interrupted to ask.

"Well, a cop starts poking around, wouldn't you be concerned? He knew your name."

"And you niggled him for more hush money?" He shrank when I stood up and growled, "How'd he provide your dole?"

So now he admitted to receiving bank transfers. "His name's Ichiro Hiraoka."

"Thick neck, big solid build? Looks like he spends a lot on his appearance?"

"Er, yeah," he said. "That's him."

"Drove a Cadillac, right?"

"No, a regular car. Blue sedan, foreign Y-number plates."

I lurched forward in surprise, making him jump to his feet—until I pulled him down again. "And there was another guy driving, maybe Chinese-American?"

"No, only the one big fellow. Japanese, I swear."

As I let out a breath, he scuttled back to the office, grabbed a cookie box from under the counter, and began sorting through bills and receipts to find a slip of paper. It was a page torn from a personal agenda with a mobile phone number written across the middle. "It went dead after I told him about you. Gave me the jitters. I'm not a bad person. There's just the one resident going around saying stuff."

I left him to dispose of the bug from 101. Upstairs, before opening 301, I tried ringing the other doorbells again. Two doors down there was a response. I asked the middle-aged man who peered out if he'd heard a commotion on July 19. I didn't think I should mention a possible gunshot.

"What? Didn't she move?" he said, scratching a stubbly chin pointed at the sailboard propped in the hall behind me. "People were in and out toward the middle of July, but I haven't seen anyone around lately, so I just figured she'd moved."

He'd heard footsteps and talking late into the night, though he didn't see any faces. The old lady and he weren't well acquainted, he said, since he didn't live here full-time. But then, as if suddenly remembering, he said, "It had to have been July 20 or 21, because I only come here on my days off. There was a big windsurfing tournament on the twenty-third, so I skipped work from the middle of the week."

I unlocked 301 and did some luminol tests in the toilet and bathroom. The drain in the bath showed a very slight reaction, though no more than normal in most homes. Next I carried a dining room chair into the bedroom to climb up and take another look at the mark on the lintel. Finding a silk sash in the closet chest, the kind that women use to belt their kimono undergarments, I looped it over the lintel and pulled down. Just as I thought, the sash fitted in the groove exactly. Something heavy had hung here. Glancing back and forth between the dent and the bullethole, I had a bad feeling about it all.

When I put the sash back, among the various clothes on hangers I noticed a boy's blue blazer. Embroidered inside the lapel was the name Hiraoka. The seams were coming undone, the designer tag so worn it was almost unreadable: Chips—a popular brand advertised as a JFK favorite when I was a student in the 1960s, though the original American tailors had long since folded and, unknown to us, a Japanese company had bought the name. An intricate hand-stitched emblem on the breast pocket showed a snake curled on a wand and an open book, a scholastic merit badge, perhaps.

Only as I laid the blazer on the bed did I realize what was missing—a family altar. I checked the living room and kitchen, even the entryway. There wasn't one anywhere.

In his initial briefing, Sato made out that Reiko Hiraoka had an older brother who died in the war, not that she was obliged to take on the family altar. But when her own son died, would any mother in those days have not kept his *ihai* memorial plaque close by?

Outside, the sun was going down. I tidied up the place, then went downstairs. The light in the entry hall was off, the super's office window had its curtains drawn.

A sea breeze blew in as I unlocked my car under the pines. The sun just grazing the horizon reflected red in the condo windows. I sat there looking at unit 301 without starting the engine. The person I was looking for was nowhere in sight, and right nearby.

44

These days a person can't just go to City Hall and get quick copies of someone's family registry like before. Laws have changed; now only the individual in question or immediate family members can request such official documents. Even when a policeman needs the stuff, he has to observe the protocol of forms and authorizations.

In the morning, I spent an hour knocking out a "Petition for Items Pending Investigation" on a word processor. Then, late in the afternoon, I set out for Yokosuka City Hall, stopping on the way to buy three likely-sounding name seals to stamp the signature blanks and make it look appropriately official.

It took me less than five minutes to obtain a copy of Reiko Hiraoka's family registry. I didn't look inside the envelope until I got back to my car in the pay lot. One entry in particular made my hand stop before I turned the ignition key.

September 11, 1975, registered marriage to US national Guillermo Kano-Law (born July 14, 1951)

There wasn't a single line about Aileen. I returned to City Hall without even bothering to lock up.

"Marrying a foreigner doesn't give the spouse Japanese citizenship," the previous clerk declared flat out.

"And what happens with the children? She adopted a daughter around the same time as the marriage."

"The spouse's child wouldn't be recorded. A completely new adoption would count separately, but that doesn't seem to be the case. Nothing is written here, so we can only assume she didn't formally adopt the girl." He stared at me like a math teacher standing tight-assed in front of a blackboard chalked up with equations, yet I persisted until finally I got what I wanted: the paperwork submitted when Aileen started elementary school. The guardian listed there was not an American parent, but Reiko Hiraoka.

Another clerk who brought me extra photocopies informed me that in order to do things by proxy this way she'd have had to apply to domestic court for certification as the carer. "What if she married an American who had offspring," he suggested, "and the husband took off, leaving the child with her? It does happen in rare instances, though I never heard of anyone raising the child on her own like this. Rather admirable of her."

"Absolutely," I agreed.

Sato lived in a mixed residential area of Yokosuka just off the old road over the hills to the Hayama coast. Shabby shophouses huddled along the main street, some completely untouched since the 1920s, half of them out of business and half of those with rusty shutters rattled down to the pavement. The street ended at a high embankment with steep stone steps leading upwards. I practically had to crawl my way up, the railing was useless. Exposed gas and water mains climbed the incline right beside me.

Sato's house was a two-story clapboard relic propped up on a steel frame. The retrofitted aluminum door opened and a stern Sato shouted that he'd heard me panting up the steps. "What's the matter, too steep for you? You're outta shape."

Just inside the door was a large square of pounded earth, with a six-mat room beyond. The *engawa* under-eaves extended into a veranda jutting out over the drop, a little something he had done, Sato boasted, when they added steel earthquake bracing. Perfect for watching the dusk settle and distant windows begin to twinkle across the hills.

After placing a cushion at a low table, he brought out a beer-logo glass from the kitchen, then poured me a strong shot of *shochu*. He didn't ask if I wanted ice or water, and I didn't tell him I was driving. "Go ahead," he just said.

I took a good sip before asking, "You live alone . . . ?"

"Ever since my old Ma died. Missed my chance to take a wife." There was little furniture to speak of and nubs of dust on the tatami mats, but the place seemed shipshape enough. A small family altar sat atop a tea cabinet. Directly above on the *nageshi* beam hung framed photos of a young man in an ensign's uniform and a fifty-something woman in kimono. "That's my old man, died in the war. Ma collapsed in her thirties and was in and out of hospital the rest of her days. Oh, there were attempts at matchmaking, but it would've been like hiring a nurse."

"So you didn't get beyond seeing their picture?"

Sato looked up at the altar. "I don't like being obliged to anyone. Better not even to bow out of it." He folded his arms and put on a stubborn face.

Changing the subject, I said, "I got a luminol reaction from Mrs. Hiraoka's car, but I don't think it's her blood."

"In the same car you found the mobile?" He was rattled, but tried not to show it.

"I'm told she had guests over for drinks at her condo on June 17, people with enough on their minds to forget a mobile phone there."

"You think some of them could've been Vietnamese? Any cause for blackmail?"

"That I still don't know. Aileen's background and upbringing were no secret, no reason for anyone from there to threaten her."

"Well then, why the hell did you come here? To say you don't know?"

"There was a bullethole in the bedroom, high up on the wall. The bullet I dug out was an 8 mm from a Nambu."

"A Nambu?" His eyes widened. "What else have you been hiding from me?"

"Sorry. I didn't have enough material in place to report."

"Sure, a sleuth can't go writing up every little bump and dent, can he? Though Investigations today, seems they report what they had for dinner." He was about to laugh, but stopped himself. Instead he asked stiffly, "And the gun itself?"

"Was in the condo, but someone lifted it."

"That guy, with the yellow truck."

I stared at him in silent admiration while he surveyed the city lights behind me. It was already dark outside.

"Think it belonged to her brother who died in the war?"

He considered this angle, then shook his head. "No, the gun wouldn't be his. Her brother got drafted at the last minute, sent straight to his death in the South Seas. Second class soldiers weren't issued pistols anyway . . ."

"Even say it was hers, would she ever have used it?"

"Not pointing at someone, no. Temperamental she may have been, but not like that."

"The pistol was a gift from a Japanese intelligence officer to an anti-French partisan who passed for a rich businessman during the Vietnam War years," I told him.

"I can think of one more provenance," he said, then fell silent for a while. I could hear the *shochu* trickle down my throat.

"There are two stories," he finally told me. "Reiko always said she got the girl through some Christian group. But there's another version, which goes that an American brought her with him and left Reiko to look after her."

"So which story's true?"

"The girl came with American citizenship, that's the only certainty. It was a point of contention with City Hall for years. Schooling was the main issue."

"Well, it seems there's a third story. In September 1975, Reiko Hiraoka married an American who was twenty-four at the time. Maybe the girl was the man's daughter, or his adopted daughter. The marriage is still on the books to this day. In fact, the only thing apparently connecting Mrs. Hiraoka and Aileen is that marriage."

No response. I emptied my glass. Before I could say no, he poured me some more.

"I didn't know any of this—" He broke off. Suddenly his eyes went wide and he looked up at the ceiling. "But why would she go on raising little Suzu?"

He stood up and pulled the string of the ceiling lamp. The room lit up, but it didn't look any bigger.

"The husband's name is Guillermo Kano-Law, a Peruvian-American," I said.

"Maybe he was one of the guests on June 17 you mentioned."

"What makes you think so? You never met him, I take it?"

"Don't know. First time I heard the name. At least he wasn't a darkie," he said sourly. In his day, in his town, probably that was the only distinction made among Americans. "But let's drop the dirt-digging. Where's all this leading to?"

"Mrs. Hiraoka and her son, were they close?"

The question caught him by surprise. "Were they *what*? Okay, he wasn't your model kid, but his mother doted on him." He assumed a defensive tone. "Sure, he could horse around, but he held his own. I mean, him going abroad, that was all on his own savings from working as an American officer's houseboy. The officer really took a liking to him, acted as his guarantor. Otherwise, in those days it would've been next to impossible for a young Japanese to visit the US."

"Did you know him from when he was little?"

His eyes narrowed and he nodded. "The squirt, for some reason he used to call me Papa. Well, folks got talking, till finally I told them to pack it in, it wasn't funny. But then, in a strange way, that made me kind of sad. Fair enough, so maybe I wasn't the Papa type. Still, if he wanted a father figure, I told him, I'd be glad to sign on. You know what he said? He said he didn't need anything so uncool! From then on, we were never that close again."

"But wasn't there still gossip?"

"Well, back then, don't ask and don't tell was the rule in drinking establishments."

"Maybe she herself wasn't sure whose kid it was."

He scowled at me. "Are you honestly saying that, at your age? A woman always knows. No matter how many men she's had, believe me, the woman knows."

I got up quietly, went over to the family altar, and opened the gilded doors. Inside were two *ihai* memorial plaques, one for each of Sato's parents.

"There's no altar at her condo," I said.

"That so?"

"Doesn't that strike you as odd? An only son and no *ihai*?"

He picked up the bottle of *shochu*, then looked puzzled, as if he'd meant to do something else. After pouring me a refill, he gave himself a slosh in his own empty teacup. "She's not alive, is she?"

"No, I don't think so, though there's nothing conclusive."

Sato crossed his arms and closed his eyes, nodding. "Handgun suicide? For what possible reason?"

"It wasn't with a pistol," I corrected. "The bullet in the wall didn't hit anyone. The gunpowder was either insufficient or old, too weak to propel a bullet through a human body." I didn't mention the hanging mark on the lintel, I couldn't see much point in bringing it up now. I sat back down at the low table.

"I get a painful feeling about this. What about the body? You must know something."

"Very likely . . . she's properly buried somewhere."

He nodded again vaguely and took a sip of his drink. I did the same.

"When I heard about your mishap, something in me snapped," he said. Among cops, a "mishap" means internal misconduct. "Then, right after they had me read the report you wrote, I heard about Reiko's disappearance."

"Yeah, it must have looked bad."

He ground his jaw. "You know, Futamura, you get to be my age saying goodbye to people isn't hard. You pat someone on the back, so long till next time, then never see them again, it's not unusual at all. But someone so close you don't even think to say next time, that's something you never get over at any age." He raised his cup, waited a breath, then drank glumly. "It's been great, felt like you and me were out investigating together again, though I've just been sitting here drinking tea and talking on the phone."

Out of courtesy, I finished my own drink before saying goodbye. There were things I still wanted to ask him, but I couldn't remember what as I slowly made my way down the stone steps.

It must have been past seven. I took the elevator up from the hotel garage where I ditched my car and cut across the backstreets toward Yori's club.

There wasn't much neon anymore, fewer bars. The *yakitori* stands were doing less business, the souvenir shops dimming their lights. There weren't half as many people about as during the day. An MP yawned in his patrol van stationed halfway up Dobuita. Posters welcomed the arrival of a missile cruiser in port, but I didn't see any sailors.

High school girls giggled past, sharing peeks at their mobile phones. Things smelled off, not from drunk GIs but general decay. To think there were women who'd raised kids on this street. For most of that time, America had been fighting its wars just over the waves. This town had been the home front, everything here faced the battlefields.

A CLOSED sign hung in the doorway of Yori's club, no reason given. On a Friday night, with a warship in port? I started to phone her, but reconsidered. I didn't really need her company, I just wanted to knock one back somewhere relaxing. And quick.

Heading back toward the garage, I passed what was once a love hotel of the rooftop Statue of Liberty variety, now half-timbered into an Irish pub. The place was thick with civvied servicemen spilling into the street and blocking traffic. Was it a brawl? Apparently not. Japanese waiters in baseball caps and lowrider jeans were ferrying out draft beer and onion rings. The sight made me feel old.

I passed by Kaput, but the alleyway was a dark blank. Even the corner bakery was closed tonight. The baker hadn't put out his cones, though no cars encroached on his streetfront. A quiet unholy night. Only the cars churning along the expressway hurried me on my way.

45

By the time I nosed into my leased parking space, it was just before eight. I hopped out and ran to the biggest bookstore in Isezakicho. A five-story superstore, yet both the history and documentary shelves combined yielded only a handful of books on the Vietnam War, all of them fictionalized accounts. The one *General History of the Vietnam Conflict* that I did find was the size of a wheel chock and every bit as expensive.

The shutters were closing when a shop assistant who couldn't help seeing me still poking around kindly located a modest hardcover, *Stolen Revolution: Why the Viet Cong Were Driven from Their Homeland*, the title Tomoda had mentioned.

Book in hand, I walked down the broad Isezaki Mall with its useless benches and unintelligible public art. Touted as a bold twenty-first century showplace, to my eyes the over-designed mercantile theme park looked more like the shambles of a fairground.

I opted for a blue-tiled pizzeria in a more placid part of town. Nothing fancy, but good enough for draft beer and a brick-oven pizza, with bright lighting and firm chairs. After eating, I ordered a grappa and skimmed through the book for crucial facts.

According to the author, Phan Bửu Kiếm, his older brother Ái Quốc's career as a businessman in 1960s South Vietnam had been a cover. His role as an undercover Liberation Army hero, however, was erased from military records once the war was over.

The Phan brothers were in fact half-brothers. Their father had been a landowner granted French citizenship by the colonial government, one of only six thousand gentleman farmers who controlled half the arable land in Cochin China at the time. Ái Quốc's mother was from a wealthy family of Hokkienese origin, but when she died young the father married Bửu Kiếm's mother, a blood relation of the last royal Nguyễn dynasty in Hue. Ái Quốc himself had no memory of his own mother, but grew close to the second wife. The two boys were inseparable.

Come June 1940, when France fell to the Nazis, the colonial government went to pieces and a puppet regime was established under Marshal Pétain. By September, the Japanese Army, having just signed a Tripartite Pact with the Axis powers, began the occupation of Indochina. Thereafter, Vietnam was pinioned between two overlords.

"The one Asian army," wrote Bửu Kiếm, "came to break the shackles imposed by the other. Many young people fell for the fairy tale of a Japanese Empire liberating us poor Asian cousins from the ignominy of white colonial rule. My brother, barely sixteen, was one of them. We heard not even a footstep of the Communists where we grew up."

The Japanese Army confiscated land from those French landowners who opposed them and gave it to Vietnamese to farm. A steady rice supply was vital for Japan.

The ousted landowners then attacked Vietnamese-run farms, among them the Phan estate. The boys' father and mother were shot and the plantation torched. Bửu Kiếm and what remained of their holdings were taken on by relatives; Ái Quốc was sent off to boarding school in Saigon.

The brothers didn't meet again for ten years. Bửu Kiếm heard from relations that his older brother had dropped out of university, but soon any word of him stopped altogether.

When finally they were reunited well after World War II, Ái Quốc explained that their relatives had cut off his support. The agreement had been they would see him through university in exchange for letting them manage the family land, but they reneged. Then one evening after he was kicked out of school, Ái Quốc made the acquaintance of a recruiting officer for the Japanese Special Forces and threw himself into anti-French guerrilla activities. From late in 1944, he underwent full-fledged training at a secret camp on Hainan Island in South China. It was there that he lost his right ear in an accident.

On March 9, 1945, the Japanese launched a coup d'état, disarmed the French Indochina Army, and placed the entire country under martial law. (Curiously enough, this was the very same date as the massive Allied firebombing of Tokyo.) As a result, Ái Quốc had a change of heart, though his work to date meant he could never openly embrace the Liberation cause. He was in tears when he told his brother this, Bửu Kiếm being already a fighter for the South Vietnamese Liberation Front.

I paused here and drank some grappa.

On August 17, 1945, the Japanese drillmaster on Hainan presented his Vietnamese trainees with pistols. The war was lost, it was only a matter of time before the officer himself would be forced to surrender his arms.

This wasn't actually in the book, but I put two and two together. It was conceivable that the pistol in Reiko Hiraoka's condo belonged to Orimasa. The *Hellboy* author would've had any number of opportunities to pick up such souvenirs. In which case, it was equally conceivable that Orimasa was in the trimmed-away section of the group photo at the tropical villa.

But there was also another person who could have brought the Nambu 14 to the condo. No, make that two persons.

I sighed at the implications. My grappa was gone and I was the only customer in the place. It wasn't even closing time, but the pizza oven was burning low. I called out. Nobody came. So I left the billed amount on the table and stood up to go.

Back home at the apartment, I didn't bother to change. I grabbed a glass of single malt, stretched my legs out on the sofa, and opened the book again.

In August, after losing the war, the Japanese Army laid down their arms, but there was no authority on hand in Vietnam to receive the weapons. Around the same time, the Viet Minh staged a nation-wide uprising, leading in September to Ho Chi Minh's declaration in Hanoi of an independent Democratic Republic of Vietnam. Meanwhile the Chinese People's Liberation Army had infiltrated from the north and a small number of British troops arrived from the south, each separately relieving the occupying army of weapons. The British soon joined forces with locally entrenched French units and attacked the Communists. The following year, Vietnam effectively split in two and a shaky truce with France ensued.

Bửu Kiếm didn't go into great detail about the sources of his brother's money. For a while after the Japanese left, Ái Quốc lost his sense of purpose. He set up a small business in Manila and saved up enough to return to Saigon.

After the humiliating defeat at Dien Biên Phu in 1954, the French began to withdraw from Vietnam. Ái Quốc made a fortune in scrap metal and rice exports, and cut a prominent figure in Saigon financial circles. According to his brother, Ái Quốc was supplying underground cells in Saigon with capital even before their reunion. Maybe so, but he also sang the praises of capitalism, built himself a grand villa in an upscale *quartier* just off the rue de Verdun, employed dozens of servants, and married three young wives all in the space of twenty years.

As the conflict evolved and indiscriminate bombing of North Vietnam escalated, American ground troops in South Vietnam rose in number to nearly half a million men, yet failed to make any decisive military gains. GIs were implicated in the My Lai massacre, forfeiting America its moral high ground. Corruption was rife throughout the South Vietnamese bureaucracy; without any firm motivation, the government and army floundered. The antiwar movement spread worldwide, mass protests pressed in on the US Congress, and Washington lost its footing. Ultimately, having suffered fifty thousand dead as of 1973, American combatants were stunned to a halt. Vietnamese deaths were said to have topped three million.

By 1975, the Liberation Front was racking up victories everywhere and, together with the North Vietnamese People's Army, laid siege to Saigon. In April of that year, US Secretary of State Kissinger testified in Congress that "Saigon is no longer defensible," and that very day South Vietnamese President Nguyễn Văn Thiệu resigned from office. On April 13, the Liberation Front entered the city and forced the Presidential Palace to end the war. News media worldwide showed Americans fleeing Saigon like rats leaving a sinking ship. Both Orimasa's novel and this book described the sense of panic and weird elation felt by the citizens amid scenes of pillaging and violence just before the fall.

Bửu Kiếm himself had spent sleepless weeks holed up in the marshes southeast of Saigon, the beleaguered Viet Cong stronghold the Americans had codenamed Birnam. By March the Communist Party leadership ordered a final onslaught, but the enemy retreated so quickly they left a huge vacuum in their wake.

Bửu Kiếm didn't learn of his brother's death until later. On March 27, Ái Quốc's villa was looted and a fire broke out. Flames consumed everything in a matter of minutes, there being no functioning fire brigade in Saigon at the time. A charred body was recovered from the ashes, but neither the identity nor cause of death was adequately investigated. Someone reported hearing gunshots before the looting. Another witness claimed to have seen an American jeep crash the gate just afterwards.

As Bửu Kiếm wrote, "Undoubtedly either the CIA or their lackeys carried out a spur-of-the-moment execution. US Embassy channels had long suspected my brother of colluding with the Liberation Army. That was an understatement. He was no mere collaborator or sympathizer; he was one of us, a true, active comrade in arms."

Two photographs were included several pages on. The first was of the teenage brothers together: Ái Quốc with upturned nose, sharp jaw line, shining eyes full of ambition, and right ear intact; Bửu Kiếm shorter, with a darker complexion and pronounced cheekbones. The second photo showed Ái Quốc in his prime, right ear already missing, his young bride holding their newborn daughter. The couple looked very happy. The colonnade in the background was immediately familiar. It was the same house, the same garden, as in the photo I had. This image was taken not three meters away from the spot where Yang and Ackerman as well as Fleet Activities Commander Glidden had posed for a parting shot with Phan Ái Quốc.

My glass was empty. The ice was all gone and the fridge had drifted light years away, so I decided to do without.

The book went on to describe Saigon under the red flag, by which time Yang, Orimasa, Ackerman, and Billy had made their exit. Phan Bửu Kiếm became a delegate to the Saigon City Assembly, but lost out in power plays and was given the brush-off. Hanoi's stance toward the liberated south wasn't much different from a bank merger: equal standing between merging partners is impossible. They were in such a single-minded hurry to unify north and south, they purged any South Vietnamese Liberation Front influence from postwar politics. Heroes like Bửu Kiếm just got in the way.

Hanoi denounced Ái Quốc as a Japanese running dog, alleging that all his contributions to the cause were nothing but clever subterfuge. "My brother was in no way the traitor that Party bureaucrats made him out to be. His entire savings were earmarked for the people's struggle for self-determination," said Bửu Kiếm in his defense, but, reading the writing on the wall, he fled the country before he also came to harm.

Many former Liberation Front guerrillas abandoned their homeland in those years. Some like him did it to escape groundless accusations, others simply jumped ship because they couldn't put up with the icy political climate. A good number defected to the former colonizers' capital Paris, others stowed away on fishing boats bound for safe havens in Thailand, Hong Kong, or the Philippines.

"Surprisingly," wrote Bửu Kiếm, "some of those who escaped to Hong Kong made contact with British intelligence operatives and were able to trade harmless gossip and dime-a-dozen rumors for UK citizenship. Party bureaucrats in Hanoi should feel just a little responsible for their part in forcing our nation's heroes into a life of tattle-telling."

Obviously many chose that route, but I couldn't help thinking he was talking about Tran. Obtaining a British passport, then coming to Japan when the crown colony reverted to China, he'd wound up grilling hamburgers at a hole in the wall, thanks to Yang and his ilk.

Then there was Tran's sister with a "pineapple" shard lodged in her head. He'd needed to save up for her operation.

That Chinatown-hating Chinaman may have been a liar, but one thing he said was right on the money. Whatever the circumstances, a needy woman is trouble.

46

I closed the book and looked at my watch. It was a little past eleven. I felt a strong urge to phone Orimasa, but as usual he wasn't answering. Maybe his machine was so full his messages didn't even play.

I dug out Inamoto's name card and called the *Zoom* editorial office. Eleven at night is hardly late for a weekly magazine crew. The man who picked up shouted Inamoto's name, then told me a moment later that he hadn't returned yet. But they were sending copy to the printers tonight, he added, so I could be sure he'd be back.

Still in my workday clothes, I grabbed a jacket and tie on my way out.

Speeding along the midnight waterfront and over two scenic bay bridges, I made it to central Tokyo in fifteen minutes. The publishing house was less than a block from the expressway exit at Kandabashi.

The main entrance, however, was shut. I pulled over to the curb directly opposite and rang the editorial office.

"Inamoto? Yes, he's in. Just a moment," answered a chipper woman's voice. "Mary Had a Little Lamb" played for a few seconds before a man came on the line. "Sorry, Inamoto's gone home." A weekly magazine editor ought to be better at lying.

I left the car and went around to the back of the building. There was a line of taxis waiting in the alley. A security guard stood at the rear door checking IDs as pairs of staffers returned from their dinner break. I mingled with the queue, flashed the flipside of my driver's license, and slipped inside.

The seventh-floor editorial office was an obstacle course of partitions and cubicles. In one brightly lit corner a *Zoom* sign hung from the ceiling. Someone was shouting into a phone, a young woman hurried past clutching a sheaf of papers. Inamoto, commanding a view of two rows of desks, sat marking galley sheets in red ink. During the minute and a half it took me to sneak around behind him, he didn't look up once, not until I tapped him on the shoulder of his corduroy jacket.

"Gah!" came a startled gasp from his throat. He didn't seem to know who I was.

"Futamura, or don't you remember?"

"Of course I do, but . . . what are you doing here?"

"We had an appointment, didn't we? When you didn't show, I came here."

He glanced about nervously. Everyone was glued to their work, too busy to notice us.

"Can we talk a minute?" I asked. "Or do I need to produce a court order?"

"No need for that, surely," he said, forcing a laugh. "I'll be in the reception area," he instructed someone or other, then nudged me toward a nook by the elevator. Pointing me to a sofa, he sat in the armchair opposite and apologized for the lack of an ashtray.

"I didn't come here to smoke," I said, and also declined his offer of coffee. He wriggled down in his seat and braced himself for my questions.

"I see you weren't badly injured. I heard you needed crutches."

"Ah, well, that was just me wanting a little sympathy," he hedged.

"Then you're not going to sue them?"

"Oh please, no. It was a simple accident."

"Not too many folks run someone down in plain view accidentally."

He wriggled some more. "Really, it wasn't intentional . . . though I am sorry I stood you up. And didn't contact you later—things got so busy."

324

"If they kept you locked in the car, I can run them in for illegal detention."

"No, please. They patched me up at their office, then took me to a hospital. Mr. Yang himself wanted there to be no misunderstanding."

"What was the make of the car?" I asked. I don't know why I asked this, I just did. Only afterwards did I realize what I was getting at.

"The car they were driving? A Legacy?"

The baker said he saw a white four-wheel drive with foreign Y-number plates, a big 4WD sticker on the back. The car that hit Inamoto was an older model white Subaru Legacy. A station wagon, but probably four-wheel drive. "Was it a Y-number?" I asked.

"The license plate? I didn't have time to look."

Whatever, the baker also saw a big guy with a smaller partner get out and head toward Kaput. Probably Wang Lun, who was short and skinny, and Hong Zhi-long aka Hole in Five, that hulk with enough of a grudge to knock me out cold then spit on my ass. The only question was why he didn't just snuff me out. Still, the scenario made more sense with those two than the clueless duo from Pearl Harbor.

A voice pleaded inside my ear, *You late. You real late. Where the money? The money! No can wait no more.*

Who had Lê Ngũ Thanh been waiting for? Suppose the hundred and fifty thousand dollars wasn't owed to him but was money his brother-in-law had stolen and stashed, unknown to anyone, there in the toilet at Kaput. Maybe Billy had been sent to look for it?

I leaned in closer. "I think you took a beating that was meant for me. Seems I rubbed Yang the wrong way the day before, but then you show up. Was the big guy at the wheel? Someone not too bright must've been driving."

"No, on the passenger side." Inamoto popped a cigarette in his mouth and lit up, then walked over to a vending machine and foraged for an empty can in the trash. "You know, Mr. Orimasa wouldn't be very pleased if he knew I was meeting with you."

"Did Orimasa ever mention a big payout? Maybe something he'd arranged to buy from Lê?"

Inamoto cleared his throat, gave me a nervous glance, and looked away.

"I'm not asking as a cop. Unless of course you'd prefer that." I went with a sudden hunch. "Maybe it was *you* had the deal with Lê? And Orimasa didn't know?"

He swallowed a denial, puffing hard at his cigarette, eyes half hidden in the smoke.

"What the hell did a Vietnamese refugee have to sell?"

This made him finally open up. "He said he had information about Aileen Hsu's parents and how they died." And in the wake of this admission, he began spilling it out. "He said he'd talk for money. Tens of millions of yen, serious money. I got him to come down a few million, but really, even at the best of times nobody would lay out that kind of cash for some gossip about a violinist."

"Was her parents' death that newsworthy?"

"In his dreams. A nude photospread of the girl wouldn't fetch that these days."

Now I was angry. "You led him on. Lê thought that money was coming, and you sat there driving a phony bargain!"

Behind his glasses, his eyes went wide in alarm. "But, well, the story changed. What I just said was a month ago. After that he came up with something else to sell, what exactly I don't know. I mean, his Japanese wasn't too good. And over the phone? I couldn't tell what he was saying. Something concerning a string of crimes, international syndicate stuff. Evidence why Billy and Tran were killed, made it sound like he knew who really killed Kennedy. As a magazine man, I'm a pushover for these conspiracy angles. In the heat of the moment I might have said I'd shell out big money for the real thing."

"Well, it was credible enough for Yang to bully you so his name wouldn't come out."

"I wouldn't know about that. Anyway, Lê was pretty vague."

"You heard about the Val-Nam development project, didn't you?"

Inamoto shook his head and started to say something, but shoved another cigarette in his mouth instead.

"Lê's neck was twisted in a knot. And you know who did it."

"Are you trying to intimidate me?" he snapped, then abruptly backed down. "Look, I'm sorry but we've got copy to put to bed. There's not even time to give it a good read."

"As if this is none of your doing. Wasn't it you told those goons he'd be waiting at Kaput? Unless you're a total idiot you knew exactly what was going to happen."

His moustache quivered. "All these wild accusations without a shred of evidence."

"There's a witness. When they came to kill Lê, they parked in front of his shop. A white Legacy. A big ape and a little guy went into Kaput. This was four or five hours after they hauled you away. Were you still in the car at the time?"

"Don't be ridiculous. I went straight home in a taxi. Mr. Yang advised me to stay put the rest of the day—"

"Those two were after me, but then they see you and change course. They figured they could nab you and still chase me around. *And* you turned out to be pretty useful."

He didn't reply. Obviously unnerved, he half levitated off his armchair.

I shifted to a calmer tone. "Lê came peddling his Aileen gossip after Billy was gone, right? These two months since you blew him off, why do you think Lê was lying low? Yang was breathing down his neck, that's why. There was big money missing. Meanwhile Lê was getting nowhere, so he came back to you with another story implicating Yang. Maybe it was all a bluff, but now Yang's sizing up just how much you know." I got up and pressed the call button for the elevator. "But don't worry," I added. "The police will keep close watch. You'll survive."

"Hey, w-wait, what's that supposed to mean? Am I under surveillance?" Fortunately he didn't follow me. I pressed CLOSE, counted to three, then pressed OPEN. A shocked Inamoto turned around with his mobile clapped to his ear.

"Be sure to tell Orimasa," I said loudly, "I'm seeing Aileen this Sunday. If I don't hear from him by then, he'll lose a big story. For his new novel, the one with lots of people dying."

He stood there bug-eyed. I pressed the ground floor button before he could reply.

It was close to three in the morning when I returned to Yokohama, but I couldn't get to sleep. Reluctantly, I fixed myself a drink, put on some music, and had another go at Phan Bửu Kiểm's book. Rereading about the years between the Paris Peace Talks and the end of the war made me wonder what Billy had been up to in those days.

According to Bửu Kiểm, America stopped recruiting volunteers for its auxiliary Military Assistance Command Vietnam early in the 1970s. Guillermo Kano-Law had enlisted in the Navy in a bid to become American prior to that, at a time when volunteers were still pressed into serving in Indochina. Those who completed their term of service alive and in one piece were granted special veterans' benefits, though tricking a permanent resident visa into citizenship required further service.

From the 1969 Peace Talks on, America steadily reduced its combatants until March 1973, when Nixon declared that an "honorable end to the war" was at hand. After that, the US kept only a few thousand military advisors in Vietnam through to 1975, the setting for Orimasa's *Hellboy in Paradise*. Meanwhile what had Billy been doing?

The Saigon PX where he worked was no mere general store. As Billy himself said, it was a window on the world. Did that window shut after the combatants left? When I was a boy and bananas were still luxury items rarely seen in Japanese markets, we thought pineapples grew in cans. And yet fresh pineapples were piled high in the Yokohama PX. It was another world. Step inside that sweet air-conditioned dreamland and you felt like a character in a Disney movie.

In his book, Bửu Kiếm expressed the same sense of awe about the Saigon PX. "A place so bright, so alive with color it made my head spin. The best smells in the world all nuzzled at my nose." Sent to scout the layout of US base facilities, he spent several hours walking around with a shopgirl working there undercover, but it wasn't long before his amazement soured. "Sugar candy," he wrote testily, "looks harmless, but rots you inside."

Our flyboy's administrative section was assigned to police this facility. His immediate superior was Chris Ackerman, and the man above him controlling the flow of all PX goods was Joseph Glidden. Did Billy bite off more than his fill of sugar candy?

Flipping through the pages, I came across a photo of John F. Kennedy with the caption "The villain who blazed the path of aggression." The young president was gazing at a globe in the Oval Office, wearing a blazer with a breast pocket badge of a snake coiled around a staff on a book.

I shut the book and finished my drink.

47

Saturday morning past ten, Tomoda woke me with a phone call. I took a shower to clear my head, put on a clean shirt, then sat by the window in the cool air. The smoke of two cigarettes escaped to join the low-slung clouds outside.

After making some coffee, I pulled a package of pancakes out of the fridge and nuked them in the microwave. A tiny bottle of real maple syrup was sleeping in the cupboard, a souvenir given to me by an import-export guy, a barstool acquaintance with offices somewhere on the harborfront. I didn't even know his name.

The pancakes were tasteless. Only the syrup had any flavor, and that was nasty. Not that I could complain, I didn't know the name of his trading company either. Let that be a lesson: never get more familiar than "Good evening" with any friendly fellow at a bar.

I scraped the pancakes into the trash, drank two cups of coffee, and went out. The tree-shaded avenue was torn up end to end with excavations for a new subway line, hardly a peaceful stroll. One grand old building that had survived wartime bombings now housed a trendy sidewalk café in anticipation of the subway opening. Only a couple of months ago it had been a foreign-affiliated bank. Soon I was sitting behind a wide glass facade, feeling like a department store mannequin. I was about to ask the waitress for coffee, but switched to a beer and a *confit de canard*. There was still over thirty minutes to go before my appointment with Tomoda.

I'd polished off everything by the time he showed up. Without a civil word of greeting, he shoved in beside me and spread a handful of computer printouts on the table. "Radioactive substances," he announced. "PCBs, dioxins, hexavalent chromium—you name it, they got it."

"What's all this?"

"It's your dirt, man, the crap from the fingers of your glove. The radioactive stuff is only in the thumb sample, the other is soil polluted with waste oil. The medical refuse up front is just a smokescreen."

A waitress came to take his order. Tomoda covered the printouts with a large envelope and asked for a cappuccino. "These readings are from the City University Science Department. They analyzed everything and mailed over the data double quick. Serious business, this."

"The stuff was on a shelf marked FAC3117, which is the US military code number for the Shibasato Warehouse District," I said.

He blinked in disbelief. "Ooh, that place has a history."

"Former arsenal, now a garbage dump?"

"And what garbage! Citizens' groups and N.G.O.s have been raising the issue for ages, but the US military gets the local municipality to haul their refuse only after they pack it up on-base. They swear up and down they take their industrial waste back to America, but I wouldn't bet on it. Why, in Okinawa up to a few years ago they were passing off depleted uranium ammunition as scrap metal."

Tomoda's cappuccino came, but he just forged ahead. "Remember, ten years back, there was that hubbub about them extending the Yokosuka Base seawall without a permit? Well, one citizens' group claimed the landfill was mixed with industrial waste."

"But there was no proof—is that what you're getting at?"

"Because inside the base is off-limits, foreign territory. And no one's been harmed, at least nothing that's been confirmed yet. But in Okinawa, the local legislature got on their case and had the Americans conduct test borings for polluted soil." He showed me an aerial photo of a road fenced off from a runway. On the embankment in between was a big dark splotch, maybe twenty meters in diameter to judge by the car driving alongside. "This hole here is a reservoir—

since filled in—and the black stuff is tainted PCB oil," he explained. "Until they were banned in 1972, PCBs were routinely used as insulating oil for electrical transformers. The Americans had been dumping the stuff here for decades, though of course heavy rain sometimes caused it to overflow into nearby streams."

"So what happened?"

"What do you think? The US military maintained they properly disposed of all the contaminated oil and dirt. Tests were conducted proving everything was safe, though to this day local resident groups don't trust their findings. And get this"—he grinned over his coffee—"the company hired to clean up the pit was a total unknown, not even an Okinawan company."

"Golden Harbor Enterprises."

Tomoda licked his coffee foam, his eyes twinkling. "You asked me to look into that warehouse at Naha Port? Turns out it's deeded to Golden Harbor. And up to half a year ago, Yang's Nanyang Perpetual Holdings had a shop in the Naha Free Trade Zone."

"Selling phony brand-name goods? Tran's sister was probably working there."

"Wait till you hear this." He leaned over and lowered his voice. "Up until last week, there was a freighter at Naha Port carrying sand from Vietnam, name of *Mineola*."

A burst of laughter shook the window as a klatsch of dressy matrons with designer daypacks walked past just outside.

"The ship's registered in Panama with a Filipino captain and leased by the US Navy for transporting 'logistic materials.' Ordinarily, that is."

"And extraordinarily?"

"Carrying things they can't openly declare, slipping through extraterritorial waters with a dummy captain at the helm. You said Tran was to pilot this *Mineola*, didn't you?"

I nodded, remembering how Notomi in Forensics had found mud under his frozen fingernails, mud with trace amounts of PCB.

"Last month, the ship was bought by a Taiwanese company," he continued, "but it's still bringing sand from Vietnam and hauling 'organic fertilizer' back from here. Same Yokohama Mizuho Pier, same Naha Port, same Val-Nam itinerary. Strange, don't you think? The US Navy lease has run out but it's still mooring there at Mizuho Pier."

I picked up a photocopy from the table, a regional map of Ho Chi Minh City and Environs. The thirty to forty kilometers between the city center and the South China Sea were crisscrossed with waterways, a network as complex as the Tokyo expressways.

"Just look how many different docks they got along the Saigon River channels," Tomoda said. "No need for any Special Economic Zone or container port just to load and unload sand and 'fertilizer.'"

"They're hauling contaminated soil to Val-Nam!"

"Uh-huh. They need landfill for all that marshland," he said, tapping the map with his pen. "And the Americans are only too happy to have a toilet to flush out their pollutants. Before it was napalm and defoliants, now it's medical waste and toxic soil."

"So why doesn't it make the news?" I asked. "Can't you go public on television with it, after I've gone to all the trouble of breaking and entering to bring it out?"

Tomoda frowned and shifted slightly to look out the window. I knew what he'd say. Neither of us were the sort of firebrand to launch a citizens' movement.

"Can you get me a pin mic?" I asked. "Something you can pick up long-range."

48

I knew it was a weekend. Did Chinese company employees still work Saturdays nowadays? By the time I was having second thoughts about calling, they picked up.

"Golden Harbor Enterprises, how may I help you?" A cheerful female voice informed me the Director would be back from lunch shortly.

Tomoda's news bureau was two shakes away. A junior technician popped out with a microphone, which he hid under my shirt with the transmitter taped to my navel. The camera fit in a nylon satchel. "It's got a pinhole lens, just point it in the general direction. Set the bag down if it looks unnatural, we can pan and zoom by remote," he said.

From there I walked several blocks to Golden Harbor, housed in the same gleaming gold monstrosity as Nanyang Perpetual Holdings. Most of the building was other businesses—a ground-floor foreign car showroom and tenant offices above. The Chinese consortium occupied the penthouse, with a private side entrance.

The elevator let me out in front of a reception counter and two young women in blazers. Judging from the number of chair positions, on weekdays there'd have been four of them to greet me. Behind them was a frosted glass partition with a fancy logotype and high relief dragon swirls that obscured the rest of the space.

"I've come to see the Director. The name's Futamura, Eiji Futamura," I announced.

"You just called, I believe?" one of the women said while picking up an intercom handset from below the counter. "Excuse me, Mr. Futamura from . . . ?"

"From beyond the baseball stadium." I pointed toward my apartment.

The woman raised an eyebrow but her smile stayed fixed. "Do you have an appointment with the Director?"

"No, but he'll want to see me. Just tell him it's about the warehouse in Chiwakacho."

The two receptionists looked at each other. The first woman put down the handset and disappeared through a panel in the glass partition. I just smiled at the other one, who responded with a brisk "Please have a seat" and promptly ignored my existence.

Almost as soon as I complied, the first one returned and led me through to a large dimly lit office with only a handful of staffers at their desks. Not one looked my way, though a legion of unattended computer screens seemed to glare at me. I was shown into a spacious reception room. One entire wall was some kind of special glass. The wall opposite featured a cabinet inlaid with mother-of-pearl and a painting of a girl acrobat. I sat on the sofa and put my satchel down beside me. There was a coffee table, but it wasn't high enough to block the lens. The video was already rolling.

I pulled out my phone and called Tomoda. Nobody else was in the room, but I kept to plan and playacted. "Listen, about tomorrow's appointment, could we do eleven o'clock at the West Exit instead?" The time was the floor, the place was the direction of the window. Tomoda acknowledged and I clicked off just as a receptionist entered without knocking and set down a cup of green tea.

"My, just like a Japanese company," I said.

Thirty minutes passed. I didn't hear a footstep. Outside the clouds hung lower, the room dimmed.

I suddenly remembered the video. It was an eighty-minute tape, maybe I ought to rewind it? I was about to check the satchel when the door opened and in came Wang Lun. He flicked a wall switch and a chandelier lit up the room.

Behind him, Yang Yun-shi wore a bespoke suit over a silk

stand-collar shirt. His long silver hair swept back as he sat down in an armchair in front of me. "The Director here is an idler," he said, turning toward the painting on the wall. "What was the point of him getting an MBA? All he cares about is collecting things like this. An unhappy-looking circus girl can't be good luck to keep around, don't you think?"

"Is that a real Picasso?"

"Something a resort developer bought during the bubble years and passed down the line. I admit Zou has an eye for these things. Well, he *is* my son." Yang cackled. "So now, what's this about Joyo Warehouse?"

"Last time we met, you mentioned you were importing sand from Vietnam."

"That's right, diatomite silica from Cam Ranh Bay. Excellent quality. Be glad to sell you some if you like. It goes for 7,500 yen a cubic meter, shipping included."

I carefully opened the nylon satchel and brought out a paper cup. "Is this what your silica looks like?"

Yang frowned, but only for a moment before reinstating a smile. "What on earth is it? It's certainly no merchandise of mine," he said after examining the contents.

"Found at the warehouse. You know the place, connected by rail to the US military pier, where you stored the things removed from Ackerman's office." It was a cheap trick on my part—a takeout coffee cup filled with dirt from the park by the baseball stadium.

"I don't know where you get these wild ideas. I only keep sand in there." He shrugged and set the container on the table, then turned to Wang standing over by the cabinet. The latter walked silently to the door and let in Hole in Five.

"Look, Mr. Futamura, I'm a busy man. If this is all you have to discuss, you'll have to excuse me. The night before last someone broke into that warehouse, and these two have a few details they wish to clarify."

"The night of July 19, Billy was hauling undeclared funds in your plane."

"I repeat, you'll get nowhere firing off outrageous claims like this."

"When I met Billy, he was up to something at Kaput in Yokosuka. This company owns the place. Whoever the so-called Director here is, you're the one in charge."

"Perhaps, but if I had to speak for every last holding we own I'd never get any work done. I grant you we've bought up properties in the area. We're planning a major redevelopment project in Yokosuka."

"That night, I believe Billy was under orders from you to find Tran, only he drank himself stupid before he could do it."

"I don't recall asking him to do anything of the kind."

"You probably didn't ask. You threatened to bury him, plane and all, in the Mekong Delta marshes if he didn't bring the guy in."

"Nonsense!" he snapped, rising out of his chair. Hole in Five moved in closer, while Wang stood next to his boss, ready to shield him.

"Just how much cash did Tran make off with?" I countered. "A hundred and fifty thousand bucks? It's been confiscated by the police."

Yang took a deep breath and, looking at the other two in turn, eased back into his armchair. "Careful now, you're playing the wrong game. I'm not who you think I am."

"Of course not, you're just small fry," I taunted. "That plane was carrying uninsurable amounts of cash and securities. If they burn, too bad. But more important, your clients might start to wonder, like maybe there wasn't anything on board at all. Can't cut multimillion-dollar deals without professional trust."

"I agree. Trust *is* the most important thing in any business. But what exactly is this speech of yours about?"

"Nanyang Perpetual Holdings' real business—exporting black

money. Transporting funds across national borders so they never come to light."

Yang stared hard at me, lips parted slightly. "A real funnyman, I see."

"That minijet was a safe with wings. Flying from base to base under Khaki Mafia cover—Japan, Korea, Hawaii, even mainland U.S.A.—carrying money wherever with no inspections or quarantine. You're an alternative APO, an airbase postal service."

"Enough, enough. You've made your point. Now if you'll excuse me," he said in a measured voice and got up again.

"Not yet. We still haven't finished talking about Golden Harbor Enterprises." I reached over and spilled the dirt onto the table.

Yang recoiled in surprise, Wang Lun caught his breath. A heavy arm grabbed me from behind the sofa. Not the slickest move the man could have made. I took hold of his arm with both hands and slid off the seat cushion, pulling his bulk up over the backrest, then let go and tumbled aside. While he was still wedged in the upholstery, I got up and slammed him in the head.

With a single sharp kick, he pushed out from the sofa and sent me sailing onto the carpet, then plowed right into me. Using my one free hand, I picked up some dirt and threw it at his mouth saying, "Here, have some of your toxic shit! Fresh from Shibasato!"

In a jumpy blur, the next thing I knew he was standing by the window holding a gun. But before he could take aim, I lunged straight at his chest and deflected his arm. I heard a shot and glass cracking like a snapped piano wire.

"*Suan le ba!*" shouted Yang. My assailant lowered his arm and spat on the carpet, which only made Yang angrier. As the muscleman's shoulders went slack, I grabbed the gun out of his hand and backed off a few steps toward the window. The bullet had only grazed the cushioned inner layer of the double-pane glass.

"Go ahead," I told Yang, "touch that dirt! Taste it! You know what it is!"

"Of course I do, it's just muck. I could eat it and it wouldn't kill me right away."

"But tons of the stuff is another story. Dumping it abroad is your main job here."

"How little you know about business. None of this is a 'main job.' Those operations are just spinoffs of the land development work we're doing in Vietnam, which I might add is helping a lot of people."

Yang then barked a command in Chinese, and the big man went to get some tissues, while Wang Lun moved the coffee table back where it had been.

I opened the gun chamber and removed the bullets, then handed it to Yang.

"It's all legitimate," he said, "other than disposing of US military garbage off-base, that is. We haven't dumped one spoonful on Japanese soil. It's all disposed of overseas and through the proper channels. There are no legal problems whatsoever."

I changed my story again. "Well, what if I told you this stuff isn't actually from your warehouse? It's from Tran's brother-in-law's car. You know Lê Ngữ Thanh, I assume?" I looked at Hole in Five wiping up his spit with a tissue. "You like to spit, don't you? Why didn't you do me in when you had the chance, when you went to Kaput to kill Lê?"

The goon turned his eyes toward Yang like a hungry kid looking at his mother.

"When Lê was murdered, a witness saw two men driving a white four-wheel drive with Y-plates. Yokosuka Investigations have already traced the license. Wasn't so smart using the same car that hit Inamoto, a vehicle that wasn't even stolen."

"Don't underestimate him," said Yang, "he's smarter than he looks."

"But not smart enough to find the blackmail note and dirt in Lê's car. There's another whole case of it."

"Futamura, I must say I misjudged you. So you traced the car for us, did you?" Judging from his expression and voice, he was clearly interested. "But why didn't you say so earlier? Why are you Japanese so circumspect? Just how much is it you want?"

"We Japanese are always waiting to be asked."

Yang produced a checkbook from an inner pocket, walked over to the cabinet to write in an amount, then tore off a check.

I took it and held the watermark up to the light. It was genuine, of course, for two million yen. In return I promptly drew him a map to the car, saying, "Last time I saw it was three or four days ago. No apologies if the police have impounded it by now."

Smiling coldly, Yang told me if the car wasn't where I said it was, he'd report it as stolen and have the bank void the check.

"So it was also you guys who killed Tran in the freezer?" I asked Hole in Five.

"You'll have to lose the questions," Yang said. "Tran made a real mess of things, as you can imagine. Surely he committed suicide to make amends?"

"Let me rephrase that. You guys must've whacked his guts before leaving him in the sub-zero. So was Billy one of yours or Khaki Mafia?" I asked, waving the slip of paper at him. He made no move to cross the dirt I'd scattered between us.

"Khaki Mafia? You must be joking."

"Or would you prefer I called it the Sneak Beak?"

"That, my friend, is just a fanciful fiction. This isn't a manga. No one in his right mind would call them a mafia. They're nothing like a triad or a *yakuza* family."

"Well, Glidden's been ordered back to Hawaii."

"Ah, so that's whose wallet you were aiming to pick."

"Think what you like. I don't expect you to understand."

For the first time, Yang's eyes cut me a slice of real emotion. "If I may beg to differ," he said without releasing his gaze, "no secret pact exists with any such ghost organization. I have a legitimate business contract with the US Forces in Japan. I don't know who put these ideas in your head, but we're strictly aboveboard. What I just paid you was an insurance premium. It'd be a serious nuisance if the media raised a stink."

"So what if Glidden gets court-martialed?"

"Don't you think it'll end with a closed-door inquiry? At the very worst, they'll let him off with a voluntary discharge. Fair enough, but still a pity at his age."

"I've seen a photo of you with your buddies Ackerman and Glidden," I told him.

"We go way back," he admitted. "Didn't I say as much last time we met?"

"You go way forward too."

"What law says old friends can't do business together? If you call that a mafia, then what about the police? Snuffing out scandals, collecting dues. What about the White House? There's a real mafia for you. Each new president making a clean sweep of staff to accommodate his own gang. Each newcomer profiting from his own portfolio of concessions." Yang leaned casually on the inlaid cabinet. "Your so-called Sneak Beak is a mere hobby compared to Washington's war industry cronies. All those companies getting in good with the administration of the hour to cash in on military budgets."

"And you wouldn't mind rubbing shoulders with them either."

"Most certainly. Military outsourcing is the wave of the future. The fourth richest man in the Philippines owned a company that had a monopoly on cleaning base toilets back when Subic Bay was still an American installation. During the Gulf War, private security in Saudi Arabia guarded US fighter planes from sabotage. Our business here is of the same caliber." He fell silent and gazed at Hole in Five humbly holding a Kleenex. Or no, Yang's eyes were trained on something far beyond the wall of glass.

As I picked up the satchel, the transmitter taped to my body slipped down to my crotch. Luckily the wire caught in my underwear and didn't fall out onto the floor. Walking very carefully, trying not to slip or shake the transmitter into either pants leg, I rode the elevator to the ground floor in a nasty sweat.

49

A block from the golden building I caught a taxi. "Where to?" the cabbie asked.

"Just circle Yokohama Stadium," I told him, twisting around in the back seat to see if we were being tailed. He didn't say a thing, he didn't even seem surprised. After the first turn, I had the driver hang a left for no reason, but saw no other car making a suspicious maneuver. I loosened my belt and peeled off the transmitter.

On the radio a comedian was talking about the women's marathon gold medalist. Why was I surprised? It wasn't as if I didn't know about the Olympics, I remembered catching a glimpse of the closing ceremony on TV the week before. But the only news I'd read in the last two weeks was a brief item about a murder in an alley off Dobuita.

I took out my phone and called Prefectural Police. Komine wasn't at his desk, but after hearing my name the desk sergeant punched me through.

I pitched right in. "About the abandoned car I reported the other day—a camouflaged vehicle belonging to Lê Ngữ Thanh. Has it been impounded?"

"Why'd you want to know?" came his usual jeering reply.

"Well, Yang now knows where the car is."

"And who was it told him, eh, champ?"

"They're going to be searching for it."

"You know, the landlord of the apartment where the victim lived was asking. Like what kind of cases do the Police Archives handle? So, uh, just what case *are* you on?"

"Listen, Yang is after the dirt that's in the car. It's radioactive waste from on base, packed in a soft-drink bottle."

"What the hell are you . . .?" The words died in his mouth.

"Lê was done in by Yang's underlings, Hong Zhi-long and Wang Lun. He was trying to put the squeeze on Yang with that dirt. And Inamoto knows this too, so you ought to protect him." I wasn't making much sense but I kept talking, not giving him an opening. "I know your team found a stash hidden in the toilet at Kaput. Well, Tran stole that money from Yang, that's what got him burned."

"You have proof of all this? One single shred of evidence you can send in?" Komine tried to pin me down by the sheer force of his voice.

"Nothing hard and fast, I just know it's the truth."

"And the woman? Who killed Tran's sister?" he asked in return.

I didn't want to answer. "I'm in a taxi, I'll call you later. Just send somebody quick. Yang's people are on their way now. Stake it out and you'll nab them breaking into the car."

"First, why would anyone tell them about the car? And second, why would anyone know what's in it? Answer me that, eh, Futamura."

"You needn't thank me."

"Don't hold your breath." He hung up.

The taxi had circled back around the stadium and stopped at a red light. "What now?" asked the cabbie. I told him to turn right, toward the café where Tomoda and I had arranged to meet up again. The driver looked this way and that over his shoulder and chuckled. "I give up, where's the camera? You're one of those TV guys, right?"

The real TV guy was sitting at the counter. "So what was that cracking noise?" he asked, half choked with anticipation.

"Don't look around. I don't think I was tailed, but those goons might still happen by."

344

Tomoda leaned in closer. "The window cracked? That gold mirror glass was so reflective, we could barely see your silhouettes when the sun went behind the clouds."

"It was a pistol. Didn't the mic pick up the gunshot?"

"Oh the audio was fine, crystal clear. I just couldn't believe anyone would fire a gun."

I set down the satchel and he pulled it over with his feet, then waited a minute before picking it up. Unzipping it on his lap, he switched off the camera. "If this baby shot anything at all, we've got the goods on them. I didn't honestly think it'd go this well."

In lieu of a response, I pulled the folded check out of my pocket and slid it across the counter. "Here, you hang on to this, a bonus piece of evidence. Granted, come Monday it'll just be a scrap of paper."

"I'll erase the part on the tape where you accept it."

"Either way, I don't care."

He frowned. "You must be beat. Better keep a cool head."

"Sure I'm tired. I don't know what I ought to be doing."

"You've come this far, d'you want to prove your friend innocent or not?"

"Prove him innocent?" I parroted. "That never really mattered to begin with."

"So then what was this all about?"

Just reaching for my coffee made my stomach hurt, so I drank some water instead. "Don't worry about me, use the tape however you like. But even if the Department doesn't bring down the lot of them, you've got to run it on the news."

"If not the news, I'll do a special program. That's a promise." He gave me a reassuring nod, took hold of the satchel, and stood up. "Who says you can't cook up news?" And with a we'll-be-in-touch wave, he walked out and cut across the avenue.

Left on my own in the café, I now knew what I had to do, but I wasn't sure how to go about it. Not quite three in the afternoon on Saturday, too early for dinner, not quite time to be doing anything.

Where else to go but a bar or my apartment?

I decided to go home, and headed south to the broadest, shortest boulevard in Yokohama. The first paved promenade in the city, laid out by a Brit at the end of the nineteenth century, the usually quiet shady street was heaped with construction materials and heavy machinery for subway works-in-progress.

Just before Yokohama Park, a minivan with tinted windows came out of a side street and suddenly braked, cutting off the way forward. The door slid open and a nondescript character in a nondescript blue suit leaned out. The tone of his voice told me his profession. "Police Detective Futamura? Get in."

He tugged me by the collar and I stumbled onto the back seat as the door slid shut.

"Eiji Futamura, formerly of Investigations, that right?" asked a pale-faced type in a leather jacket from the front seat.

"And you all are parking meter maids?" I asked back.

A shortwave radio crackled, but the driver quickly switched it off. "Just answer the questions," said the blue suit, crowding in next to me past a doorstop in a gray suit.

"You realize what you done, buddy?" the leather jacket said, flashing his badge.

"You oughta know better, snoop," added the blue suit.

For as long as I can remember, Public Security agents have looked down on us detectives as cops-and-robbers halfwits.

Out of nowhere the gray suit reached over and poked me upside the head. "Thought you could wheedle a little extra severance pay out of your Chink pals, eh? Well, aren't you like one of the family. You got no idea how long we been plugging away here."

Had they been keeping watch on Yang's place? From where? Tomoda had gone to the café on his own and left separately too. Had these suits seen us through the big glass facade?

"What did you have to talk about with Yang?" demanded the leather jacket.

"So you tapped the phone, did you?" They'd listened in on phone conversations, then just noted who went in and out of the building. They never actually planted any bugs inside. I guess that made me feel better, I wasn't losing my powers of deduction. "Stakeouts are easier that way, especially on a Public Security budget."

The gray suit tugged at my head. "How about we cross the river? Won't Komine be envious when he hears you spent the night in our camp!" Spoken without a hint of humor. Public Security operations all over Japan report to Tokyo, not to local police departments.

"What happened to your bag?" the gray suit said out of nowhere. "You had a satchel."

I scanned their faces. These clowns didn't have a clue about Tomoda. They must have lost me once, then picked up my trail again after I left the café.

"Look, I've got no idea how much money Yang makes, or how many people he rubs out." I stretched and fished out a cigarette. "But today's my day off, so yeah, let's take a holiday spin up around the Imperial Palace or wherever."

We didn't cross the Tama River. The driver did two loops around Yokohama Stadium, then headed for a condo one block from the ginkgo-lined Yamashita Park waterfront and hiked me up to the seventeenth floor. Spacious digs for upwards of three hundred thousand yen a month, easy. Depending on the unit, the high-rise probably afforded a nice view of the harbor, but this side was facing the chaos of Chinatown. In a gap between the lowered shades, a video camera trained a huge telephoto lens at Yang's gold-glazed eyesore front and center.

There wasn't much furniture, only a large desk cluttered with wireless equipment, folding chairs, wall-to-wall bookshelves and not a single book. The leather jacket and blue suit proceeded to interrogate me about why I'd gone to Yang's place. They didn't ask about Billy or Tran's sister or Lê Ngũ Thanh or Paulie in Okinawa. They didn't know about me accepting the check or my contact with Tomoda. For close to four hours, all they could do was lay threats to my pension without giving me any reason or even a glass of water.

"You know why we let you see here," the leather jacket said finally on the way to the elevator. One last snipe, meaning, I supposed, that if Yang ever got wise to this place, they'd tell the Kanagawa Police I was the leak. Or maybe they'd do it anyway. Fine by me, I'd still get my pension. To bring a disciplinary discharge down on my head, the big boys would have to go public with just cause and share the blame. Komine might yell to get it out of his system, but the career climbers above him would never come down a peg for the likes of me.

Strangely enough, none of this fazed me in the least. It just made me more concerned about the freewheeling violinist. In two weeks, I hadn't found one trace of hope for her. Just the opposite, I'd pushed things toward the worst possible conclusion.

50

A salty tang was in the night air. I joined a tide of young people drifting in from the waterfront toward the neon splash of Chinatown. It was past seven by my watch and I was hungry.

Surprisingly close by, the yellow sign of the Karlingchen Hofbräu reminded me of Billy's promise to meet back there. Why did that bother me? I told myself it was my empty stomach getting cranky, but the torn hundred-dollar bill in my wallet knew better.

I pushed through the door with its stained-glass panel to find two groups of customers in the outer restaurant section. Four college students at one table and a family at another, a couple with two nearly adult children, everybody nice and quiet.

"One for dinner?" asked the waiter. Without thinking, I shook my head and was shown through the swinging doors to the bar. Immediately my hunger evaporated. The old German lady was looking up at the Nankai Hawks slugging it out for the league pennant on a portable TV tucked into the liquor shelf. There was no one else in the place.

"Still got any of that juice left?" I asked.

"Lots," she said, baring her teeth. It took a while for me to recognize it as a smile.

"Gimme two."

"*Ach.* I hope you not say it is someone's funeral."

"One drink wouldn't make a dent. But with two, when I've finished one I've still got a whole drink left."

Brunhilda turned down the TV a little, flipped over her cocktail shaker, and started making Papa Dobles. I stood there watching her and drank the first one. After a sip of the second I sat down on a stool.

"Is alright?" She sounded a little worried. "Better with fresh grapefruit?" The old woman pursed her lower lip and nodded before returning to the ballgame. Then, with her back turned to me, she asked, "What about him? That happy drunk friend of yours."

"Still up in the air."

I drank my second glass. The sweet juice plastered the rum to my tongue. A small roar came from the TV. The opponents' first batter hit straight up the center infield and made first base.

"Do you want I should turn it off?" she asked.

"No, I don't mind baseball."

"Me neither. I don't like soccer, never a break to go the toilet."

"Baseball's designed so they can run commercials when teams change sides." The next batter bungled into a double play. "I could do better with my eyes closed," I commented, then added, "Two more please. With fresh grapefruit, no sugar."

Silently she brought out fruit from the kitchen and squeezed it on a juicer. "You say you play basesball," she said as she picked up the shaker. "Why you quit?"

"I hated switching back and forth between the plate and the field. If only I could've stayed up at bat, I might still be playing."

"Strange man. Maybe you should be—what they call it—designated hitter?"

"I was a catcher, all I did was signal and scheme behind the opponent's back."

"That's your job, what you do."

"If it was a job, it'd be ten times worse."

Brunhilda shrugged and filled two glasses. "So you never want go professional?"

"Wanting to isn't enough." I tossed back my third glass. How many times had I answered the same question the same way?

A cheer rose from the liquor shelf and for a moment the television set seemed to dance. Jersey number 9 was trotting to first base, the words HOME RUN superimposed across the screen. The Hawks had secured a one-run lead.

"I like basesball, but do not support any team."

"Strange lady. A noncommittal German."

"*Schtumpf!* I am born in Shanghai, as subject of Imperial Japan," she protested. "Just because I sell potato salad and beer does not make me German. Back home the border claim our village this way, that way, but when my father arrive in Japan, we are Poles. They have beer and potatoes in Poland too!" Scowling as if she'd squashed a stinkbug, she turned to the TV and didn't look around until I'd finished my fourth glass.

I ordered another two and scanned the row of barstools. I counted them. I read all the liquor labels on the shelf. None of it filled the vacuum. So I finished my sixth glass.

"Well?" she asked, a rather reserved query for her.

"Good stuff, but not the sort of thing I'd drink by the dozen."

"Maybe not right time of year."

My thoughts exactly. I considered ordering a martini, but stopped myself in solidarity with the vanished bar of the Hotel New Grand. Why couldn't I press charges against the hoteliers who robbed me of my martinis and slap the management in handcuffs?

"Anything wrong?" asked Brunhilda, though her real name was probably Ludzmila.

"Nah, I'm just drunk," I said. "Vodka please, a double Stoli."

Again without a word she dug a bottle out of the freezer and filled a crystal tulip to the brim. I got off my stool to drink standing up. The glass emptied itself.

I drank another. The back of my knees grew heavy, my joints wouldn't lock. I asked for the bill and reached for my wallet. That's when I saw the folded half-Franklin.

"You wouldn't by any chance accept this?" I said, smoothing out the torn bill.

351

"Accept *that*?" she snorted, her eyes buried in folds. "Specially not hundred! So many fakes these days."

And so, it occurred to me, that night's drinks had not been on Billy. The old Polish Kraut lady bid me "Sleep well" as the swinging doors creaked behind me. There wasn't a soul in the outer restaurant.

I walked to the waterfront park to catch a cab. Low clouds spread the glow of city lights above the ginkgo trees. The night air now smelled like rain, but for as long as my eyes remained open I didn't feel a drop.

51

Dockyard Garden is a hull-shaped imprint in the stone of the Yokohama waterfront. Formerly Japan's oldest stone dry dock, long abandoned in a corner of the shipyards, it was made over into an amphitheater when the wharves and cranes and adjacent freight terminal were razed in the 1990s to make way for yet another soulless glass-and-steel complex.

For Aileen's concert tonight the hundred-meter-long sunken plaza was rigged up like a ship with masts of lighting equipment and speakers. Temporary seating filled the deck area facing a round stage constructed on a pond at the prow, and the top of the grand staircase that replaced the dry dock gates at the stern served as the ticket entrance.

Wearing a lightweight coat over a striped suit, Orimasa looked down into the pit from the catwalk above. It was still early, the sky bright, the seats only half filled, but I wasn't surprised to see him. Inamoto had done his editorial duty and passed on my message.

"I didn't think you were a classical buff," I called out to him.

The big man turned slowly, his face in an oddly bashful smile. "Why do you think I like French movies? It's the music." He leaned a heavy elbow on the handrail, bowing the clear acrylic guardwall slightly. "Remember the Shin Hasegawa TV series when we were kids? Did you know they used to shoot episodes around the yards here?"

"And did you know," I asked back, "some punk tried to swipe a letter from my mailbox? A punk who hates dogs, says he knows you."

Orimasa ignored me. ". . . And Eiji Yoshikawa, the author of *Musashi*, he used to be a shipbuilder here, too."

"Don't duck out of it. You invited me to lunch that time to pump me for information, didn't you? Like what was I doing showing up at Reiko Hiraoka's condo and talking to her daughter? Must've surprised you. The super told me he'd contacted her 'nephew Ichiro Hiraoka' about me. Maybe one of these days I'll go show him a photo of you."

Orimasa turned around, but still didn't look at me. "No need for that."

"You went there to help out your 'aunt,' didn't you? Once by day to check out the place, then again with a pickup truck after dark, like a regular moving business pro."

"Moving business?" He was finally taking notice. "What's that supposed to mean?"

"You hauled away a big cardboard box. And maybe there was some repair work too? Called out on a rush job to fix a bullethole in the wall, were you?"

He put on a pained expression. "I talk myself blue about covering up, and still the punk screws around."

"Well, he's a jerk, what do you expect? He also lifted a gun from the condo, the pistol that fired the shot. A souvenir from a Phan Ái Quốc, sound familiar? Why would she even have that? Aileen said she came to Japan with only a violin, so whoever brought her over must've smuggled it in. Now who the hell do you think would do that?"

"Why don't *you* tell me? Is it someone I know?"

"A happy-go-lucky drunk with quirky tastes who'd choose an old Imperial Army gun over all the other trophies out there."

Orimasa's bulk let out a sigh as he scowled over the handrail at the people taking their seats in the amphitheater below.

"Kudo asked me to tell you he's hanging in there," I said. "Send him a care package, why don't you? He's not coming out any time soon, though he didn't rat on you, so he does have his good points."

Young people ambled by, laughing. The loudspeakers announced the performance would begin shortly.

"Must be stress," I told him. "Treat him like a dumb mutt, so he takes it out on dogs."

"Just like you're taking out who-knows-what on me."

"It's not you, it's the drunk who had you lie to me. On June 17, he visits Reiko Hiraoka's condo together with a few of his friends. Who I don't know, but it must've been a big deal because she serves them sashimi and saké. Only he ends up forgetting his phone, and when I run into him later at Kaput, he's drunk out of his skull."

The first seating call sounded. "Hey, gotta buy me a ticket," said Orimasa, moving off.

"Wait, the best is yet to come. July 19, surely you remember the night Billy died?" His feet stalled, an annoyed hand gripping the handrail. "Earlier that day Mrs. Hiraoka finally tries to contact him. Only she doesn't know how to get in touch, so she tries the numbers in the call record. She's worried, because that last time at her little banquet he was acting strange—him and whoever was asking for so much money."

"I'll hand it to you, leave the sleuthing to the sleuth. But how does this relate to me?"

"One of the numbers she calls belongs to Tran's sister, who still needs a million and a half yen for an operation. Now I don't know who told her to do what, but that same day witnesses see Mrs. Hiraoka with the woman's husband at a bank in Yokosuka, where she withdraws the daily limit of five hundred thousand yen."

Orimasa glanced around, visibly agitated. "So what is it you're saying?"

"I don't think Billy killed Tran's sister at all. Sounds to me more like he was looking out for that family. With maybe a little help from you in the persuasion department?"

"You're shooting in the dark. Wasn't me."

"Yeah, all you did was keep Reiko Hiraoka under lock and key."

"That's not going to fly either."

"Okay then, under protection, at Billy's request. What else did he tell you to do?"

His eyes narrowed. "Futamura, you deserve a medal. But if you really want to do right by Billy, you should leave him lie like he wanted."

"If this was all just about clearing his name, I'd have walked ages ago. I'll do what I have to even if it goes against him."

Orimasa nodded slowly, aging before my eyes. "You win—he did ask me. Said he'd be back in eighty-eight hours, so meantime could I please look after her."

"Billy also had you tell her about Tran and his sister, didn't he?"

"Like I told you before, he called from Yokota before he took off. Then six hours later his plane crashed in Taiwan."

"Very neat and tidy," I said with a sneer. "Less tidy is when Tran's sister gets killed the same day Mrs. Hiraoka fronts money for her. And it gets messier. The husband's got a third of what his wife needed now that she's dead and still he's desperate to squeeze out the rest— from all the wrong people. Never even realizes that Tran already stashed more than enough in dollars right there at Kaput. What the hell was the guy going to do with that kind of cash on his own?"

"How should I know? It's not like I ever met the creep." He gave me a good long look. He seemed to be telling the truth.

At the final seating call Orimasa leaned over the handrail again to scan for unclaimed seats. Viewed from above, the big stone blocks of the dry dock walls rose like a pyramid in progress. Portholes glowed here and there through the granite, lit from an underground shopping mall as the sky grew dark. The house lights dimmed and the stage lighting came up. Undercurrents of cello and contrabass buoyed a lead-in solo from the speakers atop the ship's bridge.

We hurried across the catwalk to the entrance. I handed over my ticket and Orimasa bought one for himself. "This is embarrassing," he muttered, descending the steps. "It's like a Takarazuka showgirl staircase."

"You go see Takarazuka shows?"

"Big fan from way back. I catch the Tokyo troupe whenever I can."

We located our places down separate aisles and sat at the very instant of total blackout. A slender body emerged in backlight, dressed in a deep crimson áo dài. There was a slow prelude, gradually building to a sudden burst of violin striking up the *allegro molto* of Weinberg's Concerto for violin and orchestra in G minor. Up it sailed, that eagle sound, past the tall buildings, high into the darkness above us . . .

I got up quickly at the intermission. I had to be sure to catch Orimasa in case he tried to lose me in the crowd, but the amphitheater had no lobby so there really was nowhere for him to go. It wasn't hard to find a man his size, scotch and soda in hand, by the refreshment cart they wheeled out at the base of the stairs. And he was surprisingly willing to talk. He even bought me a drink.

Something about his role in the story bothered me all through the first half of the concert, something he wasn't saying. "The photo taken at the villa in Saigon," I ventured. "Billy tore you and him out of the picture, right? That must mean something. If anyone's batting for him, it's you."

"He saved my life," he told me quietly. "You said maybe Billy brought the gun to Japan as a souvenir. I'll tell you this, we weren't sightseeing in Saigon. Ái Quốc might sometimes drive us around in a Cadillac, but that pistol of his almost killed Billy and me."

"Phan Ái Quốc drove a Cadillac?"

"A big white convertible with red leather seats." He paused to collect his thoughts. "I suppose we should've suspected Ái Quốc was a Viet Cong sympathizer, but it sure surprised me. We'd been planning a little job, then he goes and rats on us to the VC."

"You mean the ARVN reserve heist? I read your book and the brother's memoir."

"Yeah, we nearly walked into an ambush there at Ái Quốc's villa," he said, fidgeting. "Just hours before the job, we paid him a little visit when Tran said the wife would be out for their daughter's violin lesson."

"Violin lessons when the capital's under siege?"

"This was a guy who lives in a set from 'Gone with the Wind' with his young trophy wife, champagne chilling whenever anyone calls. Ái Quốc had a pipeline to all the goodies in Macy's Saigon through Tran," he explained. "But his obliging PX stock clerk was also our key to the villa. Tran and I hid in the garden while Billy took up position in one corner of the parlor watching Ái Quốc and Ackerman. Next thing I hear a *bam!* Tran is bleeding. Billy jumps out the French window in front of me when another shot whacks his right hand and nicks my shoulder. Billy switches hands and fires blind, but somehow he scores a left-handed hit. Lying on the tiles is Ái Quốc's wife, with the pistol nearby."

"That scene wasn't in your novel." I had to assume Phan Ái Quốc got killed as well.

"C'mon, it's fiction. In the book, I'm the main character, but in actual fact there were dozens involved, playing multiple roles. Tran himself turned out to be a VC mole. When the OSS military intel boys issued a warrant for his arrest, we all practically shit in our khakis."

I tried to work it out. "So Tran conned you that evening, leading you all into a trap at Phan's before the heist? And Phan almost took Tran down with you? All for what? How much gold bullion was there?"

"Wasn't any gold. The take wasn't worth that much either," he admitted. "It was a scam, a get-rich-quick thing Yang concocted."

Now I was really confused. "Yang? And yet years later, he hires Tran, who double-crossed him?"

"Better an honest enemy than a dishonest relative. Guess you had to be there."

This was some weird war zone camaraderie. Maybe even sworn enemies get all warm and fuzzy after decades. "So then, tell me this, how did Tran soak Yang for a hundred-fifty thousand dollars."

"Got me there," he said. "That you should've asked Billy."

"Speaking of Billy," I persisted, "Mrs. Hiraoka's family registry says she married Guillermo Kano-Law, Aileen's father by adoption. Explain that."

Orimasa made a do-I-care face. "Around Yokosuka, plenty of GI bastards got registry issues. Your Khaki Mafia's a mutual aid society for that sort of thing. You pay your dues, they'll help you pull strings to adopt a daughter."

"And smuggling a child in from Vietnam was an easy fix."

"Well, if that's smuggling, then how you got a copy of the registry can't have been too legal either."

A buzzer sounded and the intermission crowd began milling back to their seats. "You're a strange man, you know?" said Orimasa, shaking his head. "Why're you doing this? It's not like you two go way back or anything."

The amphitheater fell silent. The aisle uplights underscored his jaw in the dark. I dug out a name card to write my mobile number on. "Here, in case Billy wants to get in touch."

"Do I look like an errand boy?" He leered at me, a flashback to his *yakuza* past, then sauntered off. I have no idea if he sat through the rest of the concert.

52

Out on the floating stage, violin to her cheek, Aileen played up a storm, until the last lingering note faded into loud applause. Without waiting for the encore, I beat a retreat as the lights came on. One of the attendants opening the exit doors in readiness for the after-show rush directed me across the underground concourse to an elevator up to a third-floor hotel banquet area.

"Mr. Futamura? I will announce you," said a woman in a backstage staff jumper before heading down a corridor, leaving me amidst formally attired men and women carrying bags of party favors. Somewhere a child was crying, a mother scolding. I stood there for ages until finally I was shown to a prep area that served as a dressing room.

The place was buried in flowers, the scent of roses choked the air. My small bouquet was laid on a makeshift dresser where Aileen sat drinking mineral water. She'd changed into a black dress layered in lace, but her hair was still up in a high swirl. A bruise showed on the left side of her neck.

"It's a kiss mark," laughed Aileen, noticing my stare.

"From a guy with a vacuum cleaner mouth."

She laughed even more. "A violin kiss mark. By the last day of a tour it's a lot worse," she explained. Then, turning halfway around on her stool, long legs wading through bushels of red roses, she added, "These are from Signor Duecento."

I went closer for a look. There was no gift card.

Aileen undid her coif and shook loose her hair. A sequin fell glinting to her feet. I looked at the hinged photo frame propped up by the makeup mirror. The left-hand picture was of Aileen in a schoolgirl's sailor suit beside a younger version of Reiko Hiraoka. On the right was a black-and-white snapshot of Phan Ái Quốc holding a girl of maybe two or three all dressed up with a fancy ribbon. I pulled out the photo Billy left in my apartment and showed her.

"It's the same man!" she exclaimed. "Mom said the snapshot was in the violin case. She was sure it was my father ... but then why isn't my mother in the picture?"

I agreed. As a keepsake, a picture of all three family members would have been the obvious choice.

"It's always puzzled me. It doesn't make sense."

"Maybe she died not long after you were born?" I reached out a hand to her shoulder. "Didn't you say something about people walking out of your life? Saying goodbye, then disappearing. One was the man in the white uniform. Was the second your mother?"

"No, they never said goodbye, it's me who does that." The nape of her neck was flushed like an athlete after a hard run. "There's something I never told you," she said, looking up from the mirror. "I'm still high on adrenaline, so now's a good time."

She stood up with my arm for support and pushed aside some roses to make room on the sofa. Even so, it was a tight squeeze for two. "I don't remember all that much. The wallpaper in the nursery is peeled away by the doorframe. It bothered me so much I couldn't sleep. I'm still looking at it when a woman comes in. I can see she's holding a gun behind her back. It's alright, she tells me, go to sleep. Then for some reason I say goodbye by mistake. I know it's wrong, but she just smiles and kisses me and leaves. Before long I hear gunshots, far off, and I bury my head under the pillow. I guess eventually I fall asleep like that, until I hear someone calling me, and I wake up. There's a wavy red light on the wall and outside the window is all red. I don't know what to do, but someone lifts me up and takes me outside. That's all I remember."

Her story matched Orimasa's. "The woman was probably your real mother."

"My first mother," she corrected. "Yes, that must have been her. But oddly enough, in my memory, I don't call her mother. I can't see her face. It might even be a dream. After all this time, I can't even tell if it really happened or not."

I showed her Billy's photo again. "You don't remember any of these other people? How about the two Americans in uniform?"

"Is my Signor Duecento one of them? Which one?"

"If you don't know, I certainly can't tell you."

She giggled, realizing it sounded silly. "How did you come by this?"

"A friend of mine had it. A wartime acquaintance of your father, apparently."

"I'd like to meet him."

"So would I. But I'm afraid he's another one that's disappeared."

Aileen gave me a penetrating look. There was a knock on the door and in stepped her foreign manager, who said something to her in Italian. Immediately, Aileen brightened up. "Good news, I can stay on another couple of weeks. My Vietnam concert is pretty well set, pending a few points of discussion."

"Discussion here in Japan?"

"The staff will go to Saigon, but most likely I get a holiday until they give me a visa. It'll take a while to get the papers proving I was born in Vietnam. I'm an American citizen. Surprised?" she asked a bit awkwardly.

"No, that much I knew. Your stepfather is Guillermo Kano-Law, right?"

"Stepfather? Oh, you mean on the family registry. Mom just borrowed his name for legal purposes. She told me when I went to London, but I never met him."

There was an uneasy silence, reminding me that I wasn't here to chitchat. Should I tell her what happened to her mother? Inasmuch as she was Reiko Hiraoka's daughter and she'd hired me, I was obliged to present what I'd found out, in whatever shape or form. For three seconds I hesitated, three long seconds.

"Can we go somewhere else and talk?" I said. "There's things I have to tell you."

"Same here. Lots of things. Promise you'll stick around until morning?"

"I'm afraid I can't," I said.

She tried not to look upset. "Well then, let's get something to eat, I'm starting to feel hungry."

I put my hand on her shoulder again and waited a moment before saying anything. "Fine, but let me talk first. About your mother's disappearance, what I have to say isn't pleasant. I think there was more between her and your stepfather than you know. She seems to have got caught in the middle of something involving a large sum of money."

Aileen gave me an incredulous look. "But I sent regular transfers to her account. She'd have told me if she needed more or had money problems."

"It was your stepfather's money problems." I tried to break it gently. "He made some foolish moves that put himself and others in danger. Three of his friends from Vietnam War days came to harm because of him. You should probably be glad you don't know him. Your mother, however, was not so lucky."

She crossed her arms and shook her head. "I don't know if I want to hear this before eating. I think I need a drink."

"You and me both," I said, "but let's steer clear of Chinatown, if you don't mind. There's people there we don't want to see."

53

For ten days after that nothing happened. By the second weekend, I'd lost track of what the hell I was waiting for. That Saturday, the day before I'd arranged to drive Aileen to Narita for her flight to Vietnam, I left the apartment at ten to grab some breakfast and walked east toward the waterfront. The sky was a pastel blue, the breeze was cool and crisp. The Silk Center had just come into view when my phone rang.

"Mister Footamoora?" drawled an American woman. "I'm calling on behalf of a mutual friend."

"Sounds like bad news. And you are . . .?"

"Chief Petty Officer Jacqueline Farigo, sir. I have an important message for you. Could you come to Atsugi Base tomorrow?"

I stopped walking. "This friend isn't by any chance a Warrant Officer Tyson?"

The woman snickered. Her voice relaxed. "Nossir, he says you're buddies. Can you be here around five?"

Without fail, I told her. She said I should just give them my name at the main gate. I wondered whether to tell Aileen there was a change of plans, but kept walking along the Yamashita Park waterfront and forgot to have lunch.

The following afternoon, I caught a commuter train from Yokohama Station and then a taxi out to US Naval Air Facility Atsugi. On hearing my name, the Japanese guard handed me a visitor's badge and gave us directions. Up a gentle slope, past a World War II twin-propeller C47 with a seahorse painted on the fuselage, we turned left at a fire station and headed past a Pro Golfer sporting goods shop straight for the runway. As instructed, I had the taxi pull over at a giant barracks.

All was still, shimmering in the sun on the asphalt. The brick structure had very few windows, but I managed to find a door that beamed a little light into the dark interior. I felt someone watching me. Sitting on a flatbed trailer hitched to a tow truck across the way was a man in aviator green fatigues and an olive garrison cap. Work clothes, but he wore a necktie and there were epaulets on his shoulders.

"A little overdue, aren't you, Billy?" I called out.

He dangled his legs over the dropped tailgate and stared at me through his sunglasses. He didn't look out of place. A little sunburnt maybe, but not burnt to death.

"Hey, buddy," he said, raising his hand to his temple. Was that supposed to be a salute or just a wave?

"You're no buddy of mine," I said. "You're no ace, either. I don't even know who you are."

He hopped down from the trailer and strolled across to shake hands. Then striding off ahead of me, he said without turning around, "Hey, I'm *sorry*."

"Sorry about what?"

"I heard you lost your job on account of me."

"It wasn't you. I never told you I was a cop."

"Yeah, that's right, why didn't you say anything? Didn't you trust me?"

"Trust?" I laughed. "Oh I trust you, for as long as we're sitting side-by-side in a bar."

"Okay, you talked me into it." We came to a rickety glass door with BAR stenciled on it. Inside, past a handful of fast-food joints under a very high ceiling, a bare iron staircase led to a wide aisle with a long laminate counter and a row of stools. Half the counter faced a liquor shelf, the other half was a snack concession serving sushi rolls and yakisoba noodles. At the far end, a window looked out onto the runway.

A huddle of ageless women sat chatting in the back. One of them grudgingly got up and came over to wait on us. Billy ordered Bacardi and grapefruit juice, saying he'd do the mixing himself. When he paid, the woman said something in Tagalog that made them all laugh. She didn't give him any change.

"No decent place to drink here, not like Yokosuka," Billy complained, reaching behind the counter for a pitcher. He sloshed together the rum and Tropicana, filled cocktail glasses with crushed ice from a pail she provided, and poured us two impromptu Papa Dobles.

"What'll we drink to?" I asked.

"No need to celebrate my resurrection. Been toasting that enough already," he said before offering anything like an apology. "Believe me, I meant to keep my promise, if it wasn't for the plane going down."

"You don't have to keep your promises, but don't lie to me. Though I suppose if you hadn't pulled that crazy stunt, we wouldn't be meeting like this, now would we?" I looked around, surprised at how loud I was speaking. "You just used me to mislead the force into believing you flew off to the West Coast, didn't you?"

"Is that so bad?"

I wanted to be angry, but had to laugh at him trying to look innocent. "Sure, Billy, I get it. So who crashed the plane for you? You must've landed in Okinawa to post that letter, then caught a ride back in a cargo plane."

"I switched places with a noncom downtiming at Kadena. That day, for some reason, Chinese fighter jets entered the Taiwan Strait and air space to the west was restricted, so he had to approach Kaohsiung from the Pacific side. Air currents off those 3,000-meter peaks can cause serious disturbance, probably ripped off the tail fin. Poor kid, wasn't even thirty."

"But somebody who dies in a plane crash in Taiwan can't very well post a letter from San Francisco, so you had Orimasa try to steal it back. No, you never intended to show your face back here. You just wanted to remove a murder suspect from the equation."

"Don't be so down on it, wasn't any big game plan, no deep thought."

A sudden boom shook the place. The windowpanes screeched. I felt the air ramming my chest. Billy went to look as one jet fighter, then another, licked the tarmac and took off. Their afterburners trailed fire in the darkening sky.

A scramble drill, he explained, returning to the stool next to mine; the locals were sure to complain again about the noise. "I heard from Orimasa," he went on, eyes still on the window. "Yang suspected me till they discovered the remains of his loot."

"By now he must know you're alive."

"Sure, but it's okay so long as he saved face. He'll reach out once things cool down a bit. Pilots with a free pass onto American bases aren't so easy to come by."

"Only your frozen Vietnamese friend won't be returning to the fold." My throat didn't even feel the alcohol as I threw back the last of my drink.

"That was in the cards, I guess," Billy replied. "Met him by chance at a bar on Dong Khoi. All of a sudden we were like long-lost pals. A merchant ship captain he said he was. I take Tran under my wing and before long he's working at the PX." He paused as another fighter blasted off the runway. "Well, after the ground troops pull out, us American advisors hold on for another couple of years. Good pay, risk compensation, but we got greedy. Some ex-GI characters were planning a big job on an ARVN depot, a picnic they said, worth four million dollars. We took Tran into our confidence—we needed an insider."

"But wasn't Tran a Viet Cong agent?"

"According to Orimasa, but he gets carried away. He can talk himself into anything."

"So how much of his story is fiction?"

"Well, first of all, who was or wasn't VC in Saigon is beside the point. The real question was whether the Charlie would take money or not. In that sense, Tran was one of us, we were all in it together. When things went seriously wrong, he even took a bullet for us." Billy waved his glass for emphasis. The scar on the back of his hand stood out, but the tinkling ice was swallowed by a jet engine.

"I heard about the shootout at Aileen's family villa. Aileen said she vaguely remembers her mother getting a gun she'd hidden in the nursery and going outside."

"Kids and their memories. We only found out later they'd skipped her violin lesson that evening because Aileen was feeling under the weather," he explained, examining his glass. "Afterwards, when I was in sickbay, Tran showed up with the orphan girl, saying could I please take her to America. Her dad was a suspected double agent, so she'd have had no chance of a decent life once the South went communist." As if in sync, Billy took a breath just as another fighter came in to land.

I tried to keep the conversation on track. "But you brought her to Japan instead."

"I also brought Tran to Japan, got him a job with Yang too, on a freighter." He unscrewed the Bacardi to pour some over the remaining chunk of ice in his glass, then stabbed a lime from a fruit bowl with his pocketknife and squeezed in a dribble of juice.

"I know. Hauling hazardous waste to Ho Chi Minh."

"What's this now?" he said. "Yang said he was importing beach sand."

"Sand in, garbage out. Count yourself lucky you didn't know. Anyhow, Tran wasn't a captain for long."

"No, his South Vietnamese license was just a scrap of paper issued by a country that went up in smoke. But it was good enough for Yang." Shaking his head, he added, "Unlucky bastard, the moment he brings his sister to Japan, the shrapnel wound in her head gets worse. Her life was in the balance, made Tran take too many risks."

"Like going after Yang's money?"

"He had to maneuver fast, like in a dogfight." Billy swooped his hand around. "When a shipment was delayed a week, close to two hundred grand was sitting there at Parklane Terrace, and Tran knew it."

"In a hidden safe in the bathroom."

"There's the snoop! Ackerman was out of Japan on business, the vacant office was supposed to be secure."

"Then how did Tran get in?"

"Copied my key." Billy shrugged like it was no big deal. He probably even drew a floorplan of the apartment for Tran. "Broke the door down and crowbarred the safe to make it look like the Chinese boys trashed the place. But he didn't take the full amount, only a hundred-fifty thou. Who the hell would do that?" His eyes turned toward the window and the setting sun at the end of the runway. "I just don't get it. With the extra cash he could've run off anywhere on the planet. But maybe, like Yang says, 'You can't scoop up more water than two hands can hold.'"

"So you *were* looking for Tran that night at Kaput."

"Yang made *me* take the blame. If I valued my life, I either had to get it all back from Tran or scrape together the money myself."

A chuckle slipped out of my mouth. I remembered Yang telling me, the first time we met, to find his missing cargo "or else."

"Wasn't no laughing matter," Billy objected. "Face is everything for the Chinaman. He even fired his own son from Golden Harbor. Jury, judge, and executioner all in one."

"So in the end Yang got to Tran first." I sighed as I said this. "But the cash stayed hidden in the toilet tank at Kaput the whole time, not three meters away from where the woman who needed it most was murdered."

"Tran didn't trust her husband, specially not about money, so he hadn't told her. But Yang's men got to her, then Lê got his too. She survived Nam, but her luck ran out here."

I mixed myself another drink, though I couldn't remember

finishing the round before. Billy's drink had also evaporated. "You're bad news. Drunks always cause problems. A mother worries herself sick over her drunk of a son and winds up dead because of him."

"Whose mother are we talking about?"

I cut him short. "William Lou Bonney can read kanji, enough to find his way to my apartment by the name on my mailbox, as I recall."

Billy scrunched up his face like he'd been sucker-punched, then looked up at me and grudgingly switched to Japanese. "Alright, you got me, I can read a little."

"You know a place called Otátoclán?" I pressed on. "Resort town in Mexico, used to be a hangout for American hippies, the kind of backwater you could smoke dope on the street. There was an accident on the mountain road leading there: a car with a young Japanese hitchhiker ran head-on into a truck and rolled over a cliff." I gave him time to unwrap his memories. "The car's owner survived, a Peruvian resident in Los Angeles by the name of Guillermo Kano-Law. The kid who died was one Yuichi Hiraoka. So how did you change places with a dead man, Yuichi?"

Billy took a deep breath and went blank. For a split second I wasn't sure who I was actually talking to. "I came to in a hospital," he began. "It was a small town, with only two or three cops. The car was a convertible. We were both thrown out of our seats, only I got caught in a tree. He fell in front of the car and got dragged down to the bottom of the ravine, where the gas tank exploded. When I woke up, everybody had us confused. My passport must've burned up in my backpack, but his was lying nearby. Sure, this was the middle of nowhere, but I'll never understand those Mexicans. Just because he was half-Japanese, I mean, we didn't even look alike! They didn't do a dental exam or run any checks on the remains or anything. They didn't even care that this 'Peruvian' didn't speak Spanish, they just sent me back to America with his passport. I'd been wanting to enlist to try for US citizenship, but I wasn't even eighteen yet. Then suddenly I'm handed an adult passport stamped with an F-1 student visa. Well, it was like a gift from heaven. Señor Kano went straight to the Navy recruitment office."

There was a loud thud that made us both jump. The women in the back laughed as they propped a fallen mop up against the wall. Someone switched on the TV and ceiling lights. The window frame glinted gold in the last rays of the sun.

"I take it you visited your mother," I resumed.

"A little while after Nam I got in touch, just to tell her I was alive. She gave me hell. Said she thought I was dead, so why didn't I just stay dead? After that I hardly ever saw her again. Stubborn woman, but that's how she wanted it."

"But the girl your mother took in, Aileen," I persisted. "How did that happen?"

"I didn't know how to look after a kid, I plain wasn't up to it. I told Mom that Aileen was the daughter of a woman I married in America, not that she believed it." Billy's gaze slipped down like ice into his drink. "She couldn't bring herself to accept me, not what I'd become, but the girl obviously needed a home."

"Aileen said a man in a white uniform brought her to Japan. Just like you to show off for a six-year-old girl. Did your Khaki Mafia pals provide you with an officer's dress whites?"

He looked uncomfortable. "I made do with an ensign's getup. Cost me a pretty penny too."

"So you adopt her to bring her to Japan, but why's the father's name Kano-Law?"

"I hadn't changed it yet, couldn't do everything at once."

"And your mother's family registry? Whose clever idea was it to make you a spouse?"

"Mom's. The red tape to adopt Aileen from me would've taken forever."

"All that just to keep the girl?"

"I owed her. I went to war but only ever killed one person, her mother." He was peering at his glass. "And for what it's worth, Mom owed Tran for entrusting her to me."

Something flickered on the windowpane. I turned to see a Japan Series baseball broadcast on the TV opposite the counter. The sound was turned off, all you could hear was the Filipinas chatting and laughing.

I had to ask. "You never flew any Navy fighter, so when did Billy become a pilot?"

"Billy was born at the Navy boot camp in Alameda, but their veterans' fund paid for civilian flight training."

"You just wanted to be American, right? Isn't that why you went there?"

He looked more at ease now. "Why else would I go?"

"I hear you. Way back, I wanted to be something else too. Seems every joker feels like he's living someone else's life by default."

Just then, my phone rang in my jacket. I knew who it was even before I heard the voice. "An appointment," I told Billy as I put the gadget away and hopped off my stool. But then, call it the detective's curse, I had one last niggling question. "Why'd you ask me that night? There were plenty of taxis on the road."

"I wanted somebody to say goodbye to."

"Orimasa helped you. Why not ask him?"

"I felt like having one last drink with you. For what it was worth."

"You may get your drinking buddies right, but you picked the wrong goodbye guy." I pulled out the torn hundred-dollar bill and laid it on the counter. "Here's my half. Can't let you pay for every-thing."

He nodded toward the exit and left the worthless money as a tip.

Billy gave me a lift in an electric golf cart. The jet exercise was over by now, and the emergency vehicles were clearing off the runway. Stars had begun to show overhead. For all of one kilometer we didn't exchange a word while the golf clubs jostled behind us. Apparently there's quite a good golf course at the end of the runway in Atsugi. Just before the gate, several men in uniforms like Billy's and Japanese servicemen were hooking up a cable to haul the old Curtis C47 away somewhere.

I spoke up. "I read that pilots feel like they've left the world behind when they get airborne. Is that what it's like?"

Billy shrugged and stopped the cart. "Kinda. Looking down on the earth from up there does make you feel like a king. A king, and all alone."

"The book also said there's no left or right or up or down in the sky."

"That's crap." He got off the cart and started walking, hands thrust in his pockets. And all of a sudden I realized I didn't like him anymore, probably for the same reason I once thought I did.

Beside the main gate stood a lookout post with a bright spotlight. "Guess you're not going anywhere now, Billy Lou Bonney or whoever you are. You're a wanted man."

"Fine, I don't feel much like going anywhere either."

"You're a criminal here in Japan, you're fenced in for good."

"Don't be ridiculous, there are US bases all over the world."

"All of them just as much of a cage."

"What makes you so sure?"

"Because of someone out there," I said, pointing beyond the chain link fence to where a black Alfa Romeo had come to a halt. The door opened and out stepped Aileen in a dark suit.

"Fuck you, Futamura," Billy swore at me. "Of all the dirty tricks . . ."

We were even, one win, one loss. "Jury, judge and executioner at your service," I said, and kept walking right out the gate.

Aileen seemed unsettled, but reached out a gentle hand. "Are you alright? You look like you've been to a funeral."

"Yeah, my own." I turned around to see Billy still standing there. I don't know why that surprised me.

"Is he my Signor Duecento?" she whispered.

"I'll leave that for you to decide."

"Then don't say a thing." She strode into the spotlight just this side of the gate, sized Billy up, then gave him a deep end-of-concert bow. Was he shaken? He didn't look too happy. Aileen, however, came back positively beaming.

Meanwhile, a tow truck was pulling the C47 across the main gate road in front of Billy. When it had passed, he was nowhere in sight.

I took out my notebook, tore off the page where I'd noted Paulie's directions to the grave in Okinawa, and handed it to Aileen. "Your mother's resting place."

"Will you come with me?" she asked.

"No, you go alone. My job was just to find her."

"Your job, was it?" She gave it a moment's thought. "I take it you don't like company."

"I'm not the one you need. You've already lost two fathers, don't let me be the third."

She turned and walked back to her car. As she opened the door to get in, her sad eyes stared straight at me. "Okay, then, no third goodbye."

The car pulled away and soon disappeared beyond the trees. It was a long hike back to the station; I should have driven here myself.

54

The trees along the tracks had all changed color. The ginkgo leaves were a brilliant yellow, flecked with red, the closer we got to Kamakura. Tomoda and I were heading south on the Yokosuka line, drinking beer in upper deck seats. I hadn't seen him in ages.

"Yang probably meant to toss Tran's body out with the garbage," he said, "if those Myanmar boys hadn't found him first. Supposed to have been food supplies for the base in that deep freeze, but I wouldn't be surprised if there was some connection with the toxic waste he was exporting."

What could I say? I couldn't help thinking of the last scene in Orimasa's novel. Who knows what was buried down there in Vietnam? Our seats shook slightly as the train pulled out of Ofuna Station. "What's happening with the TV program?" I asked.

"Tons of busywork, but the program will happen. It's been approved."

Strange to say, I didn't care what the final verdict on Yang's crimes was, or even if no verdict were ever handed down at all.

"Everything's the American presidential election these days. Trying to air US military dirty laundry will only seem like a bit of window dressing."

"Ah well, so what's up today?"

"Don't ask," he said, smirking. "They want me to report on some centenarian toad that's been living in the pond at Tsuruoka Hachiman Shrine for decades."

"Where's the camera?"

"Gone ahead by car. I just need to show my face, beats staying at the Bureau."

A flock of housewives with daypacks sat behind us, chirping away like sparrows in an autumn ricefield.

"You know," he leaned over to confide, "Nanyang Holdings HQ's been put up for sale. And Golden Harbor's got a new Japanese boss who promises to sort out the business."

"What about Yang himself?"

"He's out of the picture. Public Security's not even sure where, but he's not in Japan. He's blown his free pass to the States, and the Kuomintang Party split-up means he's lost his backing in Taiwan too, so he can't bribe his way with the local authorities there. Meanwhile, our Public Security is obviously gunning for him." Tomoda leaned even closer and gave me a probing look. "Speaking of which, Tokyo can't be too pleased that Kanagawa Investigations have charged Yang's goons with the murder of Lê Ngữ Thanh. Wonder who could have put them up to that."

"Like they say, whoever spits at heaven. Only this time, it wasn't heaven, it was my ass the goon spit on. DNA testing from saliva's pretty straightforward, probably from the wife's body too. What doesn't figure is why he'd bring a trunk all the way from Yokohama to pack the corpse in ice, then drive it all the way back and dump it in Ackerman's garage. Leaving tracks like crazy, was the idiot trying to attract attention?"

"You're the detective," said Tomoda. "Isn't irrational behavior your specialty?"

I smiled. "Not anymore. I quit the force, I don't need the head-aches."

His smile went deadpan. "You're the idiot. Why'd you have to go and quit?"

"Even if Billy wasn't guilty, the fact is I was breaking the law drunk driving on duty. If they didn't axe me, one of you media types was bound to squawk."

Tomoda withheld comment and looked out the window. The trees had taken on a deeper coloring as the train slowed toward Kita Kamakura. As soon as the station was announced, the matrons bustled down the steps to the carriage door.

"Big personnel changes in the US Pacific Fleet, too," Tomoda continued. "Fleet Activities Commander at Yokosuka got booted, and all his hangers-on have been wiped off the slate. Waste disposal's apparently going to a listed public contractor. It may not be a full spring-clean, but it's a step in the right direction."

"Well, either way, you've done your bit," I said. "Unless you want to go dig up Birnam Wood down in Vietnam."

The train stopped and let out a crush of people. Then a bell rang and we shook into motion again.

"You shouldn't have quit," repeated Tomoda.

"I screwed up. I should've told the guy I was a cop, but I didn't."

"Not saying you're a cop at a bar is just common sense. At least you don't mind talking to strangers."

I nodded. Billy was that way too. No matter what kind of person he turned out to be, I used to enjoy drinking with him.

"Guess you knew Komine was planning to post you to some precinct out in the middle of nowhere."

"Escorting suspects to court and back isn't my idea of fun. I only ever enjoyed chasing down real criminals," I said. "I'm no career cop, I'm just not cut out for it. Never much liked the job to begin with, so quitting suits me fine."

After a short tunnel, hills hemmed in the tiny old houses along the valley. A railroad crossing signal dinged closer, then donged past, and Kamakura came into view.

"How about a bowl of soba?" asked Tomoda.

"I thought I told you, I'm meeting someone."

He blinked his disappointment as he got up. He reached out a hand. "I'm being kicked up north, to Tohoku. Seems I haven't done my share of menial office work either."

I stood up and grabbed his hand while the train braked.

"Guess we won't be seeing each other," he said.

"We'll meet up," I assured him. "Just pop back down when you get a chance."

"Sure thing." He turned to get off the train. The last I saw of him was the slouch of his back.

On past Higashi Zushi, as the train tunneled across the peninsula through to the Tokyo Bay side, I bitterly regretted not taking him up on that bowl of noodles.

From Yokosuka Station I walked along the seafront. The warships had vanished from the far bank. I turned in at the steps up to the main entrance of the shopping center, but there was no trace of Yamato's shoeshine booth, only a square of discolored pavement.

I crossed the pedestrian bridge over behind the hotel. In the building under construction at the head of Dobuita they had started paneling the interior. A sign advertised for tenants.

A four-ton truck parked in front of Private Princess made Dobuita more impassable than ever. Movers shouted back and forth as they hauled out a huge liquor cabinet, with Yori in a knit dress right behind.

"Couldn't you just leave it for the next owner?" I asked her.

"They say it's going to be a ramen shop. The age of hostess bars is over."

"And no one gets their shoes shined these days either."

"You talking about Yamato? What do you think happened to his place?"

"Don't ask me two things at once," I joked. "He owes me a polish."

"Maybe those Navy spooks got him a commendation, over in Hawaii?"

"Well, I hope he gets full retirement benefits. He was a hell of a lot more on the ball than they were." I smiled remembering his witness-stand pose, his boater and carry-all tool box. I couldn't quite picture him in dress blues with gold stripes and a medal pinned on his chest, but an aloha shirt would suit him fine.

After the movers left we walked along Dobuita. Most eateries had their shutters down, but the taco stand was open, so we sat outside in the sun and drank Coronas with lime. The old dog snoozed on the sidewalk across the way. After two beers each, I proposed we switch to tequila but Yori shook her head. "That's a no-no," she said, pressing a finger to her lips. "Even for a freelance cop."

"But I'm really free now," I told her. "I quit the force."

Her eyes widened in delight. "Wow, you finally said goodbye to the boys on the beat!" She went inside and returned with two Havana Clubs on the rocks.

We clinked glasses to celebrate, Yori crinkling her nose in a big smile.

"So what lies ahead for you?" I asked.

"I'm moving to New York. My Billy's getting his discharge. Father of a friend of his owns a shop in lower Manhattan, and they want to turn it into a Japanese restaurant."

"Your Billy can cook Japanese?"

"Uh-huh, he's real good at it now. He makes great taco rice."

When we finished our drinks, Yori said she was meeting Billy, so I walked her across the main drag to the Yokosuka Base gate.

"Where are you going to live in New York?"

"Maybe Harlem? It's got to be nicer than Dobuita."

"You don't like it here?"

"Do you?" She bobbed her head like a baby. "Anyway, hold off on getting me that Indian fabric for now."

"Just write and tell me when you know how much you need." I handed her the very first of my new name cards.

A Yokosuka policeman eyed us from his post beside the gate. A hired security guard eyed us from inside the gate. Whose laws allowed him the pistol at his waist?

Someone called out her name. There inside the heavy-duty chain link fence waved cornhead Billy. "I'll be going," she said, placing a hand on my shoulder to press a warm goodbye kiss to my cheek. Then she turned and ran straight to her sailor.

The security guard followed Yori with his eyes. The policeman stared at me standing there like an idiot. What the hell was I waiting for? Another drunk pilot to fall from the sky and invite me for a drink? I didn't even hear a jet engine, I was alone.

That was the last I ever saw of Yori and her Billy boy, the last I saw of anyone I knew there. From that day on, every familiar face was gone. All except *them*. The world has yet to invent a way to say goodbye to Americans.

TRANSLATOR'S ACKNOWLEDGEMENT

The translator wishes to thank Stephen Shaw for his tireless editorial efforts and sage advice.

TOSHIHIKO YAHAGI, born in Yokohama in 1950, is Japan's premier writer of intellectual noir and political satire. Recipient of the 2004 Yukio Mishima Award, his multi-genre career spans everything from manga artist to action film director, and he is the author of more than two dozen bestselling novels. *The Wrong Goodbye*, from the on-going Detective Eiji Futamura series, is his first work to appear in English translation.

ALFRED BIRNBAUM translated most of Haruki Murakami's early novels, including *A Wild Sheep Chase* and *Hard-Boiled Wonderland and the End of the World*. His work has received the 2001 Sasakawa Foundation Translation Award, among other honours.